MILTON, SPENSER AND THE EPIC TRADITION

Milton, Spenser and the Epic Tradition

PATRICK J. COOK

Ashgate

Aldershot • Brookfield USA • Singapore • Sidney

First published in hardback (ISBN 1 85928 271 7) under the Scolar Press imprint, Ashgate Publishing Ltd.

Published by
Ashgate Publishing Ltd   Ashgate Publishing Company
Gower House   Old Post Road
Croft Road   Brookfield
Aldershot   Vermont 05036-9704
Hants GU11 3HR   USA
England

Hardback edition reprinted 1997

British Library Cataloguing-in-Publication Data

Cook, Patrick J.
    Milton, Spenser and the epic tradition
    1. Epic poetry — History and criticism
    I. Title
    809.1'32
Library of Congress Cataloging-in-Publication Data

Cook, Patrick J.
    Milton, Spenser and the epic tradition/Patrick J. Cook.
    Includes bibliographical references and index.
    1. Epic literature, European — History and criticism. 2. European literature — Classical influence. 3. Milton, John. 1608-1674 — Criticism and interpretation. 4. Spenser, Edmund. 1552?-1599 — Criticism and interpretation. I. Title.
    PN694.E6C88 1996
    809.1'32 —dc20   95-52877
                                                        CIP

ISBN 0 7546 0048 3 (paperback)

Printed in Great Britain by Galliards, Great Yarmouth

Contents

Introduction

This book is intended to complement the welcome abundance of comparative studies that in recent years have extended our understanding of the epic genre's function and evolution in Western culture. It is grounded in the neglected fact that European epic rose from a Near East dominated by sacred cities, and in the even more neglected fact that the means by which these cities encoded their ideologies through ritual, architecture and other codes of power determined the nature of a genre that became the most prestigious literary instrument for reflecting and influencing European culture. My discussion might be said to begin where Stephen Scully's recent *Homer and the Sacred City* ends, and readers interested in the cultural matrix in which European epic took form should consult Scully's finely researched volume, to which I gladly acknowledge my debt. Starting with an attempt to consider how Homer forged culturally inflected spatio-temporal distinctions into a generic system, the present work proceeds to examine how later poets made use of this system in new cultural contexts.

The culture from which epic derives is dominated by the sense that the sacred city is the centre of the world or omphalos, to employ a Greek term for a universal phenomenon that carries many names. Omphalic space is conceptually simple: it is organized according to two features, a delineating boundary and a central cosmic axis. There is a crucial distinction between, on the one hand, the cosmic order within the walled city and within the bounds of the realm for which the walled city serves as both orienting center and synecdoche, and, on the other hand, the profane and chaotic reality outside. What historians of religion call the *axis mundi* functions both horizontally and vertically. The city is sacred not only because its walls delineate cosmos from chaos, but also because through it passes the vertical pole connecting the cosmic planes. In pre-Homeric texts the world generally begins at and emanates outward from the axis, which then serves as a point of centripetal attraction and the cherished source of contact with the divine. In Homer, and thus in European epic, this cosmogonic function of the centre has largely disappeared, but the axis retains its centripetal force. The axis also orients vertically, functioning as a validating image of the rigidly hierarchical social order of early Near Eastern civilization.[1]

A claim that epic incorporates this kind of spatiality into its generic system might be taken to entail a view that it is a conservative genre, an instrument for legitimizing and promoting a rigidly hierophantic and hierarchical culture. As I hope the following pages demonstrate, such is not the case. It is a genre largely about relations of dominance and submission, and one of its most fundamental activities is what sociologists and anthropologists call 'vertical classification', valuation through assignment to a vertical hierarchy.[2] But an act of vertical classification, though it relies upon a universal human tendency to value the high over the low, rarely is as simple as it might at first appear. As Peter Stallybrass observes in a recent study of 'the world turned upside down' topos, the high-low opposition 'can only be understood contextually', and representations that invite analysis according to the opposition can easily 'conjure up conflicting discursive frameworks'.[3] To recognize the religious basis and original cultural function of epic spatiality is not to recognize what the poet does with it.

My own description of writers' deployments of conflicting discursive frameworks is in part a response to Mikhail Bakhtin's infamous description of epic as a monologic genre that suppresses all discourses not supporting and supported by the cultural hierarchy. I am indebted to Bakhtin for his concept of the chronotope, the spatio-temporal framework distinguishing one genre from another; this book describes the omphalos-based epic chronotope and traces its evolving use. Bakhtin's view of epic, however, is profoundly mistaken. He asserts that 'the represented world of the heroes stands on an utterly different and inaccessible time-and-value plane' from our own and that 'there is no place in the epic world for any openendedness, indecision, indeterminacy'.[4] I believe that, however one calculates their ideological bottom lines, any open-minded reading of the six epics covered here will reveal Bakhtin's description to be a foil contrived to enhance what he takes to be the contrasting dialogic brilliance of the novel. Whatever their ultimate message may be, these works are filled with discursive tensions, conflicts, indeterminacies, and a recurring theme of the chapters that follow will be the relentless questioning and challenging that lies at the heart of epic's didactic rhetoric. The problem of the one and the many is a defining element in all areas of Greek thought in the centuries after Homer. The ancient Greeks acknowledged both the analytic power of this opposition and the ultimate indeterminacy of thought conducted using it. Homer too would likely assume that the monologic inevitably reveals its dialogism, the dialogic its monologism. The genre he founded certainly does. Despite our extremely limited knowledge of epic and its predecessor genres and analogues before Homer, it is probably safe to say that it is this characteristically Hellenic habit of thought that turned epic from a celebratory into an intellectually exploratory genre.

The title of this book contains an explanation for its selection of poems to examine. This is not a comprehensive history of the epic genre, but a description of a tradition that evolved through a small number of key texts that actively, one is tempted to say heroically, reworked their generic inheritance and then passed it on, greatly enhanced, to their successors. Many figures that might have been included are not for purely practical reasons of scale, both the scale of my own discussion and the scale of their contributions. Both reasons must suffice for Roman epics after Vergil, the medieval and Renaissance experiments and accomplishments in heroic poetry before Ariosto, and English works that contribute distinctive features to the *Faerie Queene* and *Paradise Lost*. Apollonius' audaciously innovative *Argonautica* deserves a place in any history of epic and could easily have found extensive mention here. If the poem had not been written, the *Aeneid* and therefore the rest of literary history would be significantly different. But Apollonius' innovations were largely passed on through Vergil, and his inclusion would add little but historical continuity and comprehensiveness to my account. Nor could the diligent historian ignore Ovid, whose undeniable influence on the epics of Ariosto, Spenser and Milton has received considerable attention.[5] I find Ovid's influence on Renaissance deployments of the epic chronotope to be real but relatively minor. His example was more useful to Renaissance theorists engaged in 'proclaiming a classic' than to poets seeking enabling innovations for their further innovations.[6] Dante enters the discussion through Ariosto, where I believe his influence was most felt, by Spenser at least, though much more could be said about his pioneering recasting of epic structures. There is also a national bias to my selection. Although Ariosto fills half of a chapter, the tradition I am tracing is basically classical and English. Like the Hydra fought by Arthur in his first appearance in the *Faerie Queene*, this book could easily grow two heads if it were severed after the discussion of *Orlando Furioso*. The English countenance it presently displays reflects a conviction that the Reformation produced a divergence in epic's evolution. There is no question that Milton was enormously influenced by Tasso's *Gerusalemme Liberata*. Aspects of this influence have been well described by Judith Kates and others, and the more limited terms of my analysis do not offer rewards commensurate with the Herculean labour required to evaluate the poem's place in the tradition.[7] Were it to grow a second head, this book would devote to Tasso's beautiful and complex epic the space it deserves. It would then proceed to Marino's *Adone*, a poem as frustrating for the modern reader as it is suggestive about the dynamics of generic evolution and interaction.

Portions of chapter 3 originally appeared in *Annali d'Italianistica*, portions of chapter 5 in *Renaissance and Reformation* and *Essays in Literature*. I wish to thank the editors of those journals for permission to reprint those materials here.

Notes

1. This type of spatiality is described most systematically and abstractly in Mircea Eliade (1959), pp. 20-65. Among Eliade's numerous treatments, see also 1988, pp. 105-29 for the world-wide architectural manifestations of omphalic space. Jonathan Smith (1987) offers the most searching critique of Eliade's concepts and the whole issue of sacred spatiality, especially in its biblical forms. For a cross-cultural survey and additional bibliography, see the collection of essays by Holm and Bowker (1994). Scully (1990) includes exhaustive bibliography on the ancient Near East.
2. Barry Schwartz's *Vertical Classification* (1981) is the basic sociological study.
3. Stallybrass (1991), p. 205.
4. Bakhtin (1981), pp. 14-16. Bakhtin most fully develops his notion of the generic chronotope in a subsequent chapter (pp. 84-258).
5. Richard DuRocher (1985) considers Milton's use of Ovid. He also glances at Spenser's use of the *Metamorphoses* (pp. 203-16). On the latter subject, see also the important work of Louis Martz (1980, pp. 203-44). Daniel Javitch (1984, p. 1029) argues that Ariosto was 'inspired by Ovid's revisions of the *Aeneid*'; see also Javitch (1978).
6. The uses made of Ovid by defenders of Ariosto engaged in 'proclaiming a classic' is the subject of Javitch (1991), chapter 4.
7. For example, by Lindsay Waters (1981), Judith Kates (1983), Roy Eriksen (1991) and David Reid (1991).

CHAPTER ONE

Homeric Origins

The *Iliad* and the Norms of Epic

The paradigmatic epic of western culture establishes its system of vertical classification quickly and emphatically. Although Achilles later regrets quarrelling with Agamemnon 'about a girl' (19.58), the conflict that opens the *Iliad* is really about who will 'rule over' whom. Forms of the spatialized vocabulary of 'ruling over' (*anasso*), containing the most basic Greek term for 'up' (*ana*), recur in this opening scene with a frequency unmatched elsewhere in the Homeric corpus. When Agamemnon rejects Chryses' offer of ransom for his captive daughter, the priest calls on 'king' ('anakti', 1.36) Apollo who 'rules over' ('anasseis', 38) Tenedos to avenge the injustice. He reminds the god that he dutifully roofed over his shrine and sent burnt offerings heavenward, stressing the vertical aspect of the power struggle, which will be decided by the strength of the participants' Olympian influence. Apollo sends plague to punish the Greeks, and the fact that punishment comes from the god 'who strikes from afar' ('eke-bolou', 1.14) helps Homer to initiate what will be a long-standing generic feature: a focus on the problem of causality. Achilles pledges to protect the seer Calchas, who announces that Agamemnon's offence has caused the god's wrath. Insulted by the challenge to his authority, Agamemnon tauntingly suggests that Achilles return home, where he can 'rule over' ('anasse', 180) his Myrmidons. Achilles responds that Agamemnon 'rules over nonentities' ('outidanoisin anasseis', 231) whose cowardly submissiveness has encouraged their king's arrogance. Nestor, who after living among two previous generations of superior heroes now 'rules over' ('anassen', 252) a third generation of lesser men, and who therefore can speak with unique authority, reminds Achilles that Agamemnon is a sceptered king who 'rules over' ('anassei', 281) a larger realm. Agamemnon charges that Achilles wants to 'rule over' ('anassein', 288) everyone. The chaotic degeneration of the Greek command ends when Agamemnon re-establishes a hierarchy, yielding to Chryses and compensating himself by taking Briseis, the captive maiden of Achilles. Achilles responds by translating figural spatiality into physical gestures that express both continued defiance and an end to this episode of one-upmanship. He dashes the sceptre to the ground, indicating his 'rejection of the royal authority and a break in the solidarity of the group'.[1] In assembly the vertically held sceptre is passed hand to hand to attendees as they are given the right to speak. Achilles' dramatic gesture both disrupts the social bond that passing it to another would continue and mimics the violent overturning that he is growing ever more tempted to inflict upon Agamemnon himself.

As the scene shifts skyward this vertical emphasis continues. Thetis rises from the depths of the sea, confers with her angry son, and ascends to where Zeus sits apart on the 'highest peak' ('akrotate koruphe', 1.499) of many-ridged Olympus. Graphically portrayed in the formal posture of supplication, holding the sky-god's knees with her left hand and reaching up to his chin with her right, Thetis pleads for a remedy and Zeus responds with a solemn nod of approbation, a gesture indicating reciprocation without the abdication of dominance.[2] Then in what G. S. Kirk labels 'a slightly inelegant zeugma', Thetis 'leapt into the deep sea from shining Olympus, Zeus into his own palace' (532-3).[3] The construction may be unusual, but its very inelegance keeps our attention directed toward the vertical dimension. Following Zeus' descent, 'all the gods rose up / from their chairs to greet the coming of their father, not one had courage / to keep his place as the father advanced, but stood up to greet him' (533-5). The action conspicuously mediates between two other scenes of standing and sitting: Achilles' sitting down in angry submission after he slams the sceptre down and Agamemnon's rising in dominance to address the assembly at the opening of Book 2. Terms are rearranged here as rising rather than sitting signifies submission, as if Homer wants us to be alert to both the vertical constants and the contexts in which these can take various forms, but in all three cases vertical change of posture is used to signify hierarchical order.[4] When Hera questions her irritable husband about Thetis' supplication, Zeus orders her to sit down in silence. Hephaestos urges her compliance, for he has felt the full impact of the thunderer's will to dominance. He reminds her of an earlier offence for which, as Book 15 (18-31) reveals, Zeus hung her from the sky with anvils on her feet. When Hephaestos tried to assist her,

> he caught me by the foot and threw me from the magic threshold;
> and all day long I dropped helpless, and about sunset
> I landed in Lemnos, and there was not much life left in me. (1.591-3)

In heaven as on earth, Homer's opening book teaches us with copious reinforcement, power relations are measured by relative vertical position.

The combination of spatial vocabulary and gesture returns in the following book when the descent of Agamemnon's royal sceptre is traced to justify his position atop the governing hierarchy:

> ... Powerful Agamemnon
> stood up holding the sceptre Hephaistos had wrought him carefully.
> Hephaistos gave it to Zeus the king, the son of Kronos,

and Zeus in turn gave it to the courier Argeïphontes,
and lord Hermes gave it to Pelops, driver of horses,
and Pelops again gave it to Atreus, the shepherd of the people.
Atreus dying left it to Thyestes of the rich flocks,
and Thyestes left it in turn to Agamemnon to carry
and to be lord of many islands and over all Argos.
Leaning on this sceptre he spoke and addressed the Argives.
(2.100-9)

'Ana' first appears as a free-standing adverb when Agamemnon stands 'up', then is woven into Zeus' status as 'king' ('anakri') and Hermes' as 'lord' ('anax'), and finally into the claim to 'be lord over' ('anassein') a vast domain. The catalogue implies that in rising Agamemnon is not just one man among many who might take the floor in assembly, but is visually enacting the claim to pre-eminence implicit in the continuity between Zeus who rules over all and his counterpart on earth. There are also problems here that seem designed to keep our attention directed to vertical distinctions. The discrepancy between 'all Argos' and the more limited domain assigned Agamemnon in the Catalogue of Ships (559-80) is one that Achilles must be pondering as intently as later generations of scholars have. A related crux, long wished away by commentators, concerns the contradiction between Hermes in his usual function as herald and his characterization as lord, which occurs only here.[5] The passage begins as a tale of divine fabrication and descent from Olympus, but transforms itself in mid-flight, as it were, into a royal genealogy, introducing in one swift and troubling stroke the heavenly descent and the dynastic genealogy as interrelated generic features of epic.[6] Supported by parallel structure, the characterization of Hermes as lord has the effect of extending a continuous dynastic lineage back to Zeus himself, strengthening the sense that Agamemnon's claim to imperial sway is natural and exclusive. The problems may of course be products of faulty composition or transmission, the last refuge of the desperate monologist, and our interpretations can only remain tentative: is the narrator shamelessly playing propagandist for Agamemnon, and if so does he wish us to observe his sleight of hand? What is beyond question is Homer's continuing interest in the forms and processes of vertical classification.

It is consistent with the vertical language of lordship that dominant cities are formidable citadels characterized by a form of *aipus*, signifying steepness as well as height.[7] Homer applies the term to the walls of Troy (6.327, 11.181), reminding us of the daunting challenge facing the besieging Achaeans, even if they can agree on who rules over whom. If *aipus* recalls the practical military reality underlying imperial sway, *makros* encapsulates its cosmic ideology. The latter term means 'long' when it refers to spears and 'high' when it refers to trees or mountains. When Homer employs it as his favourite epithet for Olympus, translators usually favour 'high' or 'lofty', but it retains as well the idea of vast extension. As the winner of the lottery that divided the world among the three sons of Rheia and Cronos described in 15.185ff., Zeus rules the entire 'wide-stretching' ('euron', 15.192) heavenly plane from his uppermost seat. Unlike other cities in the poem, Troy has walls characterized by the Olympian epithet ('teixea makra', 4.34), a sign of the interrelated vertical and horizontal dimensions of its imperial grandeur. Priam's city would be recognized as an omphalic capital by the audiences of the Epic of Gilgamesh or the Book of Isaiah.[8] Here as in other Bronze Age cultures the *axis mundi* passing through the sacred city is a visible fact. Imitating the structure of Olympus above, the city is arranged so that the royal family and patron gods inhabit a complex of temples and palaces at 'highest Pergamus' ('pergamo akre', 5.460; 6.512), the city's central acropolis. Height implies sacrality, proximity to the heavenly realm, and sacrality in turn legitimizes imperial expansiveness, for the space outside imperial bounds is profane and chaotic. It is in this important sense that all empires are universal, for an external empire is a contradiction in terms outside the order that only the expansive centre can impose. Long before Ovid indulged Augustan imperial fantasies by declaring that 'the space of the Roman city and the Roman world is the same' ('Romanae spatium est urbis et orbis idem'), the same idea underlies Odysseus' claim for Agamemnon's universal fame, which is 'as widely dispersed beneath the sky as the city was which he destroyed' ('megiston hupouranion kleos esti / tossen gar dieperse polin', *Od.*, 9.264-5).[9] Within the *Iliad*'s realistic dimension the surrounding countryside is populated by various peoples allied to the Trojans, but in its cosmic symbolism the vastness of Troy's walls suggests the imperial reach that embraces these secondary and apparently subject nations, just as its walls now contain their soldiers united to repulse a threat to the Trojan order.

Height similarly implies rule and grandeur on the personal scale. Though realism can intrude to produce contradictions for serious or humorous effect, and the relative shortness of Odysseus is one of the poet's more interesting uses of casting against type, the height of rulers and great warriors allows them to stand out among the crowd.[10] Because the warrior's task is to drive his opponent headlong (*prenes*, from *pro-*, forward + *en*, face) into the dust, this sign of high status is also a provocation, an invitation to cause a spectacular fall.[11] The tall hero who 'rules over', or at least aspires to, possesses a corresponding horizontal reach through his 'great-heartedness'. Because the concept of magnanimity has undergone an involved historical evolution and has been an important epic feature, it is necessary to stress that for Homer the 'great-hearted' terms *megathumos* and *megaletor* do not imply generosity. In the *Odyssey*, the vastly wealthy Neleus, the persecutor of the seer Theoclymenus' forebear, merits being called 'great-hearted' (15.229) not through largesse but through its opposite, his insatiable drive to seize others' goods by force. Since *mega-*, like *makros*, signifies great extent in any dimension, the epithets manage to express a mindset of aggressive territoriality and at the same time can be translated 'high-hearted' or 'proud'. This translation would be especially appropriate on the battlefield, where the terms can enhance a taunt or indicate a provocation to heroic one-upmanship. Unsatisfied with his brother's response to the fall of a companion, Ajax observes, 'now great-hearted Hector has killed him. Where are your arrows of sudden death?' (15.440-1). Hector's own great heart will brook no competition, and when he sees the wounded but 'great-hearted' (16.818) Patroclus trying to escape, the epithet helps to explain the vehemence with which he slays him.

Homer establishes the horizontal parameters of the space ordered around the Trojan axis systematically, but more gradually than the vertical parameters. Excavations reveal that Troy was organized on a radial basis around the high citadel, following a typical Bronze Age urban form.[12] The *Iliad* manifests the ordering power of the cosmic axis by reducing motion within Troy to centripetal and centrifugal: what really matters occurs at either the wall or the central acropolis, and within the city the only motion meriting description is passage from one to the other. Similarly, for the Greeks on the surrounding plain the only motion that matters is radial progress toward or away from Troy. Books 6-7 can serve as a convenient text for considering how the poem makes horizontal distinctions. As the Trojans retreat following the *aristeia* of Diomedes, Nestor exhorts the Danaans not to 'hang back' ('metopisthe', 6.68) to strip armour, but to continue pressing ahead. Hector then reverses the Trojan retreat by inspiring the troops to 'turn and stand facing' ('elelichthesan kai enantioi estan', 106) the Argives, who now 'give way backward' ('hupechopesan', 107). Following this rapid alternation of directions, Hector returns to the city to seek more divine help while the battle rages. He is next seen before the Scaean gate (237), then entering Priam's palace at the city's central temple-palace complex on Pergamus (242), where he prays to Athena at her temple 'on the peak of the citadel' (297), and visits the palace of Paris. Learning that his wife has gone to the gate, he hastens 'backward the same way' ('auten hodon autis', 391) over the well-built streets to the gate. Despite her plea that he remain inside, he goes to battle while Andromache returns homeward 'often turning back' ('entropalizomene', 496) to gaze. Meanwhile, Paris has 'come down from high Pergamus' (512) and the two brothers sweep out from the gate, appearing to their cohorts like a fair wind to weary seamen (7.4-7), propelling them once more toward the Greeks. Seeing their success, Athena descends from Olympus, landing at the oak tree outside the gate. Apollo sees her as he 'looks down from Pergamus' (21) and rushes out to meet her. The advantage in battle shifts back and forth. In its repetitive combat, as David Quint rightly comments, the *Iliad* 'suggests unending warfare' and descends into a kind of historical unintelligibility.[13] But out of the larger movements of this mêlée there also arises a clarification of the hero's relationship to the space he inhabits. All horizontal action, indeed all perception, takes place on a line drawn through Pergamus, the gate, and the Greek encampment. It is precisely this rigorous restriction that allows us to experience the peculiarly Homeric pathos of warfare that, despite its remarkable energy and variety, remains almost hopelessly repetitive.

As the exemplary Nestor and Hector demonstrate in this sequence, a primary duty of the Homeric hero is to keep himself and his forces moving in the right direction along this line. If the vertical dimension is epic's clearest register of power and value, horizontal action is where the genre most fully encodes ethical imperatives in spatio-temporal terms. The imperative to penetrate to the centre, or to resist this penetration, makes epic time strongly teleological; it is concerned with tracing a linear trajectory from one known point to another. This teleological aspect of epic has recently become a critical commonplace, especially where epic, usually the journey variant rather the siege variant modelled on the *Iliad*, is placed in opposition to non-teleological, repetitive 'romance'.[14] But it is in fact in the *Iliad*, the poem that establishes the basic generic norms of epic, that forward orientation and progress become the essential heroic rule. The idea pervades the poem's vocabulary and action. Achilles first breaks into speech to express alarm that the Greeks will be 'driven backwards' ('palimplagchthentas', 1.59) if they do not propitiate offended Apollo. Warriors acquire heroic status by being 'forward fighters' (*promachoi*) and 'the foremost' (*protoi*). They emulate Hector who, as his wife attests, would 'never stay back where the men were in numbers / but break out far in front' ' ('protheeske', 22.459). Columns of men are called *stikhes*, which is related to *steikho*, 'to move forward'. Those who don't live up to the ideal encoded in this lexicon of forwardness are shirkers who shamefully 'stand off' (*aphestanai*). The announced subject of the poem, the wrath of Achilles, takes on significance in the overall plot only to the extent that it either prevents him from moving forward, leaving him standing off in his tent while others establish their heroic credentials, or with the death of Patroclus motivates him, as he puts it, to be seen once again 'among the front fighters' ('meta protoisin', 15.151).[15]

The vertical and horizontal fundamentals of omphalic space generate a set of secondary features that poets beginning with Homer incorporated into epic's generic system. The opposition of right and left, to choose an example prominently featured throughout the genre's history, is not a piece of free-standing symbolism, although it is often discussed as if it were.[16] The gesture of supplication, which requires that first the left hand embrace the knees and then the right hand reach for the chin, reveals how conventions of augury, which viewed omens on the right as propitious, are incorporated into a larger chronotopic system. Epic not only values, but defines as two mutually implied aspects of the same event, vertical ascent and the horizontal approach to the centre. In epic up and down, central and peripheral, forward and backward, right and left are all homologous oppositions, interrelated components of a coherent 'table of opposites'. As Emile Benveniste explains, the Greek term for suppliant, *hiketes*, 'is derived from the verb *hiko*, to come, arrive'.[17] The suppliant's relationship to the giver of mercy structurally mirrors the hero's relationship to the omphalic centre, the high point he strives to approach. The suppliant's embrace is a movement inward, upward and from left to right. The coherence of the larger chronotopic system grows clearer when we observe that favourable omens on the right signify progress in the quest for, or defence of, the centre (e.g. 9.236, 9.274. 9.320, 13.821). Similarly, motion from left to right, as when Hephaistos pours drinks beginning from the left (1.597) and when the herald compares lots proceeding from left to right in the Achaean assembly (7.184), sustains proper hierarchical order. Understanding the homologous nature of oppositions in the epic system helps us to understand as well how Homer can avoid Bakhtin's alleged monologism. Consider Hector's dismissal of the eagle that appears on the left as he prepares to lead the charge across the defensive ditch of the Achaean camp in Book 12. The unpropitious nature of the omen is clear, and Polydamus recommends a prudent pause. But Hector is rising to his personal height of heroic forward momentum, and by the book's end he will smash spectacularly through the Greek gate with a huge stone. Now he threatens to kill Polydamus if he should 'turn away' ('parthamenos') from battle or cause others to 'turn away' ('apotropseis', 249). In pressing forward despite a clear warning from the gods, is Hector being courageous, or rash, or somehow both? Andromache's description of Hector's drive to break out far in front, it will be recalled, comes after Hector has been slain, reminding us that the heroic imperative can err through excess. Every reader's answer and ultimate assessment of Hector will depend upon a variety of factors, but it is important to recognize that large ethical questions are being posed through the clash of oppositions that the poem has framed as homologies. Homer's heroic code is quite simple in its parameters but not in their application.

Linear motion directed centripetally or centrifugally finds its most basic opposites in unheroic reversal of direction, halting in mid-course, standing off or swerving aside. Two other forms of motion, to-and-fro and circular, also figure prominently in the *Iliad* and *Odyssey* in ways that later epics will develop. Both come in positive and negative versions. Early in the *Iliad* the to-and-fro motion of armies can be positive. The poem's very first set of extended similes compares both forces to a variety of animals swarming 'here and there' ('hai men . . . hau de', 2.90; cf. 462 and 470). Here Homer registers awe at the vastness of the assembling forces, who fill up the available space as a horizontal sign of their leaders' sway, and at the momentous nature of the events about to occur. The closely related lexicon of 'wandering' (*phoiton*) is also employed positively early in the epic, as when Menelaus 'ranges through the ranks' ('homilon ephoita', 3.449) like a wild beast searching for Paris, who is in bed cavorting with Helen.[18] His motion has a lateral component, but he also continues progressing in the right direction. Later in the poem, as we shall see, this kind of motion unambiguously indicates a lack of control that even in these early instances may be present as ironic undercutting of the primary message. The circle embodies cosmic order in the course of encircling Ocean, the cycles of years and days, the paths of the stars. Human imitations include Achilles leading his Myrmidons in procession around the tomb of Patroclus (23.12ff.), the 'sacred circle' ('hiero . . . kuklo', 18.504) of consulting elders, and the warrior's round shield — the shield of Achilles, with its depiction of a cosmos in plenitude, makes the macro-microcosmic correspondence explicit.[19] Achilles ominously parodies his own pious example when he drags the body of Hector around Patroclus' tomb (24.14ff.), outraging not only the squeamish modern reader but most of the gods observing from above as well. Hector's circling flight around Troy with Achilles in pursuit contrasts with his earlier, rigorously rectilinear behaviour on the battlefield. As Achilles in Book 22 speeds across the plain on a 'straight course' ('ithus', 143) toward him, Hector stands steadfastly alone outside the gate, ignoring his parents' plea that he come inside the walls; that would be precisely the kind of swerving from battle for which he has threatened to kill Polydamus. But in a moment of weakness Hector does swerve, and this type of unheroic motion becomes another, establishing a precedent for the circular motion that in later epic will represent a shameful abandonment of the heroic path. Following this spectacular chase, circular imagery becomes more personal and problematic. After Hector's death Priam, as he himself tells Achilles, remains sleepless and 'rolls' ('koulindetai', 22.414, 24.165, 24.640) in the muck in his courtyard brooding over his sorrows. In this motion he echoes the sleepless Achilles, who 'revolves' ('estrephet', 24.5) in bed thinking of his past with Patroclus, and then finds relief only in dragging the body around his beloved friend's tomb.[20] Beyond the clear oppositions of warring Greek and Trojan forces, all parties are being rolled together by fate.

In making restless Achilles not merely revolve, but revolve 'this way and that' ('entha kai entha', 24.5), using one of his interchangeable formulas for to-and-fro motion, Homer adds even more ironic linkages between characters.[21] This kind of motion has evolved in the course of the poem into the diachronic manifestation of the crooked, a category that Zeus assigns to the negative side of the table of opposites when he condemns men who make 'crooked' ('skolias', 16.387) judgements in the agora. In its most recent occurrence before this, Nestor used the to-and-fro formula negatively, contrasting the skill or *metis* of the successful helmsman and charioteer who can keep on a straight course ('ithunei', 23.317; cf. Achilles' 'ithus' toward Hector) with one who wanders 'here and there' (320). With Nestor's precepts in mind, Marcel Detienne and Jean-Pierre Vernant describe the importance of this navigational skill for both Homer and ancient Greek culture in general:

> To direct, to correct, to guide a straight course, *ithunein*, are commonplace expressions in the terminology connected with navigation but by their very banality they stress the importance in the art of the pilot of the combination of skill in foreseeing where the route lies and the ability to keep one's sights set on one's ultimate destination. Despite the roundabout, oblique or tortuous path dictated by the shifting of the wind, the intelligence of the navigator is capable of guiding the ship straight, never deviating from the course decided upon in advance.[22]

The *metis* of the Trojans fails them when they are driven by Achilles into the river Xanthus, where they chaotically swim 'this way and that' and are 'spun' ('helissomenoi', 21.11) in the eddies. This lexical web contributes to a growing sense that the fates of characters are progressing outside the ordered causality they and we understand. The punishment of the Trojans in the river is inflicted on sleepless Achilles. Their punishment in turn can be seen as payment in kind for the bizarre mistreatment of Patroclus' corpse. The arrival of Ajax in Book 17 forces Hector to cease trying to decapitate his fallen foe, but the day-long battle enacts a substitute mutilation, for Patroclus is pulled by both parties 'this way and that' (17.395). Again distinctions blur as responsibility for this unintended outrage falls to neither party, but to the simple, brutal fact of war itself. In the bleak vision of the final books undirected motion consistently suggests an ominously spreading breakdown in the capacity to impose order. It is the indecisive to-and-fro of nine years' combat writ small in a world dominated by the second of Zeus' two urns, the one from which he sends bane, driving men wandering ('phoita', 24.533) over the face of the earth.

A common factor in the opposition of ruler and ruled and the opposition of repetitive actions and a course maintained through *metis*, themes respectively opening and closing the *Iliad*, is the relation of the part to the whole, the many to the one. Aristotle in the *Poetics* praises Homer for producing one large action out of many; through omitting incidents between which there was no necessary or probable connection, 'he constructed his *Odyssey* round a single action in our sense of the phrase. And the *Iliad* the same'.[23] Of course this is an insight a reader can arrive at only after the protracted labour of assembling details into coherence. The reader's labour parallels that of the hero within the text, who must find the will to, or understand how to, integrate his efforts into the collective action. At least since Bruno Snell argued that the early Greeks had no concept denoting the individual as a psychic whole, statements like the following by Jan Bremmer, based largely on an analysis of Homer, have become commonplace: 'the early Greeks, like other Indo-European peoples, did not primarily consider themselves to be independent individuals but rather members of a group'.[24] Bremmer's 'primarily' partially redeems his observation, but this implicit acknowledgement that the individual / group dichotomy is not an either / or opposition is still misleading. For Homer the hero is always both an individual and a member of a group, and these two aspects of existence are often in conflict. The founding author of the epic genre does not simply proceed with his story in a world where the group's primacy over the individual could be assumed, but repeatedly poses the relationship between the two as a problem.

The problem of one and many in Homeric warfare can be approached most economically by considering contradictory recollections by Nestor and Odysseus. Nestor recalls that on Achilles' departure for Troy Peleus enjoined his son 'to be always best in battle and pre-eminent above all others' (11.784). In this straightforward definition of the heroic imperative, Peleus assumes that to be best ('aristeyein') is logically connected with vertical superiority ('upeirokhon', from *uper* or 'above'), though he does not specify the precise nature of this connection. Odysseus, in contrast, recalls Peleus recommending, 'but curb your proud spirit within your breast, for friendly-mindedness is better' (9.255-6). Cooperative friendly-mindedness ('philophrosune') is here opposed to the proud — or most literally both 'high' and 'extensive' — spirit ('megaletora') that strives for pre-eminence above all others.[25] As the discussions among the Greek leaders in Book 9 focus on how Achilles might be reconciled, the argument over who will 'rule over' whom that dominates Book 1 is replaced by arguments over Achilles' pride, which is characterized repeatedly as *mega* (cf. 109, 496, 675). In Homer's own terms, if the Greek effort is to succeed, a way must be found to reconcile Achilles' needs to be competitively pre-eminent and cooperatively friendly-minded. We might say that the *Iliad* is about the transformation of Achilles' wrath from an obstacle to reconciling the one and the many into a solution. With the death of Patroclus Achilles re-directs his wrath away from Agamemnon and toward his group's foes. The result is a reconciliation of private and public causes. If Homer allows these causes to diverge again in the excesses that follow the slaying of Hector, this separation reminds us that the reconciliation is inevitably difficult and unstable.

The epic problem of reconciling the individual and the group is embedded in Homer's rich imagery of discipline. After all the quarrelling and assembling in the Greek camp, a simile opens Book 3 to announce the poem's first engagement in battle:

> Now when the men of both sides were set in order by their leaders,
> the Trojans came on with clamour and shouting, like wildfowl,
> as when the cranes escape the winter time and the rains unceasing
> and clamorously wing their way to the streaming Ocean,
> bringing to the Pygmaian men bloodshed and destruction. (1-6)

Although Homer is justly renowned for his impartiality, his irony at the Trojans' expense is severe at this strategic place in his narrative. The Trojans are at cross-purposes, literally attacking but in figure retreating, defending the centre yet fleeing toward the cosmos-surrounding waters of Ocean. The word for their 'escape' or fleeing, ('phugon', 4) is a favourite Homeric sneer at cowardice, as in 22.1, when the terrified Trojans having 'fled' into the city leave Hector alone outside, and their cacophony is at least as suggestive of just such a terror-driven rout as of an attack. Their representatives within the simile slaughter a diminutive people who contrast with the tall Greeks on the plain. It is no mere accident of formulaic composition that Homer will soon after this simile place Priam and Helen on the wall to marvel at 'great' ('megas', 167) Agamemnon and 'great' ('megas') Ajax 'towering above the Argives with his head and broad shoulders' (226-7), while in between these twin towers they descry an Odysseus who is 'shorter by a head' (193) for emphasis and perhaps comic effect. After applying in line 1 of the simile his strongest signifier of spatial order, *kosmethen*, Homer introduces the perennial epic ideal of unanimity when he starkly contrasts the Trojans' disorder with the Greeks' successful integration of part and whole: 'But the Achaian men went silently, breathing valour, / stubbornly minded each in his heart to stand by the others' (8-9). Despite his implied advice to Achilles about maintaining pre-eminence, Nestor has derived from his multi-generational experience an especially fine mode of military organization, one reconciling the urge to be foremost with discipline:

> First he ranged the mounted men with their horses and chariots
> and stationed the brave and numerous foot-soldiers behind them
> to be the bastion of battle, and drove the cowards to the centre

so that a man might be forced to fight even though unwilling.
First he gave orders to the drivers of horses, and warned them
to hold their horses in check and not be fouled in the multitude:
'Let no man in the pride of his horsemanship and his manhood
dare to fight alone with the Trojans in front of the rest of us,
neither let him give ground, since that way you will be weaker'.
(4.297-305)

In discipline and unanimity Nestor's men are inferior only to the
Myrmidons, who lack cowards and whose phalanx is compared to a strong
wall of close-set ('pukinoisi', 16.212) stones. Leading this exemplary force
in Achilles' absence are Patroclus and Automedon, 'both of one mind, to
fight in the forefront' ('hena thumos echontes, / prosthen', 219-20).

This insistence on the value of unity or wholeness transfers easily from
the group to the individual. Intact city walls and disciplined phalanxes
likened to 'close-set' walls find a smaller counterpart in the intact individual warrior, whose armour too is ideally 'close-set'.[26] The formulaic
arming scene, a ritualized assembling of parts which usually forms a prelude to the warrior's *aristeia*, manufactures piece by piece epic's ultimate
emblem of the integral individual.[27] When the warrior issues forth in his
close-set armour, his job is of course to destroy the integrity of enemy warriors, phalanxes, and enclosures. Epic's concern with individual integrity is
displayed in the gruesome anatomical detail of its battle scenes, in which
warriors are not simply dispatched but mutilated with relish.[28] Epic heroes
are obsessed with such violation. Although eager to mutilate their foes,
epic armies will also postpone the carnage to bury the dead, to prevent
their dismemberment by the carrion dogs and birds that haunt every hero's
imagination. The thematic importance of these animals is suggested by
their inclusion in the *Iliad*'s opening sentence. Homer's physiology of internal, 'psychological' organs opposes the intact, well-fitted, functioning
composite to the dissolute, dysfunctional organism. Norman Austin rightly
comments that 'it is in the descriptions of physiological dissolution, in fact,
that we have the clearest representation of the living person as an organic
whole'.[29] Represented by the collapse into liquidity, an image that will play
a prominent role in epic tradition, this dissolution is caused by physical attack, by what we would now call genetic predisposition, or by fear, as when
frightened Priam's *noos*, that mysterious mental organ, 'flowed together'
('chuto', 24.358) when he encountered Hermes on the way to Achilles'
tent, an internal condition corresponding to his external 'loose' ('gnamp-
toisi', 359) limbs.[30] As Austin explains, in Homer 'a man's body is a piece of
construction that disintegrates when struck at a vital point, or when subjected to violent emotional shock, as when Ate took Patroklos' *phrenes* and
unloosed his limbs (*Il.*, 16.806). In the same way, the individual mental organs are imagined as structures that can disintegrate under shock'.[31]

Within the non-corporealized aspect of mental activity orderly unity is equally desired. Ratiocination in Homer begins as self-division and ends in a single act of will. Achilles establishes the paradigm at the peak of his opening quarrel:

> . . . And the anger came on Peleus' son, and within
> his shaggy breast the heart was divided two ways, pondering
> whether to draw from beside his thigh the sharp sword, driving
> away all those who stood between and kill the son of Atreus,
> or else to check the spleen within and keep down his anger.
>   (1.188-92)

His better judgement prevails in the form of descending Athena, who recommends the latter alternative. Homer's two interchangeable words for pondering, *mermerizo* and *ormaino*, are usually translated to indicate 're-volving in the mind', but this is an anachronistic distortion of their true connotations in the *Iliad*, as is 'pondering' as well, with its implied metaphor of weighing, though the scale image amplifies a pondering-of-al-ternatives scene in 16.658. Related to *mermeros*, which means 'such as to cause anxiety, baneful, evil', the first term (which is used in 1.189) captures the anxiety of the Homeric ponderer, who invariably performs this mental action in response to a perceived threat to himself or to someone he cares for. 'Mermerizo' is often teamed with the spatial term *diandikha* (*dia-*, 'across', + *andicha*, 'asunder'), a pairing that associates anxiety with a mind divided in two, as we might expect from Homer's habit of representing mental debate over two defined alternatives. One might say that the thinking warrior pre-emptively self-divides figuratively before suffering or inflicting this fate literally. The second term derives from *ormao*, whose meaning ranges from a very general 'incite, urge' to a specifically military 'rush, make an onslaught'. It captures not the cause of pondering, but the effect, which is to translate the divided mind caused by a threat into a res-olution and then into an action. As in the example of Achilles confronting Agamemnon, this action most often consists of destroying, or refraining from destroying, another individual's integral self.[32]

It is but a short conceptual leap from removing self-division through pondering and maintaining a straight course through navigational *metis* to the process signified by the peculiar Homeric term *suntithemai*. Readers familiar with Homer only in translation will be surprised to find that a word always translated as something like 'hearken' or 'take thought' or 'consider' is the origin of our 'synthesis' and literally means 'put together'. In the *Iliad* it indicates the fact that one has made, or a request that one make, an important inferential connection. Mysteriously hearing the voices of the gods (7.53), the seer Helenos 'puts together' (7.44) the plan discussed by Athena and Apollo to rouse Hector to single combat. Homer associates prescience, navigational *metis* and this kind of putting together when he introduces Calchas, who 'knew what was, and was to be, and had been, / who guided into the land of Ilion the ships of the Achaians / through that seercraft of his own that Phoibos Apollo gave him' (1.70-2). Understandably cautious when he introduces his diagnosis of the plague's cause, the seer asks Achilles to 'consider' (1.76) or literally 'put together' his public accusation of Agamemnon, a plea that Achilles understand his need for protection. Achilles is up to the task of assembling the seer's full meaning, the causal sequence that he intervenes to prevent. The term's only two appearances in the *Iliad* not involving seers are even more revealing of the way Homer's characters engage in mental assembly. Paris tells Hector to 'put together' ('suntheo') his lame excuse for staying in his room with Helen after his ignominious disappearance from the battle-field: 'It was not so much in coldness and bitter will toward the Trojans / that I sat in my room, but I wished to give myself over to sorrow' (6.334-6). Apparently unable or unwilling to put this together, Hector makes no response and departs. How, after all, could he respond to such an irrelevancy? A similar instance occurring on the other side of the battle line furthers the suggestion that non-seer heroes may be willing to demand this challenging mental assembly by their listeners only when they desperately need a way to save face. Even after we make allowances for changing values, Agamemnon is clearly outrageous when he tells Achilles and the others assembled to 'put together my discourse' ('sunthesth . . . muthon', 19.84), to be persuaded by what he says to excuse him for quarrelling over the captive maidens. When he blames Ate, Delusion, for his error, the psychological allegory holds together. But the example he offers presents unusual challenges for assembling his words into a coherent excuse. In a provocative return to the language of the opening quarrel, he tells of Zeus blinded by Ate in the service of Hera, who manages to twist Zeus' proclamation that his descendant born that day 'shall be lord over all those dwelling about him' (19.105 and repeated in 109). Zeus seems to intend that his son Hercules begin his traditional role as *kosmokrator*, world-ruler, but Hera delays his birth and has the more distantly related Eurystheus born early to 'rule over' the Argives (124) — and over Hercules, who must take up the Labours for an inferior king. The parallel between Hercules' subjection to Eurystheus and his own to Agamemnon is so close that Achilles cannot fail to put them together, and we are left wondering just what kind of mental assembly allows him not to take offence. Perhaps he yields to the gods over human standards of justice; Agamemnon's speech would then assemble nicely with his genealogy stretching back to Zeus. Perhaps his dismissive 'it is not fitting to stay here and waste time' (19.149) indicates that he is no longer interested in merely verbal one-upmanship and therefore parallels Hector's eloquent silence. We should note also that the story requires further assembly with other passages that have been left hanging with question-provoking incompleteness: with Zeus' punishment of Hera for this deceit (15.14ff.) and of Hephaistos for trying to help her (1.586ff.). Homer has extended a narrative sequence and causal chain backward through three widely separated passages, placing severe demands that his audience stretch to comprehend an event not directly related to the war. In his first introduction into epic, Hercules brings with him new demands for mental assembly, a role that he will continue in the genre for centuries.[33]

The *Iliad*, it is no exaggeration to say, consists of interrelated variations on the theme of wholeness and division carried out on multiple scales and levels. Consider only the principal turns in the war between the opening quarrel and Achilles' return to the collective effort. The initial Greek effort falters while Achilles sulks and his Myrmidons 'wandered to and fro through the camp, not fighting' ('phoiton entha kai entha kata straton oude machonto', 2.779), their motions adding up to nothing while their fellow contingents speed with unified purpose across the plain. When the disciplined Myrmidons join the effort under Patroclus, the Greeks are but one step — the participation of their foremost warrior — away from complete unity. The success this enhanced unity brings them causes division or unity to become the issue debated urgently on high. Zeus declares 'my heart is divided in two in counsel as I ponder' ('dichtha de moi kradn memone phrenin ormainonti', 16.435) sparing Sarpedon or allowing this favourite to be slain. Hera notes that removing him from battle would mean breaking ranks with the other gods, who might also be tempted to intervene. When Zeus opts for divine solidarity over intervention, Sarpedon falls to Patroclus like an oak felled to become a ship's timber (16.484), a proud unity destroyed to become a subordinate part in a whole that represents eventual Greek success. His corporeal integrity dissolves as his lungs come out with the spear and the Greeks strive to 'work shame upon his body' (559). Watching the ensuing battle Zeus once more becomes self-divided and ponders ('mermerison', 647) the fate of Patroclus, then reconciles competing demands by promoting an appropriate unity on both sides: he grants continued military success to the unified Greeks but he also orders Apollo to restore Sarpedon's physical integrity. Now it is Hector's turn to grow divided in mind (712), pondering whether to retreat or advance until Apollo bids him seek out Patroclus. Patroclus' death is handled with great care to emphasize the dissolving integrity of his armour. First Apollo knocks his helmet to the ground, 'as if it stands for the hero's own head lying in the dust'.[34] Next come the shield and corslet, as Homer reverses the standard sequence of his arming scenes.

Following the disarming of Achilles' alter ego, Homer provides us with elaborate images of recovered unity in the newly forged armour of Achilles and the second grand council where, with Achilles willing to 'put together' Agamemnon's face-saving excuse, the Greek leaders reconcile. From here the poem moves steadily toward Trojan defeat and dispersal, even if it never arrives.

The Revisionary *Odyssey*

When the author of the *Odyssey* returns the Achaean heroes to their homes, he retains the chronotopic terms of the earlier epic: the forward pressing hero, the centre-periphery structure of omphalic space, the vertical axis as an index of power and value, the recurring problem of the one and the many.[35] But as readers have long noticed, no doubt from the very beginning, this poet is intent on revising and questioning values contained in the *Iliad*. This revisionary effort is nowhere more evident than in the two appearances of the earlier poem's central hero. When Odysseus encounters the shade of Achilles in Hades, the language of 'ruling over' once again comes to the fore. To the living hero's attempt to console his fallen comrade by pointing to his lordly position among the dead, Achilles responds:

> O shining Odysseus, never try to console me for dying.
> I would rather follow the plow as thrall to another
> man, one with no land allotted him and not much to live on,
> than be a king over all the perished dead. (11.488-91)

In the voluminous commentary on the passage, it appears to have gone unremarked that this speech recalls the opening quarrel of the *Iliad*. Achilles' dissatisfaction with universal 'rule over' the shades ironically echoes both Agamemnon's accusation that Achilles would 'rule over' everyone and Achilles' response that Agamemnon 'rules over' nonentities. The problem now is that success in the game of one-upmanship means nothing when both superior and subordinate are nonentities. The grand epic project of vertical classification has become irrelevant for Achilles, a sentiment he expresses in the mutually cancelling 'up' (*ana-*) and 'down' (*kata-*) of his striking phrase for 'rule over the dead', 'kataphthimenoisin anassein'. The issue is again foregrounded when the shades of the slain suitors hear Achilles addressing Agamemnon:

> Son of Atreus, we thought that all your days you were favored
> beyond all other heroes by Zeus who delights in the thunder,
> because you were lord over numerous people, and strong ones,
> in the land of the Trojans, where we Achaians suffered hardships.
> And yet it was to you that the destructive doom spirit
> would come too early; but no man who is born escapes her.

> How I wish that, enjoying that high place of your power,
> you could have met death and destiny in the land of the Trojans.
> So all the Achaians would have made a mound to cover you,
> and you would have won great glory for your son hereafter. (24.24-33)

'Anasses' emphatically ends both lines 26 and 30. With the former Achilles reminds Agamemnon of their quarrel and offers a mock deference death has made meaningless and therefore palatable. The phrase that ends line 30 and names what Agamemnon would have enjoyed is obscure. One commentator offers 'in enjoyment of the royal honours, the royal state which you held'.[36] I would propose the inelegant but more emphatic 'enjoying your ruling over', for the disillusioned hero is calling attention to the concept itself, to the urge to dominate that once fuelled their conflict. In so doing he questions its continuing validity, and probably not only for the dead.

It should not be surprising to find that the *Odyssey* contains both an abundance of unquestioned references to the inherited epic ideal of royal hierarchy and an unmistakable interrogation of the concept. If the former is both a generic convention and a reflection of Mediterranean reality at the time of composition, the latter responds to the gradual evolution of early Greek citadel culture into the culture of the polis. Vernant describes this change as the substitution of the public agora for the omphalos of 'mythical space':

> Alongside the private, individual houses there is a centre where public matters are debated, and this centre represents all that is 'common', the collectivity as such. In this centre every man is the equal of his fellow, no man is subject to another. . . . This is the birth of a society where one man's relationship with another is conceived in terms of identity, symmetry, reversibility. Human society no longer forms, as it did within the mythical space, a world on different levels with the king at the top and beneath him a whole social hierarchy where status is defined in terms of domination and submission.

The individual hearth, Vernant continues, 'represents, as it were, the omphalos of the house', and with the introduction of the permanent agora, 'a hearth is set up which stands for the political community as a whole'.[37] The *Odyssey* does not introduce the common hearth, but its participation in some intermediate stage of the evolution Vernant describes is evident in its diminished reliance on vertical classification. In a series of literally flatter settings, the hearth, albeit usually the royal hearth, replaces the towering citadel as the omphalic centre, the threshold replaces the city walls as a site of contention, and even the ritual of supplication changes in meaning. Whether Achilles' dissatisfaction with 'ruling over' expresses the poet's approval or disapproval of contemporary trends, and I think it can be read either way, the world the Homeric heroes return to differs significantly from the one they left.

The location in which we first encounter Odysseus, Calypso's Ogygia, appears to be entirely flat. Nevertheless, the island begins gathering omphalic associations as soon as it is introduced. Located at the 'omphalos of the sea' ('omphalos thalasses', 1.50), it is inhabited by a daughter of the axial Atlas, 'who has discovered / all the depths of the sea, and himself sustains the towering / columns which bracket earth and sky and hold them together' (1.52-4). We observe there the arrival of a god from Olympus. But the reader coming to the *Odyssey* from the *Iliad* might well be struck by the fact that Hermes does not descend to the centre, where he could then descend again outward to the periphery in the manner of Apollo. In one example of the poem's new focus upon the horizontal, Hermes does not explicitly descend, but carries out his mission in a way that teases us into noticing its unconventional spatiality:

> He stood on Piera and launched himself from the bright air
> across the sea and sped the wave tops, like a shearwater
> who along the deadly deep ways of the barren salt sea
> goes hunting fish and sprays quick-beating wings in the salt brine.
> (5.50-3)

On arrival Hermes 'stepped out of the dark blue sea, and walked on over the dry land' (5.55-6). The messenger god pauses at the entrance of Calypso's dwelling, enjoying the sights, to be sure, but also reinforcing for us the sense of sacred enclosure. The dwelling is a 'great cave' ('mega speos', 57), with the familiar Homeric modifier now even more polysemous, adding connotations of depth to height and breadth. From the threshold, he looks to Calypso at the hearth, where a great fire blazes, filling the isle with the fragrance of cedar. Even if we miss this subtle suggestion of the cosmogonic outpouring featured in pre-Homeric Near Eastern omphaloi, we soon notice four fountains dispersing water in sundry directions from the goddess' cave (70). As soon as Hermes approaches the centre we learn that Odysseus is oriented in an opposed manner. When we first lay eyes upon the hero, he is seated on the beach weeping and looking out at the barren waters toward his homeland (82ff.). From this prototype of epic counter-centres, we have been informed at the poem's opening, he wishes only 'to catch sight of the smoke leaping up from his land' (1.58-9). The centripetal motion traced on Calypso's isle by Hermes has been defined as centrifugal motion in the hero's quest, and the epic line of action and attraction has been inscribed between the hearth of Ogygia and the hearth of his own great hall.

After his escape from the navel of the sea, Odysseus sails his raft to Skheria, which presents another unique combination of vertical and horizontal: he first sees its 'shadowy mountains' (5.279) and then 'it appeared as a shield on the dark sea' (281). Odysseus' entry into the court of

Alcinous resembles the visit of Hermes to Ogygia in the attention Homer calls to horizontal motion. First there is the much belaboured entrance from sea to land, during which Odysseus must perform two supplications. Arriving at Alcinous' palace Odysseus lingers at the bronze threshold while fifty lines are used to describe his gaze passing across the exterior walls and door, twice 'from the inner room to the door' (87, 96), and on through the courtyard to the seasonless garden with its twin springs emanating water outward. Then he steps lightly over the threshold, presses on to the throne room, begs for help at the queen's knees, and sits down in the ashes of the hearth.

The *Odyssey's* manipulation of the epic chronotope in response to evolving cultural demands is also evident in the new model of supplication introduced in Skheria, a utopian realm where we might expect ideals to be most fully realized. In the *Iliad*, the supplication of Thetis is part of an elaborate demonstration of the vertical supremacy of Zeus, and supplication in the human realm is a desperate and almost always rejected substitute for the defeated warrior's very physical, headlong subjection in the dust. The *Odyssey* points to a change through the repeated supplications of the hero's entrance. First he declares himself a suppliant to the river where he seeks shelter. 'I approach your knees and your current' (5.449), he announces, leaving the reader bemused about the anatomical possibilities. The naked and begrimed hero then prudently chooses not to grasp the knees of Nausicaa, but to declare from a distance, 'I am at your knees, mistress' (6.149). In his next supplication, Odysseus embraces the knees of Arete (7.142). The series provokes comparisons with the earlier epic. In physical incompletion and in the reversal of the gender relations of the *Iliad's* prototypical supplication, these actions indicate that the ritual no longer signifies the kind of voluntary submission that might substitute for martial defeat. The horizontal aspect has become more important than the vertical, the approach of the suppliant and the location at threshold or hearth more significant than the acknowledgement of dominance and submission. Moreover, as the two shoreline interchanges suggest, the poem is replacing literal supplication with a superior, figurative version. Consider also the acceptance by Telemachus of Theoclymenos as a suppliant, which occurs without gesture and consists simply of a declaration followed by an invitation to board the ship returning to Ithaca (15.277). Certainly the power relationship of the participants has changed, for if the suppliant still asks for mercy he also claims a right to inclusion. Victoria Pedrick observes that suppliants in the *Odyssey* are generally successful because they enjoy the protection of Zeus, while 'no warrior in the *Iliad* is ever stopped from rejecting an enemy's pleas for his life by fear of Zeus'. Pedrick describes the situation at Skheria:

The wandering suppliant also has clearly defined rights in this epic. According to Nausikaa, he is entitled to food and whatever else he asks for (6.191-93); her father even apologizes for her lack of courtesy in failing to escort him into the city (7.299). Gifts are also owed to the suppliant, apparently as a sign that he is no longer considered an outcast, but a guest (8.544-47).[38]

In its evolution toward the accessible hearth of the democratic polis, however, the omphalos still preserves forms of hierarchical dominance and submission, as we can see in the fact that the setting where Homer elevates the suppliant's relative position is also the poem's setting that most frequently recalls the *Iliad*'s rigidly hierarchical citadel culture. Alcinous of the 'high-roofed house' is described as 'ruling over' his people more times than any other king.[39] One can only wonder if Odysseus notices a similarly anachronistic combination when he marvels at 'the agoras and the long and wide walls' ('agoras kai teichea makra / hupsela', 7.44-5).

In the last of the three settings defining the hero's trajectory, Odysseus restores order to Ithaca through an elaborately choreographed series of movements inward from the threshold toward the hearth. Arriving at the palace with the swineherd, he first sits down 'on the ashwood threshold, within the doorway' (17.339). After eating, at Telemachus' suggestion he proceeds into the hall, begging from left to right (propitiously clockwise) around the circle of suitors. He receives the suppliant's welcoming 'gift' from Antinous in the form of a thrown footstool, then ends his initial foray by returning to the threshold. Next he must battle the beggar Iros for possession of the threshold. With ironies they cannot appreciate — nor can we fully, until we see the full pattern of his hearth approaches and witness the roasting sausage becoming an image of mental activity — the suitors add as a prize in the contest access to the hearth; the winner can 'come up, and help himself' to a goat paunch roasting at the fire (47). Strangely, as if to emphasize the importance of his final arrival at the centre, Odysseus after his successful combat returns to the threshold, prompting Antinous to bring the sausage to him. He finally completes his movement inward later in the evening when Penelope interviews him from her seat 'close to the fire' (19.55), a location Odysseus specified when arranging the interview with Telemachus (17.571). He repeatedly characterizes himself as a suppliant at the hearth of Odysseus (14.159; 19.306; 20.232). When he achieves this status literally, his position at his own hearth uncannily coincides with the near collapse of his disguise. As the narrative fills with elusive hints of recognition, Penelope invites him to remain all night at the hearth. But Homer, for no apparent reason beyond continuing a sequence of symbolic movements, which in turn continue epic's use of the folkloric three-fold repetition evident in Hector's flight around Troy, has him sleep outdoors in the forecourt (20.1). Thus when Telemachus the next morning 'with crafty thought' (20.257) — crafty in what? — seats his father once again inside the hall at the threshold, we can expect a third and doubtless climactic intrusion. Mirroring the order of Odysseus's first incursion, the bow contest proceeds 'from left to right' (21.142) as the suitors proceed sequentially toward Odysseus and the threshold, where Telemachus has placed the bow. Unable to string the bow, the frustrated suitors then carry the bow to the hearth to warm it (183). This in turn leads to another significant and dramatically contested journey, as the goodly swineherd begins to carry the bow to Odysseus, the suitors intimidate him into returning it, Telemachus threatens him, and he finally traverses the hall. After Odysseus strings the bow and shoots through the axes — a feat suggestive of epic's valorization of linear progress — the true battle begins. Odysseus springs from his seat to the great threshold (22.2), slays the suitors, and seats himself by the tall pillar. Eurycleia can now report to Penelope, 'he has come back and is here at his hearth, alive' (23.55).

The moralized teleology of epic time is no less evident in the journey variant of the epic plot than in the Iliadic siege. If in the *Iliad* warriors must avoid shirking and such untimely diversions as collecting spoils while the battle continues to rage, now the hero's most serious temptations are either deviation away from the true path or, as Spenser puts it, sitting 'down to rest in middest of the race' (*FQ*, 1.7.5.4). One of Odysseus' great tasks is to overcome repeated temptations to stop or divert his direction. The crew must not succumb to the allure of the lotus, nor their commander to the sirens' call or the creature comforts of Phaeacia. But the *Odyssey* poet does not simply imitate the earlier poem's imperative to fare forward. One of his great innovations is to reinterpret the largely synchronic problem of the one and the many in the earlier epic into a largely diachronic problem. The hero's success depends first upon his ability to replace the kind of wandering recounted to the Phaeacians, which leaves him at Homer's version of the antipodes, into the directed movement of the journey that begins when he enters the narrator's direct representation in Ogygia. Even more than this, unlike Achilles or Agamemnon, the wily hero of the *Odyssey* depends on his ability to strategize. From the moment of his landfall on Ithaca, he must carefully weigh cause and effect, rejecting actions that do not contribute to the larger action, such as yielding to his urge to kill the insulting Melanthios (17.235ff.). Athena praises him for not rushing into the hall to see his wife and son (13.333ff.), an action that he admits would have made his homecoming resemble the unfortunate Agamemnon's (383ff.). Instead, assisted by Athena he patiently organizes his ragtag force and assembles the various components of successful combat: infiltrating the hall as an elderly beggar, instructing Telemachus on how to deprive the suitors of their weapons, setting up the bow-stringing contest, arranging for a servant to

close the door to the courtyard. It is true that, as in the *Iliad*, success requires unified movement in the ranks. Eurymachus recalls Nestor when
he urges his cohorts to 'take thought of warcraft' (22.73) and attack
Odysseus 'in a body' ('athrooi', 76) using the tables as shields for their
phalanx. But the suitors fail to follow through on the suggestion, and soon
Athena, waving her aegis, makes them resemble a herd of cattle stam-
peded by the darting horsefly (300ff.). The more important contrast now,
however, is not between unified and disunified forces, but between the
force that follows the successive steps of a plan and the force that cannot.

Odysseus as strategist represents the development of an idea already
present in the *Iliad* into the indispensable component of heroic success.
The development is evident in this poem's more frequent use of the term
suntithemai, to put together or hearken. Theoclymenus continues the
term's association with seers when he tells Penelope to hearken (17.153)
to his announcement that her husband has returned, but in the *Odyssey* it
is most often used by the hero himself. Odysseus must regularly craft narratives that elicit the listener's putting them together in a certain way. He
uses the term to challenge Telemachus to consider Odysseus' favour with
the gods (16.259), to discern the swineherd's loyalty (15.318), to warn
Amphinomous away from association with the suitors (18.129), to find out
how Penelope will respond to his own story and the fact of his return
(19.268), to plumb the mind of old Laertes (24.265).[40] The concept of
metis, cunning intelligence, also takes on a new importance. As Detienne
and Vernant point out, in the earlier poem *metis* has a temporal dimension,
for the wise man 'can explore in advance all the many avenues of the future, weigh up advantages against disadvantages and make decisions with a
full knowledge of the situation'.[41] Polydamus, whom we have observed futilely trying to restrain Hector in *Iliad* 12, weighs an ill-omened future
against a present heroic imperative and draws the right conclusion. When
the same prescient warrior advocates returning to the city after Achilles'
terrifying war-cry announces his return to battle, Homer calls him 'wise'
and describes the nature of his wisdom: he can 'see at the same time both
past and future' (18.250). The *Odyssey* explicitly assigns the ability to see
past and future together to an even more minor character, the 'old hero
Halistherses' who tries to reconcile the suitors' kin to Odysseus after their
death (24.452). But it is now the central hero who embodies *metis*.

With this revised emphasis comes a new potential for the meaning of
circular motion. Odysseus is 'polutropos', the man of many turns, in a
negative sense, for he must helplessly endure much spinning about on the
sea of fortune. This is doubtless the primary connotation of the epithet in
the epic's opening, where we hear that he 'wandered many ways' ('mala
polla / plagchthne'). In its other occurrence, when Circe wonders if he is

the polytropic hero whose arrival Hermes had foretold (10.330), positive connotations have come to the fore. For the goddess whom later allegorists will identify with temporal cycles and who may in Homer already bear circular associations, the hero's many turns resemble the many skills and devices of his related epithets, *polumetis* and *polumechanos*.[42] Detienne and Vernant explore the post-Homeric connection between *metis* and the circular bond, most notably in the image of the enclosing fishnet and the military manoeuvre of encircling the enemy.[43] This aspect of polytropic Odysseus appears in his elaborate contrivance to contain the suitors within the great hall. More importantly, especially in view of Vergil's reworking of Homeric epic, the mind's circling has come to represent the act of strategizing, of seeing the past, present and future together as the site of a coherent plan. Homer suggests more than a practical inspection when Odysseus, in an apparent fixation that attracts the suitors' puzzled attention, turns the bow round and round ('anastrophon', 21.394) before stringing it. We have been prepared in the previous book to recognize in this motion a corresponding internal movement. Seeing the treacherous women who have slept with the suitors, 'much he ponderered in the division of mind and spirit' (20.10). After addressing and subduing his heart, he remains tossing and turning in bed:

> ... But the man himself was twisting and turning,
> And as a man with a paunch pudding, that has been filled with
> blood and fat, tosses it back and forth over a blazing
> fire, and the pudding itself strains hard to be cooked quickly;
> so he was twisting and turning back and forth, meditating
> how, though he was alone against many, he could lay hands on
> the shameless suitors. And at this time Athene, descending
> from the sky, came close to him, and wore the shape of a lady.
> (20.24-30)

Joseph Russo comments:

> The man "himself" (αὐτός) is more than the sum of his parts and remains too upset to hold still. The passage seems to represent an advance from the standard Homeric conception toward a more modern one, as the poet presses the word αὐτός into service to denote the "whole" psychological entity in opposition to its constituent impulses.[44]

Concurrent with this new sense of self-integration we witness a new image for the hero's mental activity. At first reminiscent of the sleepless Achilles, Odysseus distinguishes himself from the earlier heroic paradigm by solving multiple problems of the one and the many: the rest of the poem is the story of how, despite being 'alone against many', he leverages his limited resources into an advantage over the host of suitors by organizing a precise sequence of causality. When we consider Achilles' first pondering scene as well, similarly issuing in the arrival of Athena, we can see that the two epics trace an evolution of heroic thought from the elimination of self-division that issues in an action to a circular motion of the mind that brings temporal processes to completion.

Epic Rhetoric: the Reader as Hero

We can follow and assess the actions of heroes in epic because epic space-time is highly rationalized. Modern scholarship has approached this essential generic feature from a variety of perspectives. Comparing the *Odyssey*'s methods of representation to the Bible's, Eric Auerbach uncovers 'a basic instinct of the Homeric style: to represent phenomena in a fully externalized form, visible and palpable in all their parts, and completely fixed in their spatial and temporal relations'.[45] E. R. Dodds finds a related basic instinct in Homer's use of the supernatural to render causality visible and palpable, observing that 'all departures from normal human behaviour whose causes are not immediately perceived are ascribed to supernatural agency'.[46] Thomas Greene remarks that 'the first quality of the epic imagination is expansiveness, the impulse to expand its own luminosity in ever widening circles. . . . Epic answers to man's need to clear away an area he can apprehend, if not dominate, and commonly this area expands to fill the epic universe, to cover the known world and reach heaven and hell'.[47] Greene subtitles his survey of celestial descents 'a study in continuity', by which he means the continuity of conventions in the epic tradition. He could just as appropriately mean spatial or causal continuity. One of the principal functions of a god's descent from Olympus is to map the epic universe's vertical dimension. Another is to provide a visible cause for a visible effect. Pondering the relationship between gods and men may lead us deeper into psychological or existential dilemmas, but the causal line of action in time and space remains clear.

Epic's expansive luminosity is an imperialism of rationality, a drive to extend the cosmic ordering represented by the sacred city, with its highly selective and precisely ordered details, ever outward from the centre. Later Greek thought will labour to rationalize space through the categories of the continuous and the discrete.[48] Homer prefigures this effort not only in his imagery of military discipline, but even more precisely in his vocabulary of craftsmanship, which depends upon notions of skilful joinery, close fit without interstices, and polished smoothness, characteristics allowing parts to be at once individually visible and fixed in their spatial relations within a whole. These ideas most clearly transcend mere formulaic usage or a primitive world's admiration for labour-intensive artefacts when they are attached to Homer's principal embodiments of cosmic order: the closely fitted houses of Zeus, Alcinous and Odysseus;

the polished stones of Priam's colonnade, Nestor's court, Circe's hall, the agora of Phaeacia, the 'sacred circle' of the agora on Achilles' shield.[49] It is this kind of ordered, rationalized space that epic projects outward, both horizontally so that we can map action on the earth and vertically so that we can locate action in a world of delineated cosmic planes. The same basic instinct of expansion through ordered continuity extends to the temporal dimension as well. The visible cause and effect of the unfolding story-line continues past actions recounted through such means as a character's retrospective narrations, 'digressive' passages, and genealogies. Summaries, prophecies and the many varieties of prolepsis similarly allow us to view the unfolding story as part of a continuous sequence extending into the future.

The close-fit nature of their stories allows the Homeric poems to serve as Aristotelian paradigms of aesthetic unity. But order characterizes epic as a product rather than a process. The assembly takes place in the reader's understanding, and the Homeric epic with its apparently unprecedented length and complexity must have presented an unprecedented challenge to the constructive powers of its original audience. The poet's complete grasp of his story and the world in which it takes place is a prerequisite for his carefully controlled release of information. By opening *in medias res* and then offering, often with considerable obliquity and at great textual distance from one another (as we have seen, for example, in the Hercules narrative), details that locate the present story in ever-expanding frameworks of past and future, the epic poet poses for his audience, as he poses for his characters, a recurring problem of relating the part to the whole, and readers have responded with vigorous pondering. We lack the facility of the seer, epic's ideal reader, to connect past, present and future effortlessly. Rather, like the non-prescient hero we must do the best we can, pressing on through the narrative, confronting and eliminating our divisions of mind, and eventually finding degrees of meaningful unity, though rarely do many readers agree on the nature of the wholes they assemble from the parts.

The assembly process can be quite demanding on the level of following the large course of events in space and time. It is even more demanding when the poet uses repetitions to link materials into more abstract or thematic structures of meaning. The most powerful device available to Homer for achieving such thematic linkages is ring composition, which probably originated in the exigencies of oral-formulaic composition, but which developed into a formidable technique for challenging the audience to reconcile the one and the many. The simple act of repeating images, actions, situations, can be exploited to produce interpretive challenges. To cite only an example that has figured prominently in our analysis of spatiality, the parallel supplications of Thetis and Priam mutually illuminate each other. In addition to the fear of dismemberment by carrion beasts, parental bonds form one of the few bases of commonality that can supersede the enmities of war, and Achilles' humane decision receives support from the example of Zeus. But beyond this obvious connection, there are others more thought-provoking than immediately interpretable. That this situational repetition forms one of the widest and most notable rings in the *Iliad* tells us a great deal about where the poem's thematic centre lies. Book divisions pose related problems. The extent to which the divisions imposed on the Homeric epics by Alexandrian librarians mark off meaningful organization continues to provoke lively scholarly dissension. It is symptomatic of epic's assertive dialogism that two recent books on the *Iliad* published almost simultaneously come, with equal confidence, to diametrically opposed conclusions.[50] No matter which view is more convincing, the book divisions can be said to be part of the epic process, for readers of the epics before they were so divided, and even listeners hearing them recited in parts, must have made their own divisions of the narrative based on what they perceived as signs of unity and closure. And of course book divisions present new opportunities for creating larger, multiple-book divisions that can enter into the play of meaning assembly, opportunities that later poets will vigorously exploit.[51] All of these are means by which the poet can issue a challenge corresponding to Agamemnon's insistence that his audience 'put together his discourse'. No less than the chronotopic features traced in this chapter, and no less than the various other devices long recognized as generic features of epic, beginning with Homer this challenge became an essential part of the epic tradition.

Notes

1. Vernant (1983), p. 165. As Vernant explains, 'one supports oneself generally on the *skeptron* which is like a walking stick (*baktron*) held upright with one end placed on the ground'. All Greek quotations of Homer are taken from the Oxford Classical Text, vols. 1 and 2 (3d ed., 1920), edited by David B. Monro and Thomas W. Allen, vols. 3 (2d ed., 1917) and 4 (2d ed., 1919), edited by Thomas W. Allen. Extended texts in English translation come from Richmond Lattimore's graceful yet literal version, which also retains the original line-numbering and much of the relevant chronotopic detail. I have tried to retain what Lattimore misses in my own translations of shorter passages. Because this book is comparative I have also, unlike Lattimore, retained the common English names for heroes and gods (i.e., Achilles rather than Achilleus).

2. For the details of the Greek supplication ritual, see Gould (1973). Without attention to spatial aspects, Kevin Crotty (1994) has illuminating comments

to offer on the connections between the ritual and Homer's poetics. Onians (1951, pp. 29, 97-8, 138-40) discusses the nod as a pledge in Greek culture.

3. Kirk (1985), p. 109.

4. Basing his discussion on the ethnographic research of Raymond Firth, Barry Schwartz (1981, p. 46) remarks that in the West, 'it is the movement of the subordinate as opposed to the nonmovement of the superordinate that encodes deference', while in 'traditional societies, where inequalities are more pronounced, the direction of movement plays a more important role'. Homer may very well be making a similar differentiation between Olympian and human practice. The gods also rise for Hera at 15.84-6. Kirk (1985, p. 109) informs us that after Homer the deferential rise of the gods 'became a common motif in the hymnodic tradition'.

5. Kirk (1985, pp. 126-7) observes that the substitution in lines 107-8 of 'left' ('elipen', 'leipe') for the more clearly intentional 'gave' ('doke', 'doken', 'dok') caught the attention of Homeric scholiasts, who suggested that this might have something to do with the well known quarrel between Thyestes and Atreus, the father of Agamemnon. If the Homeric text can sustain this degree of subtlety, does Hermes as 'argeïphontes', usually assumed to mean 'slayer of Argos', continue the play of irony? Since Homer does not mention Argos, the giant who guarded Io from amorous Zeus, the scholia assume he didn't know the story (Kirk, 1985, p. 127). The epithet resonates provocatively with such details as (1) the problem of identifying 'Argos' in 108 and in the Catalogue of Ships, where it can mean anything from the Peloponnesian city to the entire Mycenaean world to the 'Pelasgion' Argos of Achilles (see Kirk, p. 128), and (2) Achilles' insulting Agamemnon as a 'people-devouring' ('demoboros', 1.231) king.

6. For two studies that approach the evolution of epic from, respectively, the heavenly descent and the issue of dynasty, see Greene (1963) and Fichter (1982). Because Fichter is interested in the particularly Vergilian variant of dynastic epic, in which the poet traces the rise of the 'noble house, race, or nation to which the poet professes allegiance' (p. 1), he does not mention Homer's intense interest in matters dynastic or, for that matter, Milton's use of the Eden myth to carry the convention to its logical conclusion.

7. Paolo Vivante (1982, p. 114) accurately describes the connotations of *aipus*: 'Even as an epithet of a mountain which is approached and reached, it brings out the sense of climbing, ascending: cp. *Od.* 19.431. It is therefore found with cities and their names: *Il.* 2.573, 538, 869, 635, etc. Notice, especially in the *Catalogue of Ships*, the recurring form of such a sentence as, for example, "they who held (or inhabited) lofty Dion." We are presented with the image of towns rising on sheer rocky heights in sites which appear impregnable'.

8. For a concise discussion of Levantine omphalic capitals, see the appendix on 'Sacred Cities of the East' in Scully (1990), pp. 141-57.

9. Ovid (1931) p. 106. *Fasti*, 2.684. I borrow Norman Austin's translation (1975, p. 89) of Homer's lines, since it captures the implication of universal extension. Odysseus' description is even richer in the original, for he indicates 'destroyed' or 'sacked the city' through 'dieperse polin', which contains the idea of traversing the city's vast expanse.

10. The Homeric heroes passed their tallness genes, or at least the myth of noble tallness, on to later generations of European aristocracy. Gulliver (Swift,

1967, p. 65) observes that the emperor of Lilliput, modelled on the Hapsburgs, is 'taller by almost the breadth of my nail, than any of his court, which alone is enough to strike an awe into the beholders'. Schwartz (1981, p. 60) reviews modern sociological literature on the phenomenon and observes that 'regularly associated with competence and power, superior height is an absolute prerequisite for those adults who would perform highly symbolic roles related to ceremonial or real authoritative function, where the issue of "appropriate stature" is explicit. . . . "Palace guards," who perform no "instrumental" duties at all, must be exceptionally tall, and their stature is often accentuated by special headgear. The tallest men tend to be placed in the front ranks of military formations'.

11. The term *prenes* is formulaic in the *Iliad* for the defeated warrior, so much so that the *Odyssey* poet's single use in the context of combat (22.296) seems designed to initiate Telemachus, the victor, into the *Iliad*'s version of heroism. Instances in the earlier epic include 2.468, 4.544, 5.58, 6.43, 6.307, 11.179, 12.390, 15.543, 16.310, 16.379, 16.413, 16.579, 17.300, 21.118, 23.25. See below on what appears to be an ironic application in Achilles lying prone and restless in Book 24.

12. Kirk (1985), p. 201.

13. Quint (1993), pp. 47-8.

14. The most important comparative wielders of the teleological epic / repetitive romance distinction are Parker (1979) and Quint (1993). Epic teleology is also commonly assumed by those not using the distinction. Sarah Mack (1978, p. 55) writes of the *Aeneid*: 'The task of the present is to move toward the future and become it. . . . The present is never an end in itself; it is merely a step toward, an obstacle in the path of, something still to come'.

15. Hans Van Wees (1986, 1988 and 1994) comments on the 'forward' quality of Homer's heroes in his splendid analyses of combat conventions.

16. The standard treatment of the left / right opposition is by Cuillandre (1943). For larger cultural contexts and some corrective comments on Cuillandre's analysis, see the studies collected by Rodney Needham (1973).

17. Benveniste (1973), p. 505.

18. Ironic undercutting might be seen here too, as the specified animal images of Book 2 give way to a beast ('theri') whose only sure attribute is wildness. For a more unambiguously positive variant (among many), see the two Aiantes as they 'wander' ('phoiteten', 12.266) the length of the ramparts exhorting hangers-back to 'press forward' ('proso hiesthe', 274).

19. For an illuminating discussion of the shield made for Achilles by Hephaestos in Book 18, see Hardie (1985).

20. The verb used for Achilles' turning restlessness also describes the first effect of Apollo's attack on Patroclus: the god's blow makes his eyes whirl in dizziness (16.792). It also is conspicuous in the simile where Hector in his attack on the Greek ships is compared to a boar or lion turning again and again on hunters who have surrounded him (12.42 and 47). Whether we regard these repetitions as part of an intentional, written text-based network of imagery or as manifestations of an oral composition's chronotopic consistency, Homer's artistry in linking the three characters in this way is remarkable.

21. The formula occurs eighteen times in the *Iliad*, fifteen times in the *Odyssey*.

22. Detienne and Vernant (1978), p. 226.

23. Aristotle (1982), p. 33. *Poetics* VIII.3-4.

24. Bremmer (1983), p. 67. See also Snell (1953), chapters 1-3.
25. On the conflict of competition and cooperation in Homer see Crotty (1994), chapter 2, and Adkins (1963).
26 Armour borrows the primarily architectural quality of being 'close-set' in *Iliad* 12.317, 15.689, 16.739.
27. For a study of arming scenes without consideration of armour as an emblem of the integral self, see Armstrong (1958).
28. Charles Segal (1971) demonstrates in exhaustive detail that Homer organizes mutilation passages into an elaborate developmental progression.
29. Austin (1975), pp. 111-12.
30. Dissolving in fright is, of course, never a positive condition in epic. The irony of Homer's description is enhanced by the contrast between, on the one hand, Priam's internal-external collapse and his herald's immediate urge to throw himself down in supplication, and, on the other hand, the hairs that heroically 'stand up' ('triches estan', 24.359) on his fluid limbs. Hermes adds to the humour by asking if Priam is venturing forth because he is untouched by fear of the fury-breathing Achaeans.
31. Austin, p. 113.
32. The varieties of Homeric pondering scenes have been discussed by Walter Arend (1933), pp. 106-15, and Pietro Pucci (1987), pp. 66-75, though Pucci limits his discussion to scenes employing *mermerizo*. The interchangeability of the two terms is especially evident in scenes where both occur, as for example *Iliad* 1.189 and 193, 10.503 and 507; *Odyssey* 5.354 and 365. *Mermerizo* more often accompanies the balancing of specified alternatives, but as the example of Zeus balancing alternatives for Sarpedon illustrates, *ormaino* is used in this way as well.
33. Hercules' other appearance in the *Iliad* fits into this sequence as well. At 14.324 Hera is distracting Zeus from the war by arousing him sexually on Mount Ida. Zeus declares his passion with a list of former passions that don't measure up, including his love for the mother of Perseus, whose descendant is Eurystheus, and for Hercules' mother Alkmene. The prototypical *kosmokrator* also makes three appearances in the *Odyssey*. Odysseus will not compare himself as an archer to the great hero (8.223). He, or rather the shade of the real hero who now resides on Olympus, shows up in the underworld (11.601ff.). His only negative Homeric appearance occurs at 21.25ff., where it is recalled that he slew his own house guest Iphitus without regard for the law of hospitality. We might find in this originary appearance of the negative Hercules further evidence of the poet's revisionary project.
34. Janko (1992), p. 412.
35. Some classicists may object that my reference to the *Iliad* as 'the earlier poem' simply assumes a chronological ordering that has been subject to much dispute. But the many critical studies demonstrating the *Odyssey* poet's allusions to the *Iliad*, most notably perhaps Gregory Nagy's *The Best of the Achaeans* (1979), seem convincing to me, and my argument that the *Odyssey* revises chronotopic aspects of the *Iliad* supports this approach. On the other hand, it is impossible to exclude other possibilities. Pietro Pucci's (1987, p. 41) more complex scenario of intertextuality, for example, is not implausible: 'In fact, it is most probable that both texts — as they now stand — were composed with knowledge of the tradition that precedes each of them and were therefore produced while they were, so to speak, simultaneously looking at each other'.

36. The translation is by Alfred Heubeck in Russo et al (1992), p. 363. The satir-
ical tone of the interchange can also be seen in Agamemnon's snide response:
'O happy son of Peleus, Achilleus, like the immortals, / who died in Troy, far
away from Argos, and around you others / were killed, Trojans and the best
men among the Achaians, / as they fought over you; and you in the turning
dust lay / mightily in your might, your horsemanship all forgotten'.

37. Vernant (1983), pp. 185-8. Despite my disagreement with Vernant on a number of specific points, all four of the chapters forming the book's section on
'The Organization of Space' would serve as useful background for my argument. Vernant locates the origins of the permanent agora of the polis in the
military assembly, where warriors could gather and exercise the right to free
speech. The armies of the *Iliad* hold their assembly or *agora* in various places,
including beside Agamemnon's ship (7.387) and outside the Trojan walls
(18.243). The Ithacan assembly addressed by Telemachus as Book 2 opens occurs in an unspecified location.

38. Pedrick (1982), pp. 132-3.

39. Alcinous 'rules over' his people at 7.11, 7.23 and 11.349.

40. In other instances in the *Odyssey*, Penelope is disturbed when she 'puts together' (1.328) a singer's tale of the Greeks returning from Troy, Athena
warns Telemachus to 'put together' (15.27) the suitors' plans to assassinate
him, and the half-asleep Odysseus overhears and 'puts together' (20.92)
Penelope's prayer. On the last instance and the remarkable series of actions
this putting together seems to initiate, see Austin (1975), pp. 119ff.

41. Detienne and Vernant (1978), p. 16.

42. The positive aspect of *polutropos* is well acknowledged in modern scholarship.
For the fullest discussion, see Pucci (1987). Judith Yarnall is sensible in considering Circe's circular associations: 'Circe (*Kirke*) is the feminine form of
kirkos, meaning falcon or hawk. *Kirkos* also has a secondary meaning — circle
— perhaps originally suggested by the wheeling flight of hawks. Though the
Neo-Platonic allegorists later based their interpretation of Circe's significance upon this secondary meaning of her name, there is no compelling
reason to follow their lead. Homer normally uses the more common word for
circle, *kuklos*; the one time *kirkos* appears in the epics with the meaning of circle it is in its alternate form, *krikos*'. It is also perhaps worth observing that
Circe is the daughter of Helios, the foremost Homeric agent of temporal cycles, and that Achilles is compared to a repeatedly swooping hawk as he
attacks Hector and the two begin their circling of the Trojan walls (*Il.*,
17.757).

43. Detienne and Vernant (1978), chapter 10, 'The Circle and the Bond'.

44. Russo et al (1992), p. 109.

45. Auerbach (1953), p. 4.

46. Dodds (1951), p. 13.

47. Greene (1963), pp. 9-10.

48. For an illuminating look at how ideas of continuity important in Homer will
later become the foundations of western science, see Michael White (1992)
on ancient physical theories of the continuous and the discrete.

49. Variants of *pukaio*, which means 'closely constructed or made, well fitted together, without breaks or interstices' (Cunliffe, 1963, p. 352), characterize
(among other structures) the house of Zeus (*Il.*, 10.355), Alcinous' house (*Od.*,
7.88 and 8.458), Odysseus' house (*Od.*, 1.333, 16.415 and elsewhere). Variants

of *xestos*, which means 'smoothed, smooth, wrought, polished' (Cunliffe, p. 284), characterize Priam's colonnade atop Pergamus (*Il.*, 6.243), Zeus' colonnade atop Olympus (*Il.*, 20.11), the stones of the sacred circle on Achilles' shield (*Il.*, 18.504), the gates of Troy (*Il.*, 18.276), the stones of Nestor's court (*Od.*, 3.406), the stones of Circe's hall (*Od.*, 10.211 and 253), the threshold and doors of Odysseus' hall (*Od.*, 18.33 and 22.72; 21.137 and 164).

50. Oliver Taplin (1992, p. 13) concludes that scholars who claim that the *Iliad*'s book divisions reflect 'the fundamental structuring of the poem' are 'demonstrably mistaken'. Keith Stanley (1993, p. 186), who provides a minutely detailed analysis of ring-composition in the *Iliad*, finds 'in each of its twenty-four books a remarkable structural integrity and an equally striking internal coherence in the groups comprising them'.

51. Kirk (1985, pp. 44ff.) considers some of the possibilities created by dividing the *Iliad* into various groupings of books. The *Aeneid* has long been subjected to such analysis. G. E. Duckworth (1962, pp. 2-15) outlines correspondences between paired books of the two halves (1 with 7, 2 with 8, etc.) and finds as well a triadic structure of four-book units. Charles Beye (1993, pp. 234ff.) is a more recent example.

CHAPTER TWO

The Vergilian Revision

Philip Hardie summarizes what appears to be an ever-growing divergence in Vergil studies: 'Modern criticism of the *Aeneid* has largely structured it-self around two opposing assessments of the poem, which see it as either a panegyric of Rome and its hero, Augustus, or as a tragedy of the individual caught up in the remorseless processes of history; an epic of optimism or an epic of pessimism'.[1] My discussion proceeds from a conclusion that we cannot fit the poem into either side of this either / or distinction without distorting its essential dialogism. There can be no question that what has come to be called the poem's 'imperial voice' speaks loudly and at times convincingly, informing us that Aeneas' translation of empire is worth the costs incurred, and that Augustus' great cultural project of preserving what was gained by continually redefining the Roman identity against a chaotic, foreign other is necessary and praiseworthy.[2] To my mind there can be no question as well that relentless murmurs of irony subvert this voice. Nor, if one is willing to acknowledge not only the *Odyssey*'s questioning of Iliadic heroism but the *Iliad*'s own willingness to undercut the stature of its heroes, should it be surprising that Vergil would seek to surpass his predecessor by intensifying Homer's dialogic complexity. Homer continually poses rather than resolves the problem of the one and many, and he finds his characters most interesting psychologically when they are puzzling over alternatives and struggling to unite parts into wholes. Vergil evinces no less interest in such problems of partial vision, the type or stage of thought that allows his poem's ideological bottom line to be calculated with false precision. One of his most effective means of dramatizing the problem, as I hope to demonstrate in this chapter, is manipulation of the chronotopic framework he inherited from Homer.

Vergil weaves chronotopic effects even more densely into the fabric of his epic than did his predecessor. A reader alert to Homer's key spatio-temporal concepts will immediately notice their teeming abundance in the *Aeneid*. Consider but one statistical comparison among many that could be garnered from the word-indices compiled by Gehring and Wetmore: while the threshold-obsessed *Odyssey* refers to this crucial symbolic location about 20 times, the *Aeneid* in less than two-thirds as many lines mentions it some 70 times.[3] Repeated reference to thresholds contributes to the uncanny ominousness of Aeneas' arrival in Carthage. Venus directs Aeneas to proceed directly to the queen's threshold ('reginae ad limine perfer', 1.389). He arrives at the threshold of Juno's temple (444), founded where the migrating Carthaginians unearthed the head of a horse, an animal whose analogous position at the centre spells doom for the Trojans in Book 2.[4] Soon he is sharing a seat at the centre with Dido, while adoring Tyrians pour in across the 'propitious threshold' ('per limina laeta', 707), a description rendered cruelly ironic when immediately followed by reference to the queen's impending destruction (712).[5] Allusions contribute to the density of chronotopic reference through a multiplier effect, drawing into play their original contexts, which are sometimes multiple, to generate similarities and differences. Protected by his mother's mist, Aeneas arrives at the central temple dome ('media templi', 505) at the centre of Dido's city ('in urbe media', 441). The reader is invited to recall both the unheroic return of Paris to the citadel in *Iliad* 3 and Odysseus' prudent arrival at Alcinous' hearth assisted by Athena in *Odyssey* 7. The two Homeric scenes, so opposed in moral implication, interact provocatively with Vergil's text to produce discomforting questions as the plot develops. Is Aeneas' union with Dido, assisted by the goddess of love like Paris' with Helen, as disastrous for Roman history as Helen's abduction was for Troy (Iarbas, we should note, finds Aeneas another Paris in 4.215)? What does the substitution of Venus for the *Odyssey*'s Athena suggest about the honourableness of the hero's intentions and the wisdom of his proceedings?

While Aeneas continues to remind us of Odysseus by narrating his travails to the rapt audience, Vergil in Book 2 strengthens the parallels between violent Homeric stories and Aeneas' arrival in Carthage. Following his own ostensibly peaceful arrival from periphery to centre, Aeneas tells the story of Troy's fall as a series of movements between these two coordinates of epic space, a series no less elaborately choreographed than Odysseus' navigation of his own *megaron*. Laocoön rushes down from citadel to gate to argue against taking the Trojan horse up to the citadel. Like Achilles hurtling across the Trojan plain toward Hector at the gate, two serpents pursue an unwavering course ('agmine certo', 2.212) toward the seer from the island where the Greeks are hiding. After slaying him they ascend the citadel to take refuge at Minerva's shrine. The horse is dragged up to the city's centre ('mediae urbi', 240), but only after halting four times at 'the gate's threshold' ('in limine portae', 242), a repetition that leads Aeneas to observe painfully that the Trojans were 'blind with furor' (242). Now that the wall has been breached, the war's decisive action consists of breaching concentric barriers encountered on the way in. As Aeneas watches from the peak of the palace roof ('ad summi fastigia culminis', 458), a location ironically highlighting his powerlessness even as it affords him a privileged, gods-eye perspective, Pyrrhus stands gleaming, like a snake having just shed its skin, 'at the first threshold' ('primoque in limine', 470) of Priam's palace. Following his father's heroic example by rushing 'among the foremost' ('inter primos', 479), he 'bursts across the threshold' ('limina perrumpit', 480), bringing him in view of the royal 'inner chambers' ('penetralia', 484), the ritually charged location where the city's sacred images are kept (cf. 297, 508, 665). Now he is once more, in a mysterious and nightmarish repetition, 'at the first threshold' ('in limine primo', 485). When Aeneas attempts to capture the full horror of the spectacle by insisting, 'I myself saw' Pyrrhus 'mad with slaughter' (499-500) 'at the threshold' ('in limine', 500), the obsessive repetition of pauses at the threshold matches the Trojan horse's four-fold halting at the city gate, though now there is no question of blindness to the significance of the events unfolding. As the city rises in flames, Pyrrhus finally completes the quest left unfinished by his father, who according to non-Homeric myth died at the Scaean gate, by murdering Priam at the altar 'in the middle of the temple and under the exposed axle of the sky' ('aedibus in mediis nudoque sub aetheris axe', 512). Aeneas and now we along with the poem's internal audience have witnessed in gripping detail the destruction of the Trojan cosmos.

The wanderings of Book 3 intervene before we observe Dido's reaction to this sensational account. The delay makes the famous opening of Book 4 all the more powerful:

> At regina gravi iamdudum saucia cura
> vulnus alit venis et caeco carpitur igni.
> multa viri virtus animo multusque recursat
> gentis honos; haerant infixi pectore voltus
> verbaque. (4.1-5)

> But the queen, long stricken now by grievous pangs,
> feeds the wound with her blood and is wasted by hidden fire.
> Often the man's valour, often the renown of his people,
> rush back to her heart. His features and words pierce
> and remain fixed in her breast.

It is a critical commonplace to note the conventional equation here of love and war and to find imagistic linkages between these and countless other lines in the surrounding books. Insufficient attention to generic features has, nevertheless, obscured the fact that the most important context for the images of wounds, blood, fire, rushed movement, and penetration is the Troy narrative of Book 2. In the kind of slippage of identities that pervades the *Aeneid*, and that must owe much to the technique of blurred distinctions we have observed in the late books of the *Iliad*, Aeneas has become in effect his primary enemy. The parallel between Aeneas and Pyrrhus established in Books 1 and 2 through the language of ingress is reconfirmed, with the setting of this action now the pitiful queen herself. The slippage of identities will continue and the reduction of scale will be reversed at book's end when Dido ignites the pyre she has constructed in her own *penetralium* (504), her 'innermost court open to the skies' ('tecto interiore sub auras', 494). There, in a highly ironic assumption of female autonomy, she becomes her own Pyrrhus and falls upon her own sword. Vergil keeps the parallel before our eyes during the subsequent lamentations:

> non aliter, quam si immissis ruat hostibus omnis
> Karthago aut antiqua Tyros, flammaeque furentes
> culmina perque hominum volvantur perque deorum. (669-71)

> even as though were falling before the inrushing foe
> all Carthage or ancient Tyre, and furious flames
> across the roofs of men were rolling, over the roofs of gods.

As Book 5 opens these figurative flames become literal. We don't know whether in fact the pyre was ever lit, but Aeneas is next seen at sea holding his 'steadfast course' ('certus iter', 5.2) but 'looking back upon city walls' ('moenia respiciens', 3) which now 'gleam with Dido's flames' (4). He is back on the right path toward the Roman centre, but his reversed position compromises his heroic stature. The parallel now evoked is Odysseus' contrary posture on Ogygia, where though prevented from pursuing his homeward trek he gazed steadfastly over the ocean, wishing only to see the smoke rising from his hearth.

As this brief examination of the opening books demonstrates, Vergil uses movement between centre and periphery no less emphatically and even more frequently than Homer. As one might expect of whatever Homeric features Vergil borrows, he also manipulates this basic epic movement in a highly involved and self-conscious manner. Where Vergil's use of horizontal dimensions differs most strikingly is in his dramatization of life without clear omphalic orientation. The *Aeneid*'s vocabulary of cosmic spatiality imitates formulaic repetitiveness, but it translates this into the repetitiveness of obsession, representing an absence and need more than a presence. References to thresholds in Book 2 highlight the traumatic nature of Aeneas' loss of his orderly world, but as the few parallels we have observed suggest, his subjectivity is only a more intense version of the subjectivity conditioning the poem as a whole. Much of this subjectivity is routinely removed by translators, who have long tended to naturalize Vergil's narrative by not following what they take to be an outmoded habit of synecdoche. *Limen* is frequently translated as doorway, *moenia* as city. But to translate in this way is to remove the careful restriction of reference defining epic spatiality and the characters' attitudes toward it. The ghost of Hector tells Aeneas to 'seek walls' ('quaere

moenia', 2.294) for Troy's household gods, to find and found a space delineated from the chaos Aeneas has already entered with the Greek
crossing of the *limina portae*, an expression whose redundancy combines
Homeric sites of contention, heightens the sense of transgression, and
proleptically transfers what is left of the city's collapsing order onto the
more fragile enclosures remaining.[6] The Trojans' and the poem's obsession with walls, evident in whatever it is that Aeneas sees as he looks back
upon Carthage, is essential to Vergil's dramatization of life in chaos.

Homer's killing field outside Troy is oriented by the formidable citadel
rising above it. Across Odysseus' Mediterranean runs a line along which
he can gaze toward his beloved hearth. In contrast, the Trojan remnant
enters life outside the walls 'uncertain where the fates lead or where it is
granted to settle' (3.7). The result is an Odyssean sequence described by
David Quint:

> The *Aeneid* thus opens by evoking a pattern not only of narrative digression but
> also of narrative circularity: of romance wandering that brings the Trojans back
> to where they started, no closer to their destination. Their progress in Book 3
> may only be apparent, and Book 3 also features a series of failed settlements
> that repeatedly force the Trojans to start all over again. They seem, in fact, to
> be caught in a vicious circle, and a regressive one at that, for in these settle-
> ments they build or find miragelike replicas of Troy. It is the Trojans' nostalgic
> attempts to repeat or relive their past that constitute their wanderings, steering
> them off course and away from the epic goal of Italy.[7]

Quint's description of psychological regression rings true, most evidently
in the infantile fantasy of a miniaturized Troy at Buthrotum. In a very important sense, however, the Trojans do not merely start all over again.
Counter to any regression runs a slow but steady improvement in regaining the epic ideal of forward-directed motion. The first stage, the journey
to Thrace where Aeneas builds 'first walls' ('moenia prima', 17), appears
to be a case of purely accidental wandering. 'I fared forth an exile on the
deep' ('feror exsul in altum', 11), and 'I went there' ('feror huc', 16),
Aeneas recalls dreamily, as if he doesn't know how it happened. The same
random 'huc feror' (78) sums up the journey to Delos, although Aeneas'
account of Apollo fixing the wandering island 'in the middle of the sea'
('mari . . . medio', 73) points to its appeal and so might suggest, to the
homesick hero as much as to the reader, a consciously or unconsciously
calculated navigation. To Apollo's cryptic advice that they seek out their
ancient mother, the Trojans can only ask 'what walls are those?' ('quae sint
ea moenia', 100); that this oracle is delivered at a sacred isle in the middle
of the sea creates another ironic contrast with Homer's introduction of
Odysseus at the navel of the ocean, from which he knows exactly where he
wants to go.[8] Anchises responds to the Trojans' reasonable question by
suggesting Crete, whose location 'at the middle of the sea' ('medio . . .

ponto', 104) must be similarly appealing to the centre-hungry Trojans.[9] The sailors respond jubilantly and unanimously to their first directed destination, 'Let us seek Crete and our forefathers!' ('Cretam proavosque petamus', 129). They again build walls (132), now eagerly, and name the city Pergamum after their fallen citadel. This may be a return to the past, but it is also a renewal of the kinds of heroic action that epic values. It is, after all, the right thing to do given what they know. When the Penates instruct dreaming Aeneas to seek Hesperia, the name's implication of a direction and 'course' ('cursu', 200) continues the Trojans' orientational progress. The Furies add further detail by concluding, 'Italy is the course you seek' ('Italiam cursu petitis', 253). It should also be noticed that new knowledge directing the Trojans away from their all-too-brief periods of comfortable settlement is not greeted with lamentation, but with joy (cf. 189). Even when, after apparently nearing their epic goal, Apollo's seer informs them that the Italy they thought so near is in fact far off in the distance (381ff.), they proceed into great perils with enthusiasm and mark their first arrival in Italy with a unanimous shout once more naming their goal (523). Only with Book 4 must Aeneas, and Aeneas alone, be admonished to 'relinquish pleasant lands' ('dulcisque relinquere terras', 4.281) and return to the heroic path. Mercury will not have to repeat the lesson.

Except in the case of Aeneas' dalliance with Dido, and perhaps even there, the major challenge facing the Vergilian hero is epistemological. The minions of Agamemnon and Priam had occasionally to ponder through to decisions, and Odysseus patiently ferreted out information necessary to devise a winning strategy. Aeneas must try to proceed forward often without knowing in which direction forward lies. This new Vergilian aspect of horizontal space is captured graphically in the image of the labyrinth. Penelope Reed Doob argues convincingly that 'the idea of the labyrinth constitutes a major if sometimes covert thread in the elaborate *textus* of the *Aeneid*', forming 'a network of allusions that gradually shape a vision of Aeneas' life as a laborious errand through a series of mazes'.[10] To her detailed description we should add that the labyrinth enters the history of epic quite naturally. Even if Homer appears not to have connected the Daedalan dancing floor of Achilles' shield (18.590-2) to the predicament of his characters, the labyrinth conveniently links the to-and-fro and circular movements developed and interrelated systematically in the *Iliad*. It inescapably invites application to the problem of part and whole. The labyrinth is the image of 'inextricable error' ('inextricabilis error', 6.27) scanned intently in the Sibyl's cave by Aeneas, who is understandably fascinated by its resemblance to his life of wandering following the loss of Trojan walls. Pointedly, he is not granted his wish to 'further study the whole with his eyes' ('protinus omnia / perlegerent oculis', 33-4), for he is doomed to remain forever unsure how to combine parts into whole, individual motions into the unified epic quest. The labyrinth, I believe, should also be recognized as the product of an incomplete, paradoxical superimposition of cosmic order onto the chaotic space against which the sacred city defines itself. In the *Aeneid* Vergil famously offers a vision of a Roman 'empire without end' ('imperium sine fine', 1.279). This is a familiar extension of the Romulan walls outward to the limit of the *orbis terrarum*, the universal circle of lands that various Roman writers in breathtaking acts of wish-fulfilment identified with the imperial domain.[11] As Aeneas wanders through a broad range of future Roman territory, Vergil allows Augustan and modern readers to experience the discrepancy between his hero's ignorance and our finely articulated map. From our divine point of view above the labyrinth we discern the relation of part to whole.[12] Even without the poet having to tell us, we can see that the turn toward Carthage will require a circuitous return from a cul-de-sac. We too should notice that it is an unpropitious, leftward turn (south from his westward itinerary), just as the propitious excursion up the Tiber turns right (east from his northward route) and therefore toward the centre. For readers willing to acknowledge the subversive currents continually undercutting this ostensibly pro-imperial text, the very phrase 'imperium sine fine', which in the system of omphalic space can shift uneasily between tautology (all empires are universal) and oxymoron (imperial order is impossible without *moenia* delimiting cosmos from chaos), might also imply the inextricable error of the labyrinth, a nightmarish space paradoxically centred but unbounded, an imperial chaos.

In its masterfully sustained ambivalence toward the imperial project, the *Aeneid* manages to reassert the *Iliad*'s relentlessly vertical model of dominance and submission and at the same time to continue the *Odyssey*'s process of revaluation. Mercury's descent in Book 4 is a set-piece clearly designed to be compared with Hermes' to Ogygia. Reversing the *Odyssey* poet's reduction of vertical reference, Vergil introduces detail after detail to emphasize that Mercury is descending the vertical axis of the world. The messenger god carries the standard Homeric equipment, but now we learn that he uses the caduceus for the vertical transport of souls down to Tartarus (4.243). The lavish description of Atlas, of which he first sights the peak and then the steep sides ('volans apicem et latera ardua cernit' (246), borrows the axial imagery of *Odyssey* 1.52-4: he 'props heaven on his peak' ('caelum qui vertice fulcit', 246).[13] From this halting point in the descent 'between heaven and earth' ('terras inter caelumque', 256), Mercury graphically 'with his whole body dives down to the waves like a bird' ('toto praeceps se corpore ad undas / misit avi similis', 253-4) before imitating the horizontal flight low over the waves ('humilis volat aequora juxta', 256) of Homer's shearwater. When he arrives he sees Aeneas playing citadel architect 'founding towers and new roofs' ('fundantem arces ac tecta novantem', 260). The passage is inserted, as Philip Hardie notes in his brilliant study of Vergilian hyperbole, in a network of references to vertical communication:

> *Fama* rises to the clouds; the ascending movement is continued with the prayer of Iarbas, which takes us to the seat of the highest god, Jupiter. . . . At this point the direction of communication is reversed, and from the highest point words now descend to earth.[14]

Especially in the second half, the poem reinvokes the full panoply of citadel culture's attributes. Latinus and Turnus both inhabit 'high halls' ('tecta celsa', 7.343; 'tectis . . . altis', 413). Tiberinus climactically concludes his dream-message to Aeneas with a guiding vision of Rome that will 'rise as the head of lofty cities' ('celsis caput urbibus exit', 8.65). Soon follows the visit to the sacred heights of Rome with Evander, 'founder of the Roman citadel' ('Romanae conditor arcis', 313). Here the Capitol, already the quaking home of a god unidentified by the Arcadians, powerfully emanates 'dread sanctity' (349-50). In line with this series of recapitulations Vergil overgoes Homer by adding a vertical dimension to the attack on the Trojan camp. In their first military success the Italians overthrow the stockade's high tower ('turris . . . altis', 9.530), and in so doing strengthen the lines of association between the poem's various overthrown and threatened towers: all become versions of the overturned Trojan citadel haunting the poem.

As in Homer larger spatial patterns are repeated on the microcosmic scale of the individual warrior. Aeneas displays the Homeric hero's great soul, but over the intervening centuries magnanimity has been refined as an ethical concept. In the *Nichomachean Ethics*, *megalopsuchia* is the crown and distillation of all virtues, the truly superior man's justification for seeking glory. Retaining much of the Homeric term's relation to vertical classification, Aristotle's ideal is a high-souled man justified in looking down on others ('megalopsuchos dikaios kataphrononei'). Aristotle uses the fact that Thetis in supplicating Zeus does not specify her past services to illustrate the magnanimous one's dislike of being reminded of services rendered him, 'since the recipient of a benefit is the inferior of his benefactor, whereas they desire to be superior'. Immediately following this allusion we learn that although the magnanimous man is above anger, ambition, and the drive to compete, he is 'haughty toward men of position and fortune, but courteous toward those of moderate station, because it is difficult and distinguished to be superior to the great, but easy to outdo the lowly'.[15] Achilles himself is an example of magnanimity in the *Posterior*

Analytics, where we learn that his intolerance of insult caused him to be 'roused to wrath'.[16] Cicero distinguishes Roman from Greek ethics by taming magnanimity much more decidedly in an influential definition that we can assume Vergil's audience shared. In *De Officiis* he seems intent on removing the vertical residue left in Aristotle. Like his predecessor, he insists that the magnanimous man is free from passion and does not indulge in anger against his enemies, but he also observes that 'greatness of spirit' regards the good deed over the fame it brings. Danger arises when magnanimity is mixed with 'exaltation of spirit' ('animi elatio'), for 'from this exaltation and greatness of spirit spring all too readily self-will and excessive lust for power' and it becomes 'difficult to preserve that spirit of fairness which is absolutely essential to justice'.[17] Aeneas is the only individual hero in the narrative present time to receive the label, and Vergil seems intent on avoiding compromising Homeric associations with the term. He acknowledges epic verticality when Jupiter promises that Venus will raise 'magnanimum Aenean' to the skies (1.260), but by assigning agency to Venus he removes any negatively Ciceronian sense of 'exaltation'; Aeneas does not actually aspire to apotheosis. After this dramatic first instance, the poem's subsequent references to magnanimous Aeneas are devoid of vertical implication and utterly untroublesome.[18] Vergil appears to be calling attention to magnanimity's traditional vertical aspect and then drawing back, leaving the audience to decide to what extent the hero lives up to the Ciceronian ideals, to what extent this essentially Stoic and Republican virtue has replaced its epic and imperial predecessor.

The most momentous development of microcosmic imagery occurs in Book 4, when Vergil extends a Homeric tree simile vertically to illustrate Aeneas' resistance to the pleas of Anna on Dido's behalf. Homer's heroes fall like trees. As Wendell Clausen notes, in *Aeneid* 2.624ff. the tree simile 'is uniquely memorable in that a city, and not merely a single warrior, is compared to a felled tree'.[19] Now the comparison is reapplied to the warrior, but the association with sacred Troy is maintained:

> ac velut annoso validam cum robore quercum
> Alpini Boreae nunc hinc nunc flatibus illinc
> eruere inter se certant; it stridor, et altae
> consternunt terram concusso stipite frondes;
> ipsa haeret scopulis et, quantum vertice ad auras
> aetherias, tantum radice in Tartara tendit. (4.441-46)

> as when Alpine winds contend among themselves
> with winds now here now there to uproot an oak tree
> stout with the strength of years; there comes a roar, and the high
> boughs strew the earth from the shaken trunk;
> it clings to the rock and, as far as it lifts its top to the
> heavenly airs, so far it reaches its roots into Tartarus.

Hardie comments: 'the full significance of the earlier description of Atlas only appears when it is read in conjunction with this simile; Aeneas in his resolution is identified with the universal steadfastness of which Atlas was a general symbol'.[20] The full significance must also include the notable reference to Aeneas as *axis mundi*: while he is carrying the Trojan gods toward their future home, he has become an embodiment of Pergamum from which they were taken and the Capitol toward which they proceed. Long before the time of Vergil, as Arthur Green has discovered, post-exilic Jews responded to the loss of omphalic orientation with a 'transference of *axis mundi* symbolism from a particular place to a particular person: the *ẓaddiq* or holy man as the center of the world'.[21] Soon after Vergil, Paul and other early Christian writers transfer Temple imagery onto Christ and the individual believer. At the moment when his hero has recovered the epic path and ended the to-and-fro movement of the early wanderings, Vergil dramatically unveils an equivalent transfer through the universally recognized symbol of the cosmic tree.[22]

Yet the figuratively axial Aeneas coexists uneasily with literally tall heroes of the Homeric mold. In the Odyssean books reference to physical stature, except for the poet's habit of calling the Trojan nobility 'proceres', literally 'tall ones', is conspicuous in its absence. In this context Aeneas as *axis mundi* is consistent with such other mythic details as his promised apotheosis. When Jupiter reassures Venus that she 'will raise aloft to the starry heaven the great-souled Aeneas' ('sublimemque feres ad sidera caeli / magnanimum Aenean', 1.259-60), few readers will be prompted to speculate about whether the god means this literally, or whether the accusative 'sublimem' has adjectival force, extending the hero vertically, or adverbial, more realistically indicating his future location. The tension between the symbolic and the palpable increases when we enter the Iliadic books. There, for example, we encounter two gigantic heroes compared in extended simile to towering trees that 'raise their heads into the sky' ('caelo / attollunt capita', 9.681-2). But these are the foolish brothers Pandarus and Bitias who by inexplicably opening the Trojan encampment to Turnus nearly condemn the imperial *translatio* to failure while Aeneas is strolling the rustic Capitol. Turnus himself is modelled after Ajax, standing 'a head above the rest' (7.784). He is matched by his principal foe. Beginning with the crossing of the Styx, we find that Aeneas is lofty not merely in a figurative sense, but is literally 'huge' ('ingens', 6.616). And we even learn that he inherited his formidable stature from a father who turned the astonished gaze of youthful Evander from huge Priam, for 'Anchises moved loftier than all the rest' ('cunctis altior ibat / Anchises', 8.162-3).[23]

For a reader willing to hear what R. O. A. M. Lyne in the title of his superb volume calls 'further voices in Vergil's *Aeneid*', the poet's most subversive meditations on empire find expression as he develops Homer's mixture of literal and figurative dominance and submission into a system of remarkable complexity. One example picked up by later writers is his image of the 'headlong' (*praeceps*) fall, which deconstructively associates Homer's positive forward-faring heroism and the negative face-forward (*prenes*) position of his fallen heroes. Like Homer's warriors, Vergil's are literally thrown headlong into the dust, a fate we might find appropriate for Aconteus, for example, who makes the first charge to break the truce in Book 11, only to be 'thrown headlong afar' ('praecipitat longe', 617). In the *Aeneid* no less danger resides in being 'headlong of spirit' ('praeceps animi', 9.685), a condition facilitating self-defeat for the hero who presses forward without thinking. Aeneas becomes a prime example when he madly chooses battle with the Greeks invading Troy over the role of imperial translator assigned him by Hector's ghost. 'Rage and wrath drove my mind headlong' ('furor iraque mentem / praecipitant'), he recalls in an interval of diagnostic lucidity, 'and it rushed up in me that to die in arms is beautiful' ('pulchrumque mori succurrit in armis', 2.316-17). 'Succurrit' is a dazzling piece of wordplay that allows a number of ideas to be provocatively juxtaposed: apparent 'succour' that is in fact not assistance to the imperial guardian but to his internal foes, the disorienting interchangeability of downward and upward motion, the return of the repressed in the seductive form of the heroic code.

As this passage might suggest, one of the poem's most important conceptual oppositions is sustained between words containing the prefixes *super-* and *sub-*. Because these two indicators of high or low position occur literally hundreds of times, they cannot be examined in detail. A consideration of two crucial concepts must serve here to illustrate Vergil's most subtle methods for encoding meaning through vertical classification. As has long been recognized, the concept of *superbia*, usually translated as pride or haughtiness, is of central importance. Anchises authoritatively defines Rome's imperial mission as 'to spare the subjected and to battle down the proud' ('parcere subiectis et debellare superbos', 6.853), refining Aristotle's description of the magnanimous man's divided approach to the high and the low. As soon as Rome's ultimate patriarch makes this pronouncement, however, the poem's interpretive difficulties multiply. Lyne's consideration of *superbia*'s first occurrence highlights one problem:

> When at 1.21f. we are told that Juno had heard 'hinc populum late regem belloque superbum / uenturum excidio Libyae; sic uoluere Parcas' ['that from this source [the Trojans] would come a people wide in power and proud in war for the downfall of Libya; for such was on the scroll of the Fates'], whose opinion does 'superbum' reflect? The epic voice's? Juno's? The Fates'? (These last two would be examples of characters' feelings conveyed in the style) Or another voice's, even Vergil's personal voice? I suppose the most obvious answer is

Juno's, but the text does not let us exclude the others — even, ultimately, the last. And that thought is provoking: in general, and especially in retrospect from 6.853, the epithet seems not one that its recipient would welcome.[24]

It is not by accident that Vergil introduces both his most important *super*-term and his technique of ambiguous point of view at the same strategic location. In several early uses of *superbia*, Vergil leaves room for ambiguity. The narrator applies the term twice to Dido's palace (1.639 and 697). Aeneas applies it to Priam's doorposts ('postes superbi', 2.504) as Pyrrhus attacks them and to Priam himself, the once 'proud' emperor of Asia (2.556). In the fullest study of *superbus* in Vergil, Robert Lloyd proposes that these are 'doom-spelling applications':

> As applied to the most sympathetic of characters the adjective is almost invariably used with hindsight from the point of view of a disastrous outcome — the sense, although here for once carrying the better meaning of *noble* or *proud*, becomes virtually 'once proud, but proud no more'.[25]

Lloyd makes a valiant effort to maintain ideological purity, but a text that associates Carthage and Troy through the ominously parallel ingress of Aeneas and Pyrrhus is likely to be associating them here too. *Superbia* generates a lexical web early in the epic that links Priam and Dido to each other; to the proud Greeks Creusa has not had to face (2.785); to the Greeks' foremost representative Pyrrhus, whose pride Andromache laments she has not escaped (3.326); to the proud African peoples pacified by Dido (1.523); and finally, as Dido describes them with significant repetition, to the proud ships (4.540) and person of the deserting Aeneas himself, who has become in her eyes a 'proud foe' ('hostem . . . superbum', 4.424). Through a mechanism resembling the psychoanalytic model of revenge, in which an offence is cancelled through imitative identification with the aggressor, those who battle down the *superbi* come to resemble their victims.[26] But with a remarkable obliquity that allows the imperial voice to be heard amidst the play of irony, the elimination of difference occurs through a circle of displacements rather than directly between two proud opponents.

The epic's second half more fully enters into the Trojan viewpoint, providing a clearer delineation between the repeatedly 'proud' Italians to be battled down and the historical agents of Roman *imperium*. Mezentius is privileged to be deemed *superbus* by both Evander (8.481) and Aeneas (11.15) — one can only wonder if Aeneas' definition has changed since his description of Priam. Most frequently it applies to Turnus, and increasingly so as the war becomes a more personal struggle between the Italian warrior and the imperial founder. In contrast to his contamination in the Odyssean half, Aeneas carves his way through the Iliadic *Aeneid* unsullied by the epithet, as if he has somehow evaded the dynamics of association and grown qualified to enforce his father's imperial dictum. But given our earlier schooling, are we not meant to observe this propagandistic denial? Several details from the middle books might linger in our memory to give us pause. One is the transfer of the epithet 'superbus' (6.817), startling to anyone aware of the role played in Roman history by Lucius Tarquinas Superbus, builder of the Temple to Jupiter on the Capitol, to the soul of his foe Lucius Junius Brutus, revered as a founder of the Roman Republic. More provocative still is the poem's second set of 'proud doorposts' ('superbis / postibus', 8.720-1) portrayed at the centre of Aeneas' shield. In a scene that conflates the October 29 BC triumph following the battle of Actium and the October 28 BC dedication of a new temple to Apollo on the Palatine, Augustus sits hanging the tributes of nations on the temple's proud doorposts. In announcing his epic project in the proem to Book 3 of the *Georgics*, Vergil describes it as a marble temple inhabited by Caesar: 'in the centre will my Caesar be and keep the temple' ('in medio mihi Caesar erit templumque tenebit', *Geo.*, 3.16). The plan is realized here at the centre of the shield, but details have been added to link the passage to its surrounding narrative. In bringing his patron outside the temple to the proud doorposts and seating him on the threshold ('limine', 8.720), Vergil expands the circle of *superbi*. Robert Edgeworth is unusual among scholars in finding the emperor's position ominous:

> Elsewhere in the poem, it is the Furies who sit upon the threshold. By depicting Augustus as sitting upon the threshold, Vergil has put him into the place of the Furies. The effect of this detail is, or ought to be, as deeply upsetting as that produced by the much-pondered reference to the Gate of Ivory in Book 6.[27]

In the proem to *Georgics* 3, Vergil rejects Hercules as a hackneyed and unworthy subject for his projected epic: 'who does not know harsh Eurystheus or the altars of unpraised Busirus?' (*Geo.*, 3.4-5). Reconsidering the possibilities, in the *Aeneid* he makes Hercules perhaps the most important figure in the representation of the paradox plaguing the imperial project. Although references to Hercules abound in the poem, the most developed story is firmly rooted in sacred Rome. Critics have long recognized the 'episodic' nature of the story of Hercules' victory over the semi-human Cacus. 'When we look at it from the viewpoint of the action', G. Karl Galinsky writes, 'the results are meager indeed'.[28] Galinsky proceeds to turn this apparent vice into a virtue. Arguing that its narrative irrelevance highlights its function as part of a network of motifs, he traces the numerous imagistic, lexical, and situational links that radiate outward from the episode throughout the poem, and especially to Books 2 and 12. His analysis supports earlier perceptions of the poem's parallel between Hercules' combat with Cacus and Aeneas' with Turnus. More recent critics have understood this homology to compromise Aeneas even as it glorifies him. As D. C. Feeney admirably acknowledges the problem:

Yet, in adopting a Herculean status, and discharging Herculean functions, he also finds himself being assimilated to some of the more forbidden aspects of his paradigm. In his exercise of *vis* and *furor*, and in his frightful solitude, Aeneas comes all too close to another side of Hercules.[29]

The episode continues the poem's demonstration that in battling down the *superbi* with strength and fury, one merges with one's foe. The long-distance displacements of the Odyssean half are here replaced by the close proximity of the proud doors where Cacus displays his triumphal trophies, the pallid faces of men hung in sad decay ('foribusque adfixa superbis / ora virum tristi pendebant pallida tabo', 8.196-7), and Alcides, 'proud' ('superbus', 202) of his slaying of Geryon. The setting inescapably recalls the proud doorposts of Augustus' triumph, the *superbus* passage in next closest proximity. For the Roman audience topographical supported textual proximity, for Augustus established the area at the head of the Scalae Caci, a stairway leading down the Palatine to the legendary home of Cacus, as the residence of emperors.[30] Moreover, as this node of thematic connections radiates outward into the poem in the manner Galinsky describes, it prompts us to apply the lesson of collapsed difference to the episodes brought together. While Vergil is developing Homer's use of Hercules to impose new demands of associational assembly, he includes an economically condensed lesson to assist the process. John Zarker argues that the Salian priests' song listing Hercules' labours (8.288-302) 'reveals the greatness of the victory over Cacus in that it is a sum of the parts of all Hercules' other glorious labours':

> Cacus is choked in the same manner as were the serpents sent by Juno; he tore apart cities just as he tore apart the cave of Cacus. Cacus was divinely born as were the centaurs Hylaeus and Pholus; Cacus is a monster as was the Cretan bull and he was huge as was the Nemean lion. Cacus is himself a Typhoeus-like figure; the heads of the Lernean dragon and Cerberus recall the three-headed nature of Cacus as related by both Propertius and Ovid.[31]

As Aeneas listens to Evander's account and the Salians' list, he is sitting on the Herculean lion's pelt (8.177) that he originally put on upon departing from Troy (2.722). Arriving with the *translatio* this echo signifies are the more troublesome aspects of the mythic paradigm. Aeneas seems unable to make the necessary connections. One can only wonder if Augustus could.

The Salians singing at the Roman omphalos call Hercules 'invictus' (293), the epithet attached to the 'unconquered' hero in his role of *kosmokrator*. This role has been taken over by Augustus, whose universal empire, the poet notes, surpasses the area covered in Hercules' voyages: 'nor in truth did Alcides range over so much of earth' ('nec vero Alcides tantum tellurit obivit', 6.801). All of this of course redounds to the glory of Aeneas and his illustrious descendant, but Vergil continues his compromising contamination as well with this part of the Herculean material. At the historical moment of the *Aeneid*, the image of Hercules remained a point of contention in the empire's highly mythologized propaganda. Julius Caesar had unabashedly taken on the role of Hercules *kosmokrator* and its 'invictus' epithet. But in the competition between Antony and Octavian following Caesar's death, Antony, who claimed descent from a son of Hercules named Anton, was more successful in appropriating the Hercules identity, so much so that Augustus later refused the title 'invictus', turning to Apollo instead as his mythological world-ruling counterpart.[32] The Salians' song must have reminded its external audience that, as in the mythic past, in the historical present the imperial mission is fraught with difference-collapsing paradox.

Vergil encodes a similar wealth of suggestion into the act of supplication. In Homer the vertical aspect of the term is realized through gesture rather than etymology. In Vergil's Latin *supplex* (from *sub-* + *plico* or 'fold') becomes a signifier systematically opposed to *superbus* and other *super-* terms. Vergil introduces this concept in Juno's opening speech, where it can continue the development of issues introduced by the reference to Trojan *superbia*. As in the *Iliad*'s opening quarrel between Achilles and Agamemnon, the conflict is framed in terms of vertical relationships, though now the implicit logic is more oblique. One way of answering the perplexed narrator's question to the Muse about the 'cause' ('causas', 8) of the Trojans' ordeal is to note that, in another instance of the proud labelling the other proud, *superbus* is a term more precisely applicable to Juno, who is obsessed with hierarchical relationships, than to anyone else. Outraged that as 'queen of the gods' (46) she has had less success than Pallas, she at once projects her own defining quality onto the Trojans and worries that, because of her failure to thwart them, humankind will no longer lay sacrifices with humble reverence ('supplex', 1.49) on her altars. Her solution is a paradoxical one. She seeks aid as a 'suppliant' ('supplex', 64) to Aeolus, who presides over a realm radically different from the flat island of the wind god visited by Odysseus (*Od.*, 10.1-12). Vergil's island is almost exclusively vertical, with a 'vast cavern' ('vasto . . . antro', 52) where Aeolus 'presses with his rule' ('imperio premit', 54) the unruly winds and sits in a 'lofty citadel' ('celsa . . . arce', 56) formed when Jupiter 'piled the mass of mountains above' them ('molemque et montis insuper altos / imposuit', 61-2). In this setting Juno's supplication identifies the principle of cosmic hierarchy with the power of repression, which is both essential to the hero who would stay on the heroic path and the source of the impulses that can turn heroes mentally headlong, as Aeneas will soon be as a direct result of her actions. Her offer of a beautiful nymph reminds one of her Homeric predecessor, who seduces Sleep in a similar way (*Il.*, 14.231ff.), but the allusion works by contrast. Aeolus inhabits a sexually self-cancelling 'fatherland, a place pregnant with raging winds' ('patriam, loca feta furentibus Austris', 51), from which all of Homer's eroticism has been removed, leaving the forms of repression without the contents. This repression is a truly cosmic operation, for released impulses would eradicate the distinctions of 'seas and lands and lofty sky' ('maria ac terras caelumque profundum', 58). Juno succeeds not through the content of her appeal but through the form. She raises herself by lowering herself, and Aeolus responds by acknowledging that she is a 'queen' (76) who can do as she wishes. Further complicating the situation is the contrast between the supplications of Thetis to her 'father' ('pater', *Il.*, 1.503) Zeus and Venus to her literal father. Vergil makes a point of recalling Homer's Zeus by placing Jupiter at the highest point in heaven ('aethere summo', 1.223), but instead of reinforcing our sense of vertical hierarchy by supplicating him, Venus speaks familiarly, even scoldingly with her father.[33] She then approaches her son Cupid as a 'suppliant to his godhead' ('supplex tua numina', 1.666), addressing him with a surprising degree of religious awe. Since Cupid functions very much like the Fury that will later infect Turnus and Amata, this supplication too acknowledges the power of unconscious forces and indicates the necessity for a more oblique approach to cosmic hierarchy. The two supplications are in fact complementary as well as analogous in form, for Cupid restores the eroticism that Vergil has so conspicuously removed from Aeolus' isle.

The response to Juno's anger recommended first by Helenus and then by Tiberinus is similarly paradoxical, suggesting that one can be higher by being lower: 'overcome with suppliant gifts' ('supplicibus supera donis', 3.439), 'overcome with suppliant vows' ('supplicibus supera votis', 8.61). As a resolution to the conflicting Homeric demands of competition and fellow-feeling, this proto-Christian paradox allows the hero to continue his quest to overcome while acknowledging another's superiority. The idea is logically more compatible with the *Odyssey*'s obligation to honour the suppliant than with the preference of the *Iliad*'s warriors for physical rather than merely symbolic conquest. Accordingly, the first human supplication — though before this Aeneas views the Trojan women's supplication on the temple wall (1.481) and recalls Priam praising Achilles for honouring 'a suppliant's right' ('iura . . . supplicis', 2.541-2) — is that of the 'supplex' (3.592 and 667) Achaemenides in Sicily. The scene is modelled on the refugee Theoclymenus' supplication of Telemachus in *Odyssey* 15, though Vergil reverses Homer's removal of physical detail by emphasizing the suppliant's physical subservience. As in the closing scene of the *Iliad* and throughout the *Odyssey*, in the *Aeneid* granting a supplicator's request enhances rather than diminishes the hero's glory. With these instances as background we can better understand the function of supplication imagery in Book 4. The despairing Dido is first shown 'a suppliant submitting her heart to love' ('supplex animos summittere amori', 414) and then asking Anna to 'go as a suppliant to the proud foe' ('hostem supplex adfare superbum', 423). The hero's unmoved response adds to our unease about him, for we experience a conflict not merely between duty and love but between two aspects of the hero's imperial mission. He cannot translate empire if he spares the subjected.

In the Italian, Iliadic books supplication to a god figures prominently as a sign of *pietas*. Aeneas supplicates the Sibyl (6.115) and Juno (8.61), Ascanius supplicates Jove (9.624), and Camilla's father supplicates Diana (11.559). Book 10 also presents the battlefield counterpart of Achaemenides' prototypical exile supplication in Book 3. Immediately following the death of Pallas, 'supplex' (523) Magus begs Aeneas for mercy. That only Magus and Achaemenides are shown physically grasping the hero's knees strengthens the association between the two scenes. Now, however, Aeneas rejects the appeal and, in a vividly portrayed action strongly reminiscent of the murder of Priam by Pyrrhus, he bends back the suppliant's head with one hand and plunges his sword in to the hilt.[34] Aeneas' return to the ethos of the *Iliad*, occurring simultaneously with his association with his people's foremost enemy, can only serve further to compromise his heroic stature. Certainly Magus makes an unfortunate appeal, offering wealth to a hero who has recently been told to shun it (8.365). But this detail only adds to the unease with which we witness Aeneas' next and final reaction to a formal suppliant. 'Supplex' (12.930) Turnus offers Aeneas one last opportunity to choose between Homeric precedents. Kneeling, with uplifted eyes and pleading hand, Turnus makes a more appropriate plea, imitating Priam's appeal to Achilles' memory of his own father. But Aeneas declines to end his epic with a grand scene of high humanity and, as Lyne comments, 'in the last seconds of the poem the new Achilles is again virtually identical in action and motivation to the old Achilles, in particular the Achilles of *Iliad* 22'.[35] Aeneas can follow the example of Pyrrhus, but he cannot rise to the humanity Pyrrhus' father finally achieves.

Between Aeneas' pious supplications to the Sibyl and Juno and his disconcerting refusal to honour the supplications of Magus and Turnus lies the visit to Arcadia. When Aeneas arrives a 'suppliant at the threshold' of Evander ('supplex ad limina', 145), he for the only time in the poem assumes the position before a human being that he assumed before the gods. Despite the differing circumstances surrounding these various supplications, the chronotopic armature of Vergil's poem turns Evander's acceptance of the hero's request into a lesson that he proves unable subse quently to apply when the relationships are reversed. This crucial bridging episode is dense with spatial symbolism. The overall trajectory of Vergil's historical narrative, the descent from the Trojan citadel that will eventuate in the ascent of the Roman citadel, is in one sense completed when Aeneas tours the future site of Rome. This is accomplished through Aeneas' heeding the advice of Helenus and Tiberinus to rise by lowering oneself. It is also in a more important sense not accomplished but only foreshadowed, and Roman history will demonstrate the wider applicability of the Sibyl's proclamation on the voyage into and out of hell: 'easy is the descent . . . but to recall your steps and pass out into the open air, that is the work, that is the labour' ('facilis descensus. . . sed revocare gradum superasque evadere ad auras, / hoc opus, hoc labor est', 6.126-8). In a paradox that has long irritated readers disinclined to accommodate the complexity of Vergil's vision, Evander's dwelling possesses both a 'humble roof' ('humili tecto', 455) and a 'lofty threshold' ('limine . . . alto', 461), details that combine in surrealistic fashion when Evander claims that, literally, 'this threshold victorious Alcides passed under' ('haec . . . limina victor / Alcides subiit', 362-3).[36] No matter how we normalize such descriptions, they retain a conspicuous illogicality pointing at once to the future glory of Rome and the paradoxical means of achieving it. It is entirely appropriate for the poem's prototype of the hero raised in apotheosis that he performs this bizarre action, just as it is appropriate that Evander is related to Aeneas through descent from Atlas, who uplifts the starry heavens (141), for Evander's humility is the means by which Aeneas will achieve his own apotheosis. Evander's initiation of Aeneas into this heroic lineage is promising but less severe: 'he led huge Aeneas under the pediment of the narrow roof' ('angusti subter fastigia tecti / ingentem Aenean duxit', 366-7). The compression is horizontal as well as vertical. From this narrow roof Evander's fame spreads through the world ('terris didita fama', 132). Aeneas' quest is not only to rise into the heavens but, through whatever humility he can muster, including the many supplications the Sibyl predicts he will be required to perform (6.91ff.), to continue the long imperial project whereby Evander's universal fame will be transformed into the universal empire of Augustus.[37]

All of these actions take place in a world of intensely cyclical time. In his survey of ancient philosophies of history, Frank Manuel concludes that 'the whole of the surviving corpus of literature inherited from antiquity testifies virtually without contradiction that cyclical theory possessed the Greco-Roman world'.[38] Although it does not contain an explicit theory of universal time in the manner of Plato, Aristotle, the Stoics or the Epicureans, the *Aeneid* is equally 'possessed'. Homer's graceful evocations of nature's cycles have been replaced by a harsh vision of humankind's vulnerability in a world rolling relentlessly onward. Helenus declares that the king of the gods 'rolls changes; and thus is the order turned' ('volvit vices, is vertitur ordo', 3.376). As the order turns, forms of human order are violently overthrown and maintaining the heroic quest, and the imperial dynastic line, becomes an unprecedented challenge. Symptomatic of Vergil's cyclical world are such expressions as Troy 'upturned from its base' ('ex imo verti', 2.625), realms and household gods 'overturned' ('versos', 11.264), live heroes rolling ('volvimur', 5.629) on the waves while the waters roll ('volvit', 1.101) the dead beneath them. Flames, smoke, and floods roll through scenes of devastation, and in their midst heroes are 'overturned' and writhe in twisting death throes in the dust. In the poem's first half turning is an unfortunate but necessary aspect of the motion needed to navigate the labyrinthine world, and logically speaking, the warriors of the second half too could turn positively, as Homer's heroes regularly do, toward heroic pursuit of their enemies. The vocabulary of turning in this context, however, applies exclusively to turning back in flight and defeat, with the suggestion that the cycles of time are the most powerful enemies of all.[39]

If Vergil was heir to generally pessimistic philosophies of cyclical history, he was also heir to a positive model of circular motion unavailable to Homer. Although the idea that the heavens' circlings reflect perfection was commonplace among post-Homeric poets and Pre-Socratic thinkers, it remained for Plato to extend the idea systematically to the microcosm. The Athenian interlocutor of the *Laws* moves easily from discussing the world soul's 'control of heaven and earth and their whole circuit' to the representation of *nous* (mind or intelligence) as rotary motion about a fixed centre. 'The revolution of intelligence', he claims, moves 'after the fashion of a well-turned cartwheel. . . . Intelligence and movement performed in one place are both like the revolutions of a well-made globe, in moving regularly and uniformly in one compass about one centre, and in one sense, according to one single law and plan'.[40] Because Plato's rotating *nous* is ultimately contemplative rather than active, there are problems in considering it a model appropriate to epic poetry. But in its focus on one centre, law and plan it forms an interesting and probably enabling precedent for Vergil's development of the *Odyssey's* addition of circular motion to the previously rectilinear *metis*.

In a pre-emptive move recalling the self-division of Homer's heroes, the Vergilian hero responds to his (and her) precarious position in the cycles of history by turning things over in the mind. In the poem's reconstructed chronology, Anchises sets the pattern in his response to the oracle on Delos, which refers cryptically to the Trojans' return to an ancient mother-land. By 'revolving the memories of old men' ('veterum volvens monumenta virorum', 3.102), Anchises connects details of history to the present circumstance and comes up with a plan for the future. Recalling Teucer's empire-founding voyage from Crete to Asia Minor, he constructs a coherent narrative of Trojan history that provides, as noted above, the Aeneadae's first directed course of travel. In Africa the son imitates the father when after 'revolving so many things' ('plurima volvens', 1.305) throughout the night Aeneas determines to 'go forth to explore the new lands' ('exire locosque / explorare novos', 1.306-7). Venus 'crosses his path in the middle of the wood' ('media sese tulit obvia silva', 314) and tells him, 'just go forward' ('perge modo') and 'proceed' ('perfer', 389) to the queen's threshold, which he will reach if he will just 'go forward and direct his steps where the path leads' ('perge modo et, qua te ducit via, derige gressum', 401). We should note the laboured abstraction of this first pondering scene encountered by the reader. We do not know what the multiple items are that Aeneas revolves. They are not the two parts of the path, into and out of the wood, which form a unified itinerary no less than do Anchises' recollected and proposed journeys. On the other hand, in some sense they are, for the hero's present trek to the centre recapitulates in miniature the long narrative of empire-founding with which Jupiter eases the anxieties of Venus immediately before the pondering scene. The very abstraction of the scene encourages us as readers to perform our own relation of part to part. At some point in this process we can understand that the poem's first two instances of pondering demonstrate an essential activity of the Vergilian hero. They also, we eventually learn, demonstrate the hero's predicament, for both acts of pondering lead in the same wrong direction.

As a result, Aeneas' first pondering scene must be corrected by a second. Following Mercury's visitation, Aeneas 'swiftly now here now there divides his mind, drives it through various parts and turns it through everything' ('animum nunc huc celerem, nunc dividit illuc / in partisque rapit varias perque omnia versat', 4.285-6). In this fuller synthesis of Homeric pondering models, the circular 'versat' unites parts into a totality, Aeneas resolves on a course of action, and within hours the Trojans are proceeding forward again. A final pondering scene (8.19ff.) finds Aeneas 'seeing all' ('cuncta videns') and again undergoing the experience of 4.285-6, which is repeated verbatim, though now with a simile appended:

> sicut aquae tremulum labris ubi lumen aenis
> sole repercussum aut radiantis imagine lunae
> omnia pervolitat late loca iamque sub auras
> erigitur summique ferit laquearia tecti. (8.22-5)

> as when from brazen bowls of water a flickering light
> flung back by the radiant form of the sun or moon
> flies widely through all places and now skyward
> rises and strikes the panels of the high roof.

Aeneas is often faulted for displaying here an inability to fix his thoughts, a shortcoming that will require Tiberinus' subsequent appearance to resolve. Medea displays this inability in the *Argonautica* (3.754ff.), the simile's source, but Vergil's changes contrast Aeneas with his notoriously unstable predecessor. As in the repeated image of mental motion preceding the simile, multiplicity gives way to totality ('omnia pervolitat'), and now this progression is accompanied by ascent, a motion to which the contradictory 'sub auras' and the intervening ceiling calls attention.[41] Tiberinus presents the practical details that realize the terms already presented: the straight, directed path upstream completes both the horizontal aspect of Aeneas' mission toward the centre and its vertical aspect, his ascent to a new lofty city. After this final orientation, Aeneas gives up pondering.

In these and the poem's other instances, the pondering hero is the active agent and mental revolution accompanies, indeed may be seen as part of, external heroic action. The pattern holds for the other characters. Venus' mental turning in 1.657 issues in Cupid's journey to Carthage. When Latinus mentally revolves matters in 7.254ff., he invites Aeneas to approach his throne. When Camilla's father revolves things in his mind in 11.551ff., he saves his infant daughter by launching her toward safety bound to his spear. Turnus in 10.285ff. appropriately ponders who will lead the attack on the Trojan camp. Even Dido, who 'turns her mind in all parts' ('partis animum versabat in omnis', 4.630) imitates heroic action in her active suicide and her ascent of the high pyre. Amata offers a spectacular example of the negative counterpart to this positive circularity, where one is the turned victim rather than the turning agent. In a memorable simile she is whipped by Allecto into Bacchic frenzy like a spinning top driven by boys with their sticks (7.377ff.). Her rotation, certainly an allusion to Hector's spinning like a top at the blow of Ajax in *Iliad* 14.413 and perhaps as well to Plato's use of the spinning top as an image of the soul in *Republic* 436d-e, suggests pondering run out of control, while her irregular motion 'through the vast city' ('immensam . . . per urbem', 377) contrasts with the successful hero's translation of internal circular into external linear motion.

For the benefit of an audience accustomed to the exaggerated gestures of the stage, the *Aeneid* works an interesting variation on these forms of motion in its imagery of rolling eyes, a gesture that William S. Anderson believes Vergil introduced into literature.[42] While Aeneas, about to depart Carthage, delivers his excuses to the outraged Dido, she gazes upon him askance, 'turning her eyes to and fro, and with silent glances scans the whole' ('huc illuc volvens oculos, totumque pererrat luminibus tacitis', 4.363-4). With his characteristic control of abstraction, Vergil specifies the object of her sight only as a 'whole'. The hero's integral body is the literal referent, but the more figurative object is Aeneas' discourse, which resists her efforts at assembly. This 'whole' initiates a sequence of fragmentation images: the disruption of her own discourse in midspeech (388), her swoon, her fantasy of dismembering Aeneas (600), and finally her own reduction to ashes, the ultimately fragmentary material that haunts this section of the poem (cf. 427, 552, 633). The implications of her rolling eyes are profoundly ambiguous. Their motion contrasts negatively with the hero's eyes, which are held steadfast ('immota tenebat lumina', 331), but she also imitates the totalizing motion of pondering so important in Book 4. Book 7 provides contrasting models that can lend support to divergent interpretations of Dido's demeanour. Rolling eyes ('volvens oculos', 7.251) are the outward sign of Latinus' inward pondering ('volvit sub pectore', 254). In the same book an equivalent expression describes frenzied Amata 'rolling her bloodshot eyes' ('sanguineam torquens aciem', 399), clearly a symptom of her involuntary spinning as Allecto's top and as victim of the serpent the fury has sent winding ('volvitur', 350) into her heart.

If the clear contrast in Book 7 complicates our retrospective understanding of Book 4, it also enriches the interpretive potential of subsequent scenes. When in the next book Aeneas receives new arms from his mother, he not only turns each piece over ('versat', 8.619), but also 'rolls his eyes across each piece' ('oculos per singula volvit', 618), as if he is trying to assemble the parts into a whole. The meaning of this procedure grows vaguely sinister when the whole scene concludes with a statement of Aeneas' unknowing response to the carnage portrayed on the shield: 'ignorant of the deeds, he rejoices in the portrayal' ('rerumque ignarus imagine gaudet', 730). The next instance occurs when Pallas, about to be slain by Turnus, surveys his killer: 'he rolls his eyes over his huge body and with fierce glance from afar goes over all' ('corpusque per ingens / lumina volvit obitque truci procul omnia visu', 10.446-7). Is the youth heroic in his pondering glance and subsequent attack, or is it madness for him to seek out such a formidable foe? We cannot be certain. Nor can we comfort ourselves with certainty when Vergil completes his sequence of images. Standing 'with rolling eyes' ('volvens oculos', 12.939) above the suppliant Turnus, Aeneas begins a process of assembling parts, as 'more and more the speech began to turn him as he paused' ('iam iamque magis cunctantem flectere sermo / coeperat', 940-1). In the course of this visual survey his glance passes to Pallas' belt stripped by Turnus as a trophy of war. Immediately both the rolling of his eyes and the corresponding mental assembly cease. The poem's imperial voice can suggest that Aeneas' compromising *furor* has now ceased as well, and that the dangerously deflective narrative of Turnus has given way to the grand narrative that has guided the hero since his last two pondering scenes. But the network of imagery enables another voice to present a contrasting interpretation. In a moment of passion Aeneas neglects an essential heroic labour, and in the partial vision that results, he at once founds an empire and violates its mission.

Notes

1. Hardie (1986), p. 1.
2. For a recent and magnificently argued consideration of this continual redefinition, see Quint's (1993) chapter on 'Epic and Empire: Versions of Actium'. My reading of the material Quint covers differs from his in that I find Vergil to be perfectly aware of, indeed conspicuously dramatizing and even deconstructing through his epic's clash of voices, the Augustan effort of redefinition. In other words, while Quint repeatedly finds that the *Aeneid* 'conforms to the prevailing ideological climate' (p. 83), I find it to be repeatedly critiquing prevailing ideological constructions.
3. Part of this intensity derives from differences between Latin and Greek languages which must in turn derive from differences in culture. The principal Homeric term for threshold is *oudos*, which is related to *odos*, meaning 'a way, path, track, passage, road'. Architecturally the Homeric threshold is a row of blocks forming the lower part of a doorway, but it is conceived more as a ritualized site of entry than a barrier to be crossed: one sits down inside the threshold. The Roman term produces connotations opposed to the Greek sense of passage through. According to Ernout and Meillet (1967, p. 359), it was associated in popular etymology with *limes*, a boundary line or course running transverse to the path of entry. Latin love poetry realizes the Roman conception when it locates the lover outside at the threshold in the *exclusus amator* convention, on which Copley (1956) is the standard work. Surprisingly little attention has been paid to threshold imagery in ancient epic. Charles Segal (1967) discusses threshold imagery as part of the *Odyssey*'s use of rites of passage. Robert Edgeworth (1986) considers the ominous associations of thresholds in the *Aeneid*.
4. The buried head also contributes to the association of Troy, Rome, and Carthage as imperial centres. The startling description of Priam's headless corpse lying on the shore after Pyrrhus' attack seems designed to invite speculation. Charles Martindale (1986, p. 144) proposes that the corpse recalls that of Pompey the Great, left headless and unburied on the Egyptian strand following his defeat by Julius Caesar. I believe that Vergil's audience would also recall the most prominent (and probably legendary) beheading in early Roman history. According to Arnobius of Sicca (1949, pp. 458-9), it was common knowledge that the Capitol was named from *Caput Auli*, the head of Aulus. After a successful rebellion against the Tarquin tyranny by Caelius and Aulus Vibenna, Aulus fell out with his brother and was beheaded. His head was buried in the hill that subsequently became the Capitol. Livy records that during the building of the temple to Jupiter Capitolinus by Lucius Tarquinas Superbus an undecayed human head was found and taken as a sign of approval for the project. The soothsayers proclaimed the Capitol 'the citadel of the

empire and the head of the world', ('arcem eam imperii caputque rerum', Livy, 1967, p. 191, I.lv).

5. Citations of the *Aeneid* are drawn from the 1969 Oxford edition edited by R. A. B. Mynors. Because all translators inevitably fail to capture Vergil's chronotopic subtlety, I have included my own English translations, which are intended to be literal rather than literary.

6. Mario Di Cesare's *The Altar and the City* (1974) is an exemplary exception to the tendency to naturalize Vergil's carefully restricted spatial vocabulary. He observes, for example, that Aeneas' 'outcry, as he observes the labours of the *Tyrii . . . coloni*, is not for a lineage, a race, or an empire; it is for *moenia*, walls which define without limiting the city' (p. 2). Avoiding the redundancy of 'limina portae', translators also avoid Vergil's combination of Iliadic and Odyssean sites of contention.

7. Quint (1993), p. 57.

8. Delos, the birthplace of Apollo and Artemis, served as an omphalic centre drawing pilgrims and panegyrics from around the Greek world from at least the eighth century BC. Its sacred status is reflected in the Homeric Hymn 'To Delian Apollo'. Odysseus (*Od.*, 6.162ff.) compares Nausicaa to the celebrated palm tree at the great altar on Delos. For evidence that Vergil's audience would have been familiar with the island's importance as a sacred centre, see Bruneau (1970).

9. Vergil is imitating here the Homeric description of Crete 'in the middle of the wine-blue water' ('meso eni oinopi ponto', *Od.*, 19.172). In the autobiography the disguised Odysseus fabricates for Penelope, Crete takes on imperial dimensions that strengthen the cosmic implications of 'meso', as opposed to the opposite, disorienting sense of being in the midst of something. Vergil's 'medio' probably contains both senses, adding to the dramatic irony. Donald Mills (1983, p. 38) believes Crete is being presented here as an omphalic centre.

10. Doob (1990), p. 228.

11. See note 9 of chapter 1, for Ovid's equation of Rome and the world. Claims that the Roman empire extends to the ends of the earth, that the Roman empire is defined by the sun's course, and so forth, abound in Roman imperial literature and in the writings of Greek admirers. A few examples: Ovid, *Fasti*, 1.85, 2.136-8, 2.684 (the last quoted above); Cicero, *Pro Cestio*, 67; Seneca, *De Beneficiis*, 3.33.

12. The important disparity between the gods' (and here our) perspective and the human-eye view is often neglected in discussions of the poem. For admirable exceptions, see Commager (1981) and Feeney (1991), p. 157.

13. Hardie (1983) surveys the Roman associations of Atlas with the world-axis.

14. Hardie (1986), p. 276.

15. Aristotle (1939), pp. 220 and 223. Aristotle describes *megalopsuchia* at length in Book 4, sections 3-4 of the *Nichomachean Ethics*.

16. Aristotle (1989), vol. 2, p. 238. *Posterior Analytics*, Book 2, section 13.

17. Cicero (1975), pp. 64-7. *De Officiis*, Book 1, sections 19-20.

18. Aeneas is also magnanimous at 5.17, 5.407, 9.204, 10.771. I find it suggestively bizarre that the second use of the term also has vertical implications: steep Acragas once produced 'magnanimous horses' ('magnanimum . . . generator equorum', 3.704). The bitter Juturna provides the poem's final usage when she complains about the 'proud mandates of high-souled Jove' ('iussa superba / magnanimi Iovis', 12.878).

19. Clausen (1987), p. 52.

20. Hardie (1986), p. 280.

21. See Green (1977) on 'The *Zaddiq* as *Axis Mundi*'. Green observes that with Christianity the imagery is applied to the individual, to Christ, and to a slightly shifted geographical locality: the centre of the world 'has moved a very significant few yards from the Temple Mount to the Mount of Calvary' (p. 329). One must also include Rome, a centre for pilgrimage from early in Christian history. Muslim orthodoxy, Green observes, resisted description of the Prophet in these terms, but 'Sufi masters from the eighth century onward speak of the *qotb*, a single holy man who is the "pole," standing at the height of the world's spiritual hierarchy'.

22. For a discussion of the cosmic tree symbol, see Butterworth (1970).

23. Aeneas is *ingens* at 8.367 and 12.441. Anchises' tallness is also observed in Hades at 6.668. Turnus too is *ingens* (10.446) when confronting Pallas.

24. Lyne (1987), p. 231.

25. Lloyd (1972), p. 128.

26. Otto Fenichel (1945, p. 511) writes that 'revenge is a special type of magical "undoing" of a humiliation, based on an identification with the aggressor'.

27. Edgeworth (1986), p. 157.

28. Galinsky (1966), pp. 18-19. Scholarly commentary on Vergil's Hercules is voluminous. Feeney's brief discussion (1991, pp. 155-62) includes references that update Galinsky's.

29. Feeney (1991), p. 161.

30. Small (1982), p. 19. Small's coverage of the Cacus legend is exhaustive and definitive. She also provides useful background for Augustus' cult of Apollo, whose temple was built on the grounds of the emperor's Palatine residence. It should also be noted here that Vergil, at the same time that he strengthens the association by portraying Cacus and Augustus at their residences, also attenuates it by moving the monster's residence from its traditional site on the Palatine to the Aventine hill. It is hard to overestimate the symbolic impact of Roman topographical references for the original audience. Augustus moved the Sibylline books from the temple of Jupiter Capitolinus to the new Palatine temple as part of his project of stripping Jupiter of his supreme authority, a project already conspicuously underway when Vergil was maintaining the traditional emphasis on the Capitol and affording Jupiter an unprecedented degree of preeminence (cf. Feeney, 1991, pp. 137-55).

31. Zarker (1972), pp. 42-3.

32. On the use of Hercules by the various rivals for power in the early empire, see Anderson (1928). In a chapter on 'Rival Images: Octavian, Antony, and the Struggle for Sole Power', Paul Zanker (1988) describes the manipulation of Hercules iconography and Octavian's eventual preference for Apollo. Especially interesting in relation to the *Aeneid* are the pictorial means used to betray Antony with his own successful appropriation of Hercules. Antony was portrayed as Hercules drawn in a chariot with Omphale. Like Aeneas looking back to Dido's Carthage, he looks backward to the object of his infatuation, a sign that supports other indications of effeminate slackness.

33. As Feeney (1991, p. 151) notices, the formula describing Jupiter's supreme vertical position recurs meaningfully in 12.853: 'The very first and the very last words in the first and last Jupiter-scenes are identical, so that we enter and leave Jupiter's realm with the same phrase'.

34. Killing the suppliant, Aeneas 'grasps the helmet in his left hand, and bending back the suppliant's neck drives the sword up to the hilt' ('galeam laeva tenet atque reflexa / cervice ornatis capula tenus applicat ensem', 10.535-6). Murdering Priam, Pyrrhus 'winds his left hand in his hair, and with the right raises his flashing sword and drives it to the hilt in his side' ('implicuitque comam laeva, dextraque coruscum / extulit ac lateri capulo tenus abdidit ensem', 2.552-3). The fact that Priam, despite just having praised Pyrrhus' father for respecting suppliants' rights, is not here *supplex* but aggressively defiant does not soften our assessment of the new Trojan Pyrrhus. We should note also that the left / right dichotomy enters to suggest an incriminating parody of the supplication ritual's sequence. For a Homeric precedent for the parody, consider that in the famous scar scene of *Odyssey* 19 Odysseus grasps the old nurse Euryclea by the throat with his right hand and draws her to him with his left. Auerbach (1953, pp. 2-3) finds the details simply to be products of Homer's method of 'externalizing', but the symbolism is inescapable: in contrast to Vergil, Homer is softening the impression of Odysseus by maintaining the supplication pattern. Another question presents itself in the scene: is magnanimous Aeneas, in the manner of a Homeric hero, provoked by Magus' name?

35. Lyne (1987), p. 112. Lyne's book contains superb analyses of the allusive connections between Aeneas and several of Homer's characters. He misses, however, the internal identification with Pyrrhus.

36. Yardley (1981) reviews recent commentators' bafflement over the 'high threshold' and 'humble roof' passages as well as earlier attempts to evade the problem. He suggests that Vergil is contrasting the grand houses of the Augustan Palatine, whose entrances deserve the epithet *alta*, with the simplicity of the past.

37. Hardie (1986), pp. 193ff. and 252ff., is instructive on the vertical and horizontal expansion of both fame and empire in the *Aeneid*. He finds extensive parallels between Vergil and Lucretius in these aspects of the epic quest.

38. Manuel (1965), p. 7.

39. Flames roll in 2.759, 4.671, 12.672; smoke in 3.206, 12.591, 12.906; floods in 6.659, 11.635. Representative instances of navigational turning in the labyrinthine first half include 1.158, 3.146, 3.532, 3.669, 5.23, 5.177. For the imagery of heroes overturned, see for example: 1.116, 6.362, 10.790, 11.640, 11.889, 12.329; for writhing, 6.581 (here the defeated Titans writhing in the abyss establish the prototype), 9.414, 9.433, 10.700 11.669; for turning-in-flight, 6.491, 8.706, 9.686, 9.756, 9.800, 10.573, 10.593, 10.646, 11.412, 11.618, 11.684, 12.462. In the last case the pattern is so pervasive that instances that might at first appear exceptions must be read ironically. Ornytus, for example, turns ('vertitur', 11.683) amidst the ranks and is heroically a full head higher than the rest, but immediately following this description he falls to Camilla, who found the combat 'no heroic labour in the turning ranks' ('neque enim labor agmine verso', 11.684).

40. Plato (1961), pp. 1453-4. *Laws* 10.898a-b. The passage was criticized by Aristotle in *de Anima* 1.3, where the idea that *nous* possesses movement is explicitly rejected.

41. The contradiction is heightened by Vergil's use of the formula 'sub auras' elsewhere only in settings open to the sky (3.422, 3.576, 4.494, 4.504, 7.768); in 2.158 the phrase is figurative, meaning 'bring to light'. The contradiction seems to me resolved in the implied hyperbole about the roof's height.

42. Anderson (1971), p. 49.

CHAPTER THREE

From Ariosto to Spenser

The epic chronotope established by Homer and refined by Vergil would not have sustained its appeal across so many centuries had it not participated in habits of thought common to both classical and Judaeo-Christian cultures. The hero's forward drive and the poet's glorification of his patron, who is the current link in the poem's dynasty and the eventual beneficiary of its action, combine to form a teleology compatible with the Christian sense of progress toward salvation. Spatially, the Christian world, centred in holy Jerusalem or papal Rome and organized vertically in cosmic planes, easily accommodates the pagan omphalic model. In the application of spatial parameters to heroic ethics, the two traditions are no less compatible. Biblical injunctions to follow the straight and narrow path fit well with Greco-Roman moral geometry; in steadfastly maintaining his linear path, the epic hero imitates both Old Testament exemplars and Plato's Phaedrian charioteer, who, as he maintains his straight course despite the sideways pull of the passions, is himself an heir to a long-held Greek preference for the straight over the crooked.

Vergilian epic's chronotopic coherence and compatibility with Christian ethics made it an unavoidable model for the aspiring heroic poet of the Renaissance. A second model forming part of the Renaissance generic repertoire inevitably found its way as well into heroic narrative. The tradition of long verse narratives initiated in France around the middle of the twelfth century, and soon after that labelled 'romans' for their use of the Romance vernacular, continued into the Renaissance. These romances constitute a distinct generic tradition because they too gave rise to a system of substantial chronotopic coherence. Romance evolved from, and in many ways continued to resemble, both classical epic and the *chanson de geste*, which shared a broad range of generic features with its classical predecessor. As a result of such extensive overlapping among generic categories, the internecine interactions of epic and romance generated the Cinquecento's most intense critical quarrels.[1] Romance also, like pastoral, distinguished itself from its generic kin through meaningful oppositions. The most exploitable set of oppositions derived from the genre's return to the cyclical temporality that had been replaced in epic's mythic substratum by a rigorous teleology. Instead of the historical or pseudo-historical setting of epic, romance creates a more fully fictional and timeless setting dependent upon cyclical patterns. Medieval romances usually begin on a specific feast, such as Easter, Pentecost, or Christmas, a detail that launches the action into the cycles of the liturgical and sidereal years, often combining divine sanction with the restorative natural energies of spring or the new year. The romance hero may be assigned quests to perform, and he may pursue them with all the goal-orientation of his epic counterpart, but these quests are subsumed within a larger cyclical pattern of repeatability rather than within the relentless teleology of epic. Or the romance hero may simply cast himself into the currents of adventure, relying upon chance more than directed labour to fulfil his heroic mission as knight errant.

Romance replaces the linear unity of epic's plots based on such overarching, goal-oriented actions as the siege, *nostos*, pilgrimage, or *translatio* with cyclical patterns of procession and return that open new representational possibilities for structures of repetition. For courtly romances, the closest relative to classical epic, the court retains a horizontal omphalic function as the origin and goal of proceeding and returning actions. But the romance centre, although it remains a source of ethical and other values, has lost most of the epic centre's function as an *axis mundi* indexing these values on a vertical scale. The vertical dimension, in fact, is generally suppressed in romance. In a world of horizontal immanence rather than vertical transcendence, gods do not descend as part of a causal sequence nudging the hero back onto the straight and narrow path. Rather, the romance hero wanders through a landscape — the forest setting popularized by Chrétien is symptomatic — in which the marvellous may manifest itself at any time, without causal origins or motivations.[2] Instead of divine interventions, we witness miracles (effects without causes) and magic of a mysterious nature. The romance court's more tenuous centring is also reflected in pervasive moral ambiguities and in the new prominence assigned to the individual, whose quest need not be subordinated to a collective project, and who receives more sustained attention because he is isolated in his quest and undergoes a more mysterious form of self-fashioning. The self remains a site of conflict. But if the epic self is shaped by the struggle between cosmic and chaotic forces, between the deflecting energies of eros and furor and the aligning forces of divine assistance and heroic repression, the oppositions shaping the romance self lack a similar evaluative clarity. Romance commonly pits the hero's familial or societal against his erotic allegiances, but it does not assign one of these unqualified moral superiority. As a result — or more precisely, as one correlative feature of romance among many in a coherent chronotopic system — romance endings are no less qualified, inconclusive, ambiguous than the endings of the great epic exemplars of antiquity. Like the epics of Homer and Vergil, which inevitably prompted continuations, medieval romances too take part in larger story-cycles. The principal closural difference between the two forms is that the inconclusive ending of epic contrasts meaningfully with the genre's teleological temporality, while romance returns less problematically to its cyclical beginning.[3]

The relationship of *Orlando Furioso* to the texts and categories of epic and romance is no less controversial in our century than it was in Ariosto's own. Patricia Parker, David Quint, and Sergio Zatti, to name only three of the most substantial recent examiners of the relationship, implicitly disagree about particular points as much as they agree that some kind of synthesis or interplay of the two forms constitutes the poem's most fundamental artistic innovation. Vergil had established a precedent with his self-conscious incorporation of pastoral into epic. It is consistent with the lowering and levelling impulses of pastoral that Aeneas' first supplication to a fellow human, highlighted so strongly through the paradox of lowly roof and lofty threshold, occurs in Evander's Arcadian realm.[4] In Vergil's revision of epic, the humility that in Book 8 reveals its pastoral connections becomes a crucial component of heroic success. But although we might read later understandings of genre backward into history and refer to 'romance' wanderings in ancient epic, for Vergil generic interaction was a real but decidedly secondary part of his poetics. The situation is very different for Ariosto, who in his satires and comedies no less than in his epic reveals a preoccupation with exploiting what Rosalie Colie calls 'the resources of kind'. The most powerful of these resources, and one that few important Renaissance poets neglected despite continuing disapproval by many theorists, was the creation of conspicuously mixed forms.[5] Ariosto's approach to creating heroic poetry responsive to cultural pressures was to allow epic to serve as what the Russian Formalists call a 'dominant', defined by Roman Jakobson as 'the focusing component of a work of art: it rules, determines, and transforms the remaining components'.[6] In *Orlando Furioso*, for the first time since antiquity, epic's set of conventions forms a dominant against which other generic conventions strike meaningful oppositions.[7] As both overt criticism and the implicit criticism of imitating poets have acknowledged in various ways from the time of its publication, clearly the most important of these oppositions, though certainly not the only ones, arise from the interaction of romance with the epic dominant. Boiardo's *Orlando Innamorato* incorporated extensive Vergilian material into a romance matrix, enhancing the appeal of Carolingian tales for humanist audiences. When Ariosto created his continuation, he reversed the process, and in doing so produced perhaps the most influential narrative of the Renaissance.

Ariosto and the Renaissance of Epic

During the very period when Ariosto was writing and revising *Orlando Furioso*, the papacy was labouring mightily to recover Rome's status as *umbilicus mundi*. Charles Stinger describes the 'translatio Templi' effected by the Quattrocento papacy as St. Peter's basilica came increasingly to be identified with Solomon's Temple and new emphasis was placed on Rome succeeding Jerusalem as a cult-centre and religious capital.[8] Even more prominent in papal ideology were new identifications of the Pope as Caesar. The Roman triumph was enthusiastically revived. The first such Renaissance ceremony, in 1466, was notably Vergilian, parading Cleopatra subdued by Augustus at Actium and praising the pontiff's 'sanctum imperium'. Julius II (1503-13) returned to cosmic centrality the Herculean epithet declined by Augustus, proclaiming himself 'pontifex invictissimus'.[9] Vida's Latin *Christiad*, begun within a year or so of the first publication of *Orlando Furioso*, likens Christ's Ascension to the triumphator's climb of the lofty Capitol. The most impressive artistic result of this ambitious *renovatio imperii* remains visible today. The ambitions of Paul III (1534-49) combined with Michelangelo's architectural genius to produce the renewed Capitol. Above the convex oval pavement evoking the cosmos and Achilles' shield stands an equestrian statue of Marcus Aurelius. Stinger summarizes the intended symbolism:

> The succession Alexander-Antonine emperor-Jupiter would have symbolized the transmission of world hegemony from the empires of Greece and Rome to the imperium of the Roman Church governed by the Farnese Pope. . . . The ancient Romans figuratively moved the umbilicus mundi from Delphi to the Roman Forum, and medieval legend transferred this to the Capitol. Thus the Marcus Aurelius as Kosmokrator-Apollo stands at the nodal point of the universe. The locus of power in Renaissance Rome again assumed a cosmic perspective.[10]

We can appreciate Michelangelo's accomplishment and at the same time be thankful that epic revived at a distance from this centre of aspiring power, indeed in a court increasingly uneasy with papal assertiveness. As he reworked the Boiardan material, developing both its imperial and dynastic aspects in order to reshape it into something more closely resembling Vergil's prestigious epic, Ariosto inevitably encountered a resistance of his material to his form. Temporally, Ferrara's Este rulers, the dynastic heirs of Ruggiero and Bradamante, are the focus of the poem's epideictic rhetoric and the ultimate beneficiaries of its heroic action. Spatially, however, the discrepancy between Ferrara's modest realm and Augustus' universal empire could only contribute to the poem's irony. Prevented from imitating Vergil's carefully unified spatio-temporal framework even had he wished to do so, Ariosto instead intensified his poem's internal generic tensions by retaining Paris' function as the poem's romance court centring characters' cycles of emanation and return and at the same time developing Carlo's capital into the poem's epic omphalos located 'at the navel of France' ('ne ombilico a Francia', 14.104.2). Out of such fortuitous tensions and discrepancies rose an enormously influential work that would restore the epic genre's relevance to a world growing more resistant to the ideological hegemonism implicit in the papacy's attempted translation of epic fiction into historical reality.

Despite his able defence of *Orlando Furioso* as an epic poem, in following contemporary categories Giraldi Cinthio unwittingly misled future readers when he entitled his work the *Discorso intorno al comporre dei romanzi*, for Ariosto is emphatic about the fact that he recognizes and is incorporating both forms within a poem continuing the tradition of Homer and Vergil.[11] As *Orlando Furioso* begins, the romance action of Boiardo's *Orlando Innamorato* appears to be undergoing metamorphosis into epic action. The poet in the opening stanza mixes romance and epic materials, announcing he will sing of women, knights and love, but the focus turns quickly to arms, the great historical conflict of Cross and Crescent, the wrath of Agramante, and Carlo as 'roman emperor' ('imperator romano', 1.1.8). Orlando has just returned with Angelica from his adventures 'in India, in Media, in Tartaria' (1.5.3).[12] More than a mere listing of Boiardo's exotic locales, this series emphasizes the fabulous nature of Orlando's exploits by progressing northward toward less familiar locations and culminating in a region that, as Michael Murrin notes, was represented by a blank space in the maps of the Este library.[13] As they are being selected and ordered into an inversion of epic's hierarchizing of locations upwardly from periphery to centre, such romance spaces are also being left behind, it would seem, replaced by a precisely located and literarily significant point of convergence 'at the foot of the lofty Pyrenees' (1.5.7), the border between Christian and pagan worlds where the Carolingian material first took epic form. Carlo, however, does not evince the epic sagacity appropriate to a Holy Roman Emperor, and the poet laments human judgement's propensity to 'err' ('erra', 1.7.2). Mixing allusions to both the *Iliad*'s opening quarrel and Vergil's opening search for the 'cause' of Trojan travail, Ariosto labels Angelica the 'causa' (1.8.7) of the conflict between the emperor's two foremost knights (1.8.7) and then has Carlo remove her from the custody of Orlando, who has brought her, in what might suggest either a retreat from or a continuation of Aeneas' *translatio* to Hesperia, 'from the Hesperides' ('dagli esperii', 1.1.7).[14] Instead of allowing 'l'arme' to rule and transform 'gli amori' (1.1.1), Carlo confuses generic motivations by offering Angelica as the reward for whoever will kill the most Saracens that day.

The named cause now mysteriously produces an unexpected effect. 'Contrary to their prayers, however, were the results' ('contrari ai voti poi furo i successi', 1.9.5), and the Christian forces are put to flight. No one gets the girl, Carlo fails to achieve victory, and the multiple actions to follow proceed without the omphalic orientation needed to unite these actions into a single succession and success. The pun on 'successi' goes to the heart of the poem's narrative method, which proliferates individual stories of knights acting alone instead of assisting in the success of the collective project, and which pushes medieval interlace techniques to a new and audacious extreme. Ariosto interrupts both individual and collective successions in a way that challenges the reader to weave an unprecedented number of threads together into a coherent tapestry, to use Ariosto's own recurring image of narrative structure, a sequence that begins with his first justification for shifting attention from one character to another: 'because I need various threads and various warps, since I intend to weave them all together' ('perche varie fila a varie tele / uopo mi son, che tutte ordire intendo', 2.30.5-6).[15] The epic poet's challenge to 'put together the discourse' is most noticeable on the level of narrative intelligibility, though of course Ariosto issues as well substantial interpretive challenges. Not the least of these is the rapid interplay of genres. Already in a series of subtle generic modulations, the poem has moved toward epic and then away, shifting focus from exotic Asia, to Carlo waiting with the armies of Christendom assembled for the great day's conflict with the infidels, to unseen defeat brought about through unspecified causality. The process will continue unabated.

The Christian defeat produces the centrifugal dispersion, characteristic of romance rather than epic beginnings, into the forest landscape that will dominate cantos 1-3 and large sections of cantos 18-29. It is appropriate that the movement into this quintessential romance setting is caused by Angelica's flight, for it is her specialized function to lead Ariosto's knights into 'error', just as she has somehow caused Carlo's judgement to err. Since the moral and epistemological aspects of this error-errancy have been explored recently by a number of critics, to consider it in further detail would be superfluous here.[16] But it remains worth emphasizing that Ariosto's forest, like his heroine, serves a very specialized purpose, and one that represents a revision of previous romance practice. Knights from Chrétien to Boiardo suffered the ordeals and entanglements of the romance forest, but they did not suffer the more systematic punishment meted out to Ariosto's wayward knights.

In Boiardo's *Orlando Innamorato*, which deploys epic features in counterpoint to its romance dominant, the moral import of the knights' dispersion is obscured by inconsistent motivation among the pagans. The grandiose desire of the Indian king Gradasso to 'conquer and destroy / All the sun sees, all sea surrounds' ('vindicere e disfare / quanto il sol vede e quanto cinge il mare', *OI.*, 1.1.7) immediately establishes an epic context

with the familiar Roman imperial imagery. His desire to complete his collection of Hector's arms (1.1.5) — he is missing only the sword
Durindana, which is in the possession of Orlando — is further evidence of
Boiardo's understanding of epic's parallel of the cosmic *imperium* and the
integral self. This opening epic alignment of the Orient, in itself an interesting reversal of the usual association of romance with the effeminate
east, sets up a counterpoint to the romance context initiated by the
Pentecostal gathering of knights, of which we hear immediately following
the pagan forces' setting sail.[17] The fears Boiardo evokes for 'our holy
faith' ('nostra fede santa', 1.1.7.6) let the reader know unequivocally the
moral alignment of this conflict. But Boiardo just as quickly drops all moral
pretence when he introduces Angelica, sent by her father who, for reasons
apparently not worth mentioning, wishes to collect heroes in his dungeon.
Helpless before their instant passion, the knights disperse and drift without
significant moral taint eastward through forests and other romance settings
to Albraca, where Angelica alternately titillates and spurns a swelling population of knights without regard to race, creed, or national origin. Only with
the second book, and the second invasion, this time by the African king
Agramante, a descendant of Alexander the Great, does a situation exist in
which the knights' collective mission might conflict with individual desire.
But despite Boiardo's delight in using Orlando to demonstrate that 'the
proudest man in the world is conquered by love, completely subjugated'
('nel mondo e piu orgoglioso, / E da Amor vinto, al tutto subiugato',
1.1.2.3-4), never more than momentarily does he evoke a conflict between
arms and love or between any other morally defined polarities.

Ariosto's application of an epic dominant to the materials inherited
from Boiardo is most evident in his imposition of a moral framework upon
the knights' flight into the forest, which is condemned in the strongest
possible terms. As the Saracen forces move against Paris, the defence of
the city takes on apocalyptic overtones. Amidst ringing church bells, the
desperate prayers of the populace, and young soldiers begging to die for
their faith (14.100-3), Paris becomes the sacred centre to be defended at
all costs. Rinaldo's exhortation to his troops explains what is at stake:

> I say, saving this city
> you will oblige not only the Parisians,
> but all the countries around.
> I speak not only of neighbouring peoples;
> there is not a country throughout Christendom
> that does not have citizens within.

> dico, salvando voi questa cittade,
> v'ubligate non solo i Parigini,
> ma d'ogn'intorno tutte le contrade.
> Non parlo sol dei populi vicini;

ma non e terra per Christianitade,
che non abbia qua dentro cittadini. (16.35.1-5)

In the siege narrative the setting becomes fully mappable according to the familiar coordinates:

Paris sits in a great plain
at the navel of France, or rather the heart;
the river passes within its walls,
and runs, and exits on the other side.
But first it forms an island, and secures
one part of the city, and the best;
the other two (for in three parts is the great land)
outside by the moat, inside by the river are bounded.

Siede Parigi in una gran pianura,
ne l'ombilico a Francia, anzi nel core;
gli passa la riviera entro le mura,
e corre, e esce in altra parte fuore.
Ma fa un isola prima, e v'assicura
de la citta una parte, e la migliore;
l'altre due (ch'in tre parti e la gran terra)
di fuor la fossa, e dentro il fiume serra. (14.104)

Ariosto displays considerable familiarity with the topography of the Parisian 'terra' or 'world'. The Seine flows northwest toward Paris, passes from east to west across the middle of the city, forming the internal enclosure of the Ile de la Cité, and then after exiting turns again toward the northwest. Thus can Agramante neatly polarize the surrounding country by moving his forces across the river 'towards the west' ('verso ponente', 14.105.6) to array them along the southern wall. He now has 'no city or country behind him not his own, all the way to Spain' ('ne cittade ne campagna / ha dietro, se non tuea, fin alla Spagna', 105.7-8). From this location Rodomonte launches the epic genre's most spectacular *aristeia*, a single-handed penetration to the very centre of the city. As he charges with epic rectilinearity up 'the street that runs straight to the bridge of St. Michel' ('quella strada che vien dritto al ponte / di san Michel', 16.243-4), the Christian forces he encounters turn contrastingly chaotic, with the narrator lamenting that he can't even call them squadrons or phalanxes ('non diro squadre, no diro falange', ₹16.23.6). Alexandre Doroszlaï rightly notes that Rodomonte's course is along the Rue Saint-Jacques, which is the most important street of medieval Paris and the 'cardo' or north-south axis of the quadrated Roman city.[18] As the initial stage of the (future, from the point of action in the ninth century) pilgrimage route to the shrine of Saint Jacques of Compostella, a route that Ariosto has made sure we know is under Saracen control, the street is repeatedly mentioned in the Carolingian *chansons*.[19] After desecrating this holy route by burning churches (16.85) and filling the main square with 'scattered human limbs' (16.89), he arrives at the great door of the 'royal palace, lofty and sublime' ('regal casa, alta e sublime', 17.10). While he batters the door the poem reaches an unmatched density of Vergilian allusion, as Ariosto fills the scene with details from the destruction of Priam's palace: the defenders hurling missiles from the roof; the women wailing inside, rushing in panic through the palace, and embracing the doors; a lengthy simile comparing Rodomonte to a serpent emerging from darkness and sloughing off his skin as fresh life surges through him. The simile allows Ariosto to fuse Vergilian and Christian symbolism, in effect echoing a character's announcement that the Roman empire is buried ('il romano Imperio, oggi e sepolto', 16.86) and that Satan is destroying the city ('Satanasso . . . strugge et ruina la citta', 16.87). The simile also removes the important description of the serpent's 'rolling' ('convolvit', *Aen.*, 2.474) his length inward as a manifestation of history's forces of destruction, for in Ariosto's generic contamination Rodomonte is here being distinguished from heroes caught in the infernal turnings of romance.

Meanwhile, Rinaldo has arrived with reinforcements from England, escorted by the archangel whose eponymous bridge Rodomonte has crossed into the city centre. While Rinaldo leads a portion of his forces across the Seine northwest of the city and then turns unpropitiously left ('da man sinistra', 16.29.5) to attack Sobrino's western watch, the rest of his forces enter the city by the northern gates of San Martino and San Dionigi (16.30.7), where they are greeted by Carlo (16.85). Despite his earlier show of heroic foresight — with the eyes of Argus he 'foresaw' ('previde', 14.107.2) where Agramante would attack — and successful defence of the southern wall, Carlo is now in the wrong quarter. Outside the walls Rinaldo's left turn seems irrelevant at first, for his subsequent *aristeia* leads to near-victory. But when renewed fighting around Paris is imminent in canto 27, we learn that he has been wandering repetitively between Paris and Orlando's domains in search of Angelica; he now abandons Carlo shamelessly in his hour of greatest need and the tide of battle turns in the Saracens' favour. Inside the walls, while Carlo's location in the north makes his judgement once again seem questionable, it does allow the action within the city to remain on the north-south axis, as his forces now rush south to the centre to encounter Rodomonte. The attack is ineffective, and Rodomonte is compared to a helmsman correcting his vessel (18.9) and then to a 'high-walled alpine castle well-founded in rock'; ('scoglio alpino / di ben fondata rocca alta parete', 18.11) able to withstand the gales that rip up mountain ash and spruce. Carlo's next tactic is to clog the central piazza with the whole population of the city. It is only when

Rodomonte perceives that he 'could come to no end' (ne possa / venir a capo', 18.17) to his killing that he turns back. Even this exaggerated hero can't resolve the problem of the one and the many in these circumstances.

Clearly designed to elicit the contemporary audience's memory of recent Ottoman attacks upon the Italian homeland, the epic elevation of Rodomonte's ferocious *aristeia* shows forth through any screen of irony we might find superimposed upon it and supports the sharp moral contrast between the defending heroes and the erring knights pursuing an ever-withdrawing Angelica in the forest. This contrast appears with utmost clarity when we compare, as the Vergilian allusions insist that we do, the high heroics of the incursion scene with Orlando's restless thoughts before his abandonment of Carlo and the Christian cause. Paris and 'the holy empire' ('il santo Imperio', 8.69) have been saved from Agramante's siege by intervention from above:

> The Creator on high bent down his eyes
> to the just lamentation of old Carlo,
> and with a sudden shower doused the fire:
> nor probably would human skill been able to quench it.
> Wise is he who always turns to God,
> for no one else can ever better assist him.

> Il sommo Creator gli occhi rivolse
> al giusto lamentar del vecchio Carlo;
> e con subita pioggia il fuoco tolse:
> ne forse uman saper potea smorzarlo.
> Savio chiunque a Dio sempre se volse;
> ch'altri non pote mai meglio aiutarlo. (8.70)

The scene's spatial terms — the horizontal enclosure of the siege, the repeated vocabulary of 'turning' upward and downward that describes the proper relationship between high Creator and creature — are echoed and transformed in the microcosmic description that follows:

> That night Orlando to his restless featherbed
> imparts many a swift thought.
> Now here now there he turns, now he gathers them
> all in one place, but he never grasps them firmly:
> as a tremulous gleam from limpid water,
> bounced from the sun or from nocturnal rays
> across the wide roof goes with a long leap
> to right and left, and low and high

> La notte Orlando alla noiose piume
> del veloce pensier fa parte assai.
> Or quinci or quindi il volta, or lo rassume
> tutto in un loco, e non l'afferma mai:
> qual d'acqua chiara il tremolante lume,
> dal sol percossa o da' notturni rai

per gli ampli tetti va con lungo salto
a destra et a sinistra, e basso et alto. (8.71)

As D. S. Carne-Ross points out, the simile is adapted from *Aeneid* 8.22-5,
where 'it is used to describe the inner tension in Aeneas' mind as he lies
awake contemplating the approaching Italian campaign'.[20] The parody is
multiple: of the honourable Christians' steadfast resistance; of the 'seeing
all' ('cuncta videns') Aeneas' preparation as he 'turns everything over'
('omnia versat') and yet casts his thoughts high but not low, much less to
the sinister left (and certainly not from right to left!); of epic's vertical and
horizontal expansiveness. Orlando's problem, Ariosto informs us with a
ribald joke layered onto an epic imperative, is that he cannot grasp firmly
the burgeoning multiplicity Angelica occasions. As a result his separation
from the epic project is inevitable. The heroes' subsequent dreams are
also meant to be compared. The prophetic visitation by Tiberinus, who
instructs Aeneas on how to locate the Roman imperial centre, contrasts
with Orlando's Petrarchan nightmare, in which he runs blindly through
the stormy forest searching desperately 'this way and that' ('e quindi e
quinci') only to receive a prophecy on the futilities of the horizontal plane:
'never hope for joy on earth' ('No sperar piu gioirne in terra mai', 8.83).
The condemnation is redoubled when these passages are seen to allude
forward to Rodomonte's Turnus-like *aristeia*. In contrast to the Saracen's
alpine castle standing steadfast among the fallen trees, Orlando in his
dream vainly seeks shelter from the storm in a landscape of fallen trees
(8.81). Nor could anything be farther from the Saracen's fiery and
unswerving incursion into Paris than Orlando's prone and watery vision of
trembling moonbeams.

While Rodomonte is elevating himself to the status of foremost epic
hero in the first half of the *Furioso*, the relentlessly linear nature of his trajectory across the walls and into the city's heart is strengthening the
contrast of the great epic battle with the errancy of the forest scenes.
Although several critics have commented on the pervasive use of the verb
'girare' in the poem, it appears to have gone unnoticed that Ariosto is employing a traditional image of infernal torment. When, for example,
Ferrau ends up where he had started after a futile search for Angelica, or
Bradamante searching for Ruggiero finds herself back at the point of departure (1.31; 23.9), Ariosto is grafting onto the epic tradition of negative
circling another tradition with origins in Psalms 11:9: 'the impious walk
in circles' ('In circuitu impii ambulant'). This is the same kind of futile
motion Dante observes in the first circle of hell in *Inferno* 3.52-4:

Looking again, I saw a banner
that ran so fast, whirling about,
that it seems it might never have rest.

Eo io, che riguardai, vidi una 'nsegna
che girando correva tanto ratta,
che d'ogne posa mi parea indegna.

In the forest and in Atlante's enchanted palace, which is a contracted architectural version of the forest, the knights are revealed to be doubly
cursed. Impious because they are away from the epic action, they nevertheless cannot free themselves from the labour that the pious Vergilian
hero must endure.

Ariosto's conversion of the romance forest from a morally neutral place
of testing and irruptions of the marvellous into an infernal space invites us
to make additional Dantean glosses upon his complex interplay of genres.
In the terms of *Inferno* 1, epic represents the 'diritta via' (both
Rodomonte's straight path and the morally 'right' choice *a dritta*), while
romance represents the 'dark wood', the 'selva oscura' entered when the
straight path is lost or abandoned. This formulation is in accord with recent work on Ariosto employing the epic-romance distinction. What must
also be recognized is that the Dantean subtext also suggests that a way can
be found back into the light, perhaps even that entering the *selva* is a necessary or at least inevitable step along this tragicomic way. Significantly,
before they return to full epic stature, the knights who contribute most to
the Christian cause are immersed into an intensified, more fully *oscura*
version of the forest. The exception is the always exceptional Astolfo,
whose idiosyncratic way of participating in the pattern is to become a tree
himself. Rinaldo's experience in the forest of Ardennes is the most fully allegorical of the series:

When he had gone many miles into
the woods, the adventurous paladin,
far away from town and castle,
where the place was roughest and most dangerous,
all at once he saw the sky grow turbulent,
the sun having disappeared in sudden clouds,
and there issued forth from a dark cavern
a strange monster in the shape of a woman.

Poi che fu dentro al molte miglia andato
il paladin pel bosco aventuroso,
dal ville e da castella allontanato,
ove aspro era piu il luogo e periglioso,
tutto in un tratto vide il ciel turbato,
sparito il sol tra nuvoli nascoso,
ed uscir fuor d'una caverna oscura
un strano mostro in feminil figura. (42.46)

To escape this apparition, which turns out to be a 'hellish fury' ('Furia infernal', 50), Rinaldo plunges even deeper into the forest:

On the saddest path, on the worst way
he went hurrying, in the thickest wood,
where the precipice was steepest, where the valley
was thorniest, where the air was gloomiest,
hoping thus to shake off from his shoulders
this beastly, abominable, horrible bane.

Nel piu tristo sentier, nel peggior calle
scorrendo va, nel piu intricato bosco,
ove ha piu asprezza il balzo, ove la valle
e piu spinosa, ov'e l'aer piu fosco,
cosi sperando, torsi de la spalle
quel brutto, abominoso, orrido tosco. (52)

Just as Vergil arrives to guide the pilgrim Dante in the middle of his way, so at Rinaldo's crisis a knight in shining armour arrives to serve as a 'guide and leader' ('guida e duca', 42.59) to lead him out of the dark wood. The knight is Wrath himself ('Ira'), now a wholesomely epic persona who by curing Rinaldo of his desire for Angelica allows his eventual return to the Christian camp. First, with careful attention to epic spatiality, he directs Rinaldo to take the 'way that ascends toward the mountain' ('quella via ch s'alza verso il monte'), which he does without a backward glance ('senza dietro mai volger la fronte', 42.57). He then heroically attacks the monster, continually driving her back until he 'makes the monster turn back to her dark hole' ('poi ch'alla scura buca / fece tornare in mostro', 42.58). Epic and romance have been overlaid to create a new kind of space. In this paradoxically liminal centre, far from the epic centre and in the dense heart of the forest, psychological change comes about through fluidly interchanging epic and romance features: the monstrous woman of the cave who is also a fury risen in epic fashion from hell, a knight in shining armour who is also a celestial guide.

Bradamante too strays down a path. Having slain the deceitful Pinabello, who had tried to kill her, she attempts to return to Ruggiero, but she is the victim of fate,

which made her stray down a path
that took her where the forest was thick and intractable,
where it was most strange and lonely,
while the sun was leaving the world to darkness.

che la fe' traviar per un sentiero
che la porto dov' era spesso e forte,
dove piu strano e piu solingo il bosco,
lasciando il sol gia il mondo all' aer fosco. (23.5)

Here she also encounters personified Wrath. In contrast to Rinaldo's experience, wrath for her has been the force leading into rather than out of the dark wood:

'Wrath,' she said, 'has separated me from my love:
if only I had marked the course,
when I set out on this wretched undertaking,
so that I could return to where I left'.

— L'ira — dicea — m'ha dal mio amor disgiunta:
almen ci avessi io posta alcuna mira,
poi ch'avea pur la mala impresa assunta,
di saper ritornar donde io veniva. (23.7)

In acknowledging and repenting her fury, she begins a process of subordinating her martial inclinations to the love that will allow her to participate in epic teleology through dynastic marriage, the ultimate vocation of woman warriors in Renaissance epic. Her eventual partner's own plunge into the 'thick woods, where the dark branches seemed densest and most intertwined' ('folto bosco, ove piu spesse / l'ombrose frasche e piu intricate vede', 45.92) ends when Leo, having persuaded the tearful Ruggiero to reveal his identity, renounces his claims on Bradamante and blesses the destined dynastic union. Finally, Orlando's wandering 'into the middle of the woods where the foliage was darkest' ('per mezzo il bosco alla piu oscura frasca', 23.124) occurs at the poem's most pivotal moment, between his discovery of Angelica's 'infidelity' and the full onset of his madness. After wandering self-divided all night in 'hell' ('questo inferno', 23.128), at sunrise he sheds all emotions but 'hatred, rage, wrath, and fury' ('odio, rabbia, ira e furore', 129) and begins the destruction of the landscape foretold in his dream. In this instance the centre of the forest leads farther downward into the inferno, but even Orlando's furor, a more intense but otherwise analogous version of a nearly universal love-madness, is a mark of his supreme heroic stature, and a necessary step in his renunciation of Angelica for a higher, epic calling.

A story line within the movement of dispersion meriting especially close attention to generic interplay is Ruggiero's voyage to Alcina's island and back. In this remarkably rich sequence, Ariosto superimposes epic and romance journeys to create a mythographic palimpsest. Critics have long acknowledged the importance of Hercules' adventures as a mythic subtext in the poem, especially in the careers of Orlando and Ruggiero. In the fullest treatment of the subject, Eduardo Saccone demonstrates that 'the Hercules of the title generates two heroes, whose trajectories are at once analogous and opposed'.[21] Ruggiero's side of the story is of particular relevance to our subject, for the allusions to the Greek heroic prototype begin (after the poet's opening compliment to Cardinal Ippolito, the son of Ercole I, as 'descendant of Hercules', 1.3) with an important geographical reference. Borne aloft on the hippogryph, Ruggiero is quickly swept beyond the confines of Europe:

> He had left by a great distance
> all of Europe, and had passed beyond
> by far the mark established
> for navigators by invincible Hercules.
>
> Lasciato avea di gran spazio distante
> tutta l'Europa, ed era uscito fuore
> per molto spazio il segno che prescritto
> avea gia a' naviganti Ercole invitto. (6.17)

As much recent scholarship has established, the mythic figure here in-voked is a favourite of Renaissance humanists. For Coluccio Salutati and the small but distinguished circle immediately influenced by his encyclo-pedic treatment of the labours, Hercules is the patron of Reason, the peerless hero whose name was believed to signify glory or the glory of struggle, the compendium of all virtues who embodies magnanimity, a trait Ariosto mysteriously reserves for Bradamante (35.72.1). In the great age of navigation it was only logical that interest would be renewed in the fact that his epic 'labours', socially constructive tasks performed in the ser-vice of King Eurystheus, embody the very notion of epic's universal expansiveness. G. S. Kirk summarizes the mythographic tradition of the labours, whose number and order contain a degree of logical arrangement well suited to epic:

> First come the six tasks in the Pelopennese, mostly the disposal or capture of remarkable beasts. The second group of six lies outside the Pelopennese and indeed covers the known world; the first three take him south, north and east respectively, whereas he goes west in two of the last triad, which is strongly concerned with the underworld.[22]

It is in line with this tradition that Ariosto calls the hero 'invitto', the ep-ithet of Hercules *kosmokrator*. Despite Ruggiero's trembling heart and lack of control, and despite the fact that it is Atlante's plan to keep his ward from a heroic destiny that is directing the hippogryph's flight, Ruggerio's epic destiny is here being comically but triumphantly announced. Ariosto's version of Atlas, the traditional upholder of the epic world, can-not succeed in his attempts to defer the operations of Fate. He has evolved into an upholder of the romance world, but he unwittingly reverts to his classical role when his attempts backfire and Ruggiero and Bradamante grow into their epic destinies through the separations he effects.[23]

After carrying Ruggiero over the ocean 'in a straight line and without ever being deflected' ('per linea dritta e senza mai piegarsi', 6.19), the winged steed mysteriously lapses into what the poem has already estab-lished as a familiar pattern. Sighting Alcina's isle, it descends 'with a great turn' ('con larghe ruote') and after a 'a revolution in a great circle' ('un gi-rarsi di gran tondo', 6.20) it deposits the hero in a romance setting. As Saccone notes, here Ruggiero makes the famous Herculean choice *in bivio* and then re-enacts Hercules' degrading subjection to Omphale.[24] He can escape only after Melissa, with her 'ring of reason' ('annello de la ragion', 8.2), her shaming reference to Ruggiero's Herculean upbringing (7.57), and her admonition to become 'an Alexander, a Julius, a Scipio' (7.59), has made him see the compound 'errors' of his ways. But we must wonder why, or rather how, the Herculean Ruggiero is so easily led astray. How is it that, despite Astolfo's warnings and the right choice 'to the right' ('a man destra', 6.60) at the crossroads, Ruggiero walks so blindly into the clutches of Alcina? One answer is that the palimpsestic landscape, a space suggestive of the refusal of Renaissance realities to respond to readable inherited models of conduct, obscures and distorts the Herculean itinerary.

The passing of Hercules' pillars invokes not only the great aetiological hero who established them, but also Ruggiero's most noteworthy predecessor in passing beyond them: Ulysses of *Inferno* 26, no longer the hero of epic homecoming, but of a romance journey away from the centre into the unmappable. To Dante's Ulysses, the pillars are markers erected 'so that men should not pass beyond' ('accio che l'uom piu oltre no si metta').[25] Nevertheless, abandoning (after a pointed reference to Aeneas) the 'pieta' owed his present family and his progeny, Ulysses sets out 'following the sun' ('di retro al sol', 117), entering the Atlantic in a 'mad flight, always gaining on the left' ('folle volo, / sempre acquistando dal lato mancino', 125-6). Upon reaching the antipodal mountain isle the ship encounters a whirlwind, and 'three times it whirled her round with all the waters' ('tre volte il fe girar con tutte l'acque', 139), plunging the overly ambitious hero and crew to the bottom of the sea. Ruggiero's auspicious journey, we might say, is undermined by the hubristic counter-voyage of Ulysses. Although he adheres to the sun's path along the Tropic of Cancer (4.50) without Ulysses' sinister deviation to the south (like Aeneas' within the confines of the Mediterranean), he too encounters disaster at the antipodes as he spirals down to Alcina's mountainous isle. Piling irony upon irony, Ariosto punishes Ruggiero for abandoning the epic, dynastic responsibilities he does not yet know he has by making Atlante send him ostensibly out of harm's way.

As if the two conflicting journeys were not enough to confuse both Ruggiero and our own understanding of epic's evaluative spatiality here, Ariosto compounds the confusion with a third palimpsestic layer. Herculean Ruggiero's correct choice at the crossroads takes him 'to the mountain' ('al monte', 6.60), but when the combination of monstrous opponents and seductive helpers has coaxed him onto the smooth and easy road leading 'across the plain' ('per la pianura', 6.60) toward Alcina's palace, the trek, mysteriously, does not grow easier. Ruggiero finds himself climbing once again:

> Somewhat hardgoing and rough
> through the middle of a wood led the path,
> which also was rocky and narrow,
> and went almost straight up the hill.
> But when they had climbed to the top,
> they came out into spacious fields,
> where they saw the most beautiful and splendid palace
> that was ever seen in the world.

> Alquanto malagevole et aspretta
> per mezzo un bosco presero la via,
> che oltra che sassosa fosse e stretta,
> quasi su dritta alla collina gia.
> Ma poi che furo ascesi in su la vetta,
> usciro in spaziosa prateria,
> dove il piu bel palazzo e 'l piu giocondo
> vider, che mai fosse veduto al mondo. (7.8)

At the top, he encounters a terrestrial paradise ('paradiso', 7.13.8) and angels who seem to be from heaven. The landscape has been transformed
into a setting of counterfeit Dantean askesis. To escape such a deceptively
metamorphosing place Herculean *virtus* will not suffice. In his aspect as
Dantean everyman, Ruggiero must cross a desert shore that recalls difficult crossings of *Inferno* 1 and *Purgatorio* 2; overcome Dantean beasts, one
of which, in a small but funny allusion, bites him on the 'left foot' ('piede
manco', 8.8.2) to render infirm Dante's crucial 'pie fermo' of *Inferno* 1.30;
and finally, like a spirit being ferried to purgatory, be carried across the
water to Logistilla's haven by an old 'ferryman' ('galeotto', 10.44.7; cf.
Purgatorio, 2.27).[26] After a refresher course in heroic virtue at Logistilla's
palace, Astolfo remounts the hippogryph to 'complete the whole circle he
had begun, to have like the sun gone around the world' ('finir tutto il com-
inciato tondo, / per aver, come il sol, girato il mondo', 10.70.7-8).
Equipped with new knowledge and the ring of reason, a symbol of his own
circumnavigation, Ruggiero can now become a Herculean hero worthy of
the great age of exploration, extending epic luminosity into the widest of
possible earthly circles, the great globe itself. All of this is accomplished,
it should be understood, on the wings of romance, by means of a circular
flight on a fabulous beast imported from a land 'far beyond the frozen
seas' ('molto di la dagli aghiacciati mari', 4.18.8). But this apparent epic assimilation of the cyclical on the large scale does not carry over to
smaller-scale action. Ruggiero's progress is soon halted as he rescues the
nude Angelica from the Orc, foolishly gives her the ring, and undergoes a
comic dis-arming ritual in which, shaking with lust, he fumbles with his
armour 'now on this side now on that / confusedly' ('or da questo or da
quel canto / confusamente', 10.115.1-2). Needless to say, this scene does

not lead to a successful *aristeia*, sexual or otherwise, for Angelica disappears and as the narrator turns to another story Ruggiero 'goes groping around the fountain like a blind man' ('intorno alla fontana / brancolando n'andava come cieco', 11.9.1-2).

Not content with the epic potential realized through Ruggiero's generically mixed circumnavigation, Ariosto balances this early journey with Astolfo's symmetrically placed excursion late in the poem. The two episodes are intimately linked, not only through sharing a dense allusiveness that has made them the poem's most discussed episodes, but also in the way they cooperate in employing geography in the service of epic expansiveness. The vehicle for Astolfo is once again the romance hippogryph, inherited as a kind of reward and *translatio* for freeing Ruggiero from Atlante's enchanted palace. Like the earlier journey, and like the poem as a whole, this journey takes the liminal Pyrenees as its point of departure (33.96). Astolfo too passes 'the boundary placed for the first navigators by unvanquished Hercules' ('la meta che pose / ai primi naviganti Ercole invitto', 33.98.1-2). But the very recurrence of this salient detail, and perhaps the now openly Dantean emphasis on the pillars' role not as neutral 'sign' but as proscribing 'boundary', highlight the fact that Astolfo's overall trajectory is perpendicular to Ruggiero's. His southward crossing of the strait avoids the transgressive implications of Ruggiero's westward crossing and introduces no confusing mythographic palimpsest. Moreover, once Astolfo has wandered eastward to the Nile, we see that the journey is intended to trace a north-to-south line along the Nile to Nubia: 'to the city of Nubia he held his course / between Dobada and Coalle a straight line in the air' ('Alla citta di Nubia il camin tenne / tra Dobada e Coalle in aria a filo', 33.101.5-6). When projected upon the map of the world, the two journeys together trace a system of perpendicular coordinates running east and west along the Tropic of Cancer and north and south down the Nile, corresponding with surprising exactness to that used in the T-in-O maps which, from the sixth century to the Renaissance, served Europe as the primary emblematic representation of the world.[27] When we add to these mappings the hippogryph's origin in the exotic Rifean mountains far north of the Urals ('nei monti Rifei', 4.18.7), Ariosto's version of the North Pole and conventionally the northern endpoint of the meridian defined by the Nile, we see that Ariosto has inscribed his action, quite literally, from the top to the bottom of the earth and all the way round. Lifted by the soaring imagination of romance, epic expansiveness has covered and mapped the world.

The descent from heaven in canto 14 is for the archangel Michael an exercise in frustration, and for Ariosto a declaration through both action and tone of, to translate Thomas Greene's analysis into my own, the 'clear

independence of Humanist and Christian traditions' (119) of epic verticality.[28] Communication between cosmic planes occurs in the world of the
Furioso. Indeed, it is quite true that the Ineffable Goodness of the poem is
a deity to whom 'the faithful heart does not pray in vain' (14.75.1-2), as
we have witnessed in his intervention to save Paris. But Michael's comic
difficulties imply that the days of easy epic commerce between celestial
and earthly planes are gone, that epic's chronotope must be supported and
complemented by romance's if the heroic poem is to represent modern reality. One of the most important functions of Astolfo's journey is to
strengthen this implication. When he reaches the southernmost point of
his journey Astolfo is not able, unlike Hercules, to 'penetrate the earth all
the way to the centre / and search around the infernal ravine' ('penetrar la
terra fin all centro / e le bolgie infernal cercare intorno', 34.5.3-4). With
the hippogryph's aid he can reach 'the earth's highest elevation' ('alla maggiore altezza de la terra', 38.24.2) and taste the apples of Eden, certainly
no mean feat, but even the divine chariot of Elias will lift him only to the
'lowest heaven' ('ciel piu basso', 38.23.7), a destination far below that usually reached by the cosmic voyagers of literature. It is consistent with the
strong contrast established here between an exuberant earthly expansion
and a carefully limited ability to leave the terrestrial plane that Astolfo re-
acts with wonder not at the earth's insignificance, but at the moon's
surprising largeness. The conventional *contemptus mundi* of celestial ascent
tales has no place in this most humanist of epics.

Astolfo's journey to the moon takes part in the poem's ultimately decisive, if somewhat unsteady, turn toward closure. With his return of
Orlando's wits from the moon the war is won, the heroes converge upon
Paris to be welcomed in a cosmos-affirming triumph (44.32) that positively parodies Rodomonte's incursion, and the dynastic marriage is
arranged. Patricia Parker asserts that this closural re-introduction of epic
structures is specious. Because St. John in the ascent episode appears to
reduce even the Gospel to the status of a literary fiction, she argues, in
Ariosto's radically sceptical vision 'the exercise of closure, under the sign
of a guiding Providence, remains a purely literary tour de force, a demonstration that the creator of this "varia tela" knows as well as the Weaver
Fates (XXXIV.89) how to bring his carefully woven "text" to an end'.[29] But
this reading begins in a contradiction that assigns John the authority to remove his own and others' authority, when in fact John is implicated in a
version of the 'liar's paradox', which prevents a liar from convincing us he
is lying.[30] Rather than ending in radical scepticism, the poem concludes by
affirming the prudential epistemology and hierarchical morality of its epic
dominant, and at the same time acknowledging that the irrational energies represented by the romance chronotope are of value, and perhaps
even invaluable.

Spenser's Legend of Wholeness

Spenser's Legend of Holiness, the subject of the remainder of this chapter, intensifies the process of generic interplay by which Ariosto revitalized the epic genre. As we follow the *translatio studii* northward to consider the effort to 'overgo' his predecessors Spenser announced in a letter to Gabriel Harvey, we encounter cultural conditions that at first might seem to invite closer adherence to the Vergilian paradigm.[31] An emerging empire expanding from a centre that was both an unchallenged seat of political power and Europe's most populous city, 'the most taut and vigorous national society in Europe'[32] was a fit subject indeed for a literary form founded on the concept of *imperium sine fine* centred in space and 'origined' in time. Unlike the Ferrarese poets, who faced an awkward, if ultimately productive, discrepancy between the limitations of a small duchy and the universality of Vergilian empire, the English poet had no need for the compromising structural manoeuvre of dividing the spatial seat of empire from the temporal origin of the patron's dynasty. But if English nationalism invited epic composition, English Protestantism presented considerable challenges in the form of new attitudes toward space and time.

Protestants of every persuasion looked at best with ambivalence upon the omphalic cosmology that underlay epic and Catholicism. On the one hand, traditional manifestations of sacred spatiality — altars and the anointed priests who presided over them, cathedrals with their cosmic architecture, the monasteries' 'paradise of the cloister', the *caput mundi* at Rome — became primary targets of the Reformers' iconoclasm.[33] On the other hand, at the same time that Protestants were denouncing such symptoms of papist ritualism and materialism, they were also infusing new life into their spiritual equivalents. Attempting to reach back across centuries of Catholic corruption to recover the purer practices of the early Church, Protestants focused on the Pauline imagery of the individual believer and the spiritual community as temple and on the Augustinian imagery of pilgrimage as movement toward the celestial city. The writer of Protestant epic, inheriting as an essential, defining part of the genre's tradition a spatiality that could easily be seen to support the Catholic world-view, would at the very least have to locate his poem's action in a setting that negotiated the relation between the literal and the figurative in new ways.

Ideological cross-currents were equally treacherous with respect to time. The reformer's diligent approach to active engagement in the world, what we now view as the proverbial Protestant 'work ethic', found a natural correspondence in epic's emphasis on ceaseless heroic labour toward a predetermined goal. In the Protestant moral vision one must always remain, like Redcrosse as he approaches Errour's den, 'resolving forward still to fare' (1.1.11). Contrasting Spenser with Shakespeare on this point is instructive. The characters of Shakespeare's festive comedy and romance generally benefit from withdrawal into the green world of cyclical time, where an openness to what the moment may bring holds greater potential for lasting benefit than does steadfast adherence to a path of predetermined action. Even for Shakespeare's tragic characters, the operation of declining fortune often involves single-minded adherence to an established plan. In this sense, we can say that Shakespeare's imagination, in contrast to Spenser's, remains rooted in the more rural, medieval, pre-Reformation reality of ritual and holiday that more sober forces were labouring to excise from the reformed commonwealth. However, the Protestant poet also faced a considerable obstacle to aligning his moral vision with epic's goal-directed temporality. The important precursors to Protestant epic — medieval forms that owed their sense of directed quest to earlier epic models, pre-Reformation Christian epics that assimilated Vergilian structures, and humanist allegorizations that translated the classical epic quest into terms compatible with Christian ethics — all relied upon the related assumptions that heroic stature was earned through labour and that the hero's itinerary proceeded from a state of sin to a state of salvation. In asserting that only faith, and not good works, was required for salvation, the reformers in effect challenged the moral validity of the epic chronotope. If justification is an unmerited, freely bestowed act of divine mercy, and if predestination blurs (or in its extreme version completely eliminates) the distinction between the state of the elected saint's soul in the world and in the hereafter, then the traditional epic itinerary is no longer an adequate imitation of life. Yet, even if central principles of Reform logically eliminated the need to earn one's salvation, Protestants hoping to promote a moral society could hardly afford to let this fact imply that good works were unnecessary. Richard Hooker, for example, the most influential Elizabethan theorizer on justification, simply warned that although 'we teach that faith alone justifieth . . . we by this speech never meant to exclude either hope or charity from being always joined as inseparable mates with faith in the man that is justified; or works being added as necessary duties'.[34] Admonitions against drawing a logical but misleading conclusion might have sufficed for the preacher, but for the Protestant poet who would educate his audience by portraying the exemplary life, there remained a fundamental challenge of reconciling the theological idea of necessary but undirected duties with the generic convention of directed heroic labour.

Developments in figural hermeneutics created challenges and opportunities no less momentous. The most significant change in this regard began when Reformers promoted the typological method to replace what

Luther found nonsensical in the medieval exegetical tradition associated with Origen and the School of Alexandria. As Barbara Lewalski has demonstrated in several studies of Protestant typology, this rejection of earlier allegorical practices as activities of human 'fancy' and violations of the literal text did not lead to more restrained and objective readings of scripture. Rather, the Protestant tendency 'to regard history as a continuum rather than as two eras of time divided by the Incarnation of Christ' encouraged the extension of typological readings beyond the conventional pattern, in which an Old Testament type foreshadowed a New Testament antitype, to more flexible approaches, and ultimately to a habit of thinking in which one continually referred to universal Christian history for exemplars, noting similarities and differences.[35] It has long been recognized that the poet who named his epic after a 'true glorious type' (1.Pr.4.7) of his sovereign exploited his culture's newly intensified typological habits. What has not been adequately appreciated is the extent to which Ariosto's method of generic interaction enabled him to do so.

As we have observed, epic's emphasis on unity and inclusiveness, manifest in such diverse phenomena as imperial expansion, the unified plot, and the integration of individual action into the collective endeavour, can be seen as well in its idealization of the hero's bodily integrity. In the first stage of his project for overgoing Ariosto, Spenser translates epic *integritas* into a specifically Protestant ideal. William Nelson points provocatively, though without further explanation, at Spenser's substantial innovation:

> Had Spenser indeed intended to represent the Red Cross Knight in the process of attaining a state of grace I can only wonder that he did not show him winning that armour of a Christian man piece by piece, the shield of faith in one episode and the breastplate of righteousness in another until, fully armed at last, he is equipped to overthrow the dragon. But the whole armour of God is already his in the first stanza of the first canto.[36]

Preferring to view the knight's armour as something 'which will not be truly his until he has earned it',[37] the conventional wisdom about Book 1 does not acknowledge the significance of the fact that Redcrosse enters the poem having already succeeded in attaining the status of a spiritually ennobled 'patron' of integral wholeness.[38] Clearly, the young and inexperienced knight has much to learn, but in fact the poem provides no evidence that he must 'earn' his salvation, a requirement that would imply salvation by works and place Spenser in conflict with a central Protestant doctrine.

Redcrosse can enter his legend in full armour because he has already experienced 'justification by faith'. As if he were anticipating modern misconceptions about the armour's symbolism, Spenser offers us an explanatory gloss in the Letter to Raleigh. When the 'tall clownishe younge man' (he has the makings of an epic hero) presents himself at court in Cleopolis, he is declaring faithful adherence to all that the order of Gloriana's knights represents. It is important to emphasize that, like the sixteenth-century Protestant who must depend entirely upon God's mercy for his unmerited justification, he does not merit the traditional courtly 'boone' that he receives, and that he is not required to succeed in his assigned good works before acquiring it. Nor is he simply granted, in the conventional romance manner, an adventure meant to test his worth, but more precisely 'the *achievement* of any adventure, which during the feast should happen' (my emphasis). Given Spenser's militant Protestant viewpoint and his consistently traditional, etymological use of the term in his poetry, there can be no doubt that by 'achievement' Spenser means precisely that: 'completion, accomplishment, successful performance' (OED 1). To indicate the workings of election, as soon as Redcrosse is granted this achievement, Una enters with 'the armour of a Christian man specified by St. Paul'. He is told that 'unlesse that armour which she brought, would serve him', (i.e., 'fit' him, denoting his elected status), 'he could not succeed in that enterprise'. And of course the armour does fit him, as we knew from Gloriana's granted boon that it would, and as we know that he is destined to succeed in his enterprise, which is at once a specific quest in aid of the distressed Una and the allegorical pilgrimage of the Christian life. Redcrosse has been distinguished from those other knights who 'for want of faith, or guilt of sin' (1.7.45) have revealed themselves as not among the elect and have been slain by the dragon of Eden. An elected saint, Redcrosse as a warrior possesses a degree of immunity from ultimate failure that was unavailable before the Reformation; the fantastic invincibility acquired in romance through magic is now a theologically sanctioned reality applicable to extra-literary history, where the nation of the elect, by definition, is destined to succeed. Redcrosse must learn his identity as England's patron saint, but the reader sees the red cross of Saint George at the moment he enters the poem.

The bloody cross inscribed on Redcrosse's shield and breastplate is a traditional attribute of the saint, but Spenser makes it much more prominent than in previous versions of the legend. Temporally, just as the Crucifixion represented the pivotal moment of human history, so in the rituals surrounding the Crusades did the symbolic act of 'cruce signari', the imprinting of the cross on the crusader's scapulary, signify his pivotal spiritual transformation. This taking of the cross became the prototype for the rituals whereby an aspiring knight entered chivalric orders.[39] In his use of the doctrine of justification by faith, Spenser has effected a Protestant revision of the symbolism of the cross toward the salvational history of the individual. Equally important is the spatial symbolism of the cross that has long been part of its promiscuous polysemy. Reformation iconoclasts destroyed the physical remnants of the papist rood, but they could not extinguish centuries of accumulated associations. Like Christians everywhere, Elizabethans could hardly fail to respond to Christianity's primary figuration of the *axis mundi*. A vast exegetical tradition emphasized the central, omphalic position of the cross, through its association with the Tree of Life, which was of the same wood as the later tree on Calvary, and through the cosmic centrality of Jerusalem, which generations of Crusaders fought to recover.[40] As early Christianity asserted its own claims to universal *imperium* the shape of the cross, the revered *species crucis* that focused meditations from the early middle ages, displaced *Roma quadrata* as an image of the cosmos it centred. The most overtly cosmological reference to the cross comes from Duessa, who in observing that the knight 'bore a bloudie Crosse, that quartered all the field' (1.2.1) offers a conventional gloss on the *species crucis*. 'Field' extends beyond the heraldic context to include the 'world' of medieval allegory as seen in Langland's 'fair feld full of folk'. 'The field is the world', Christ explains in interpreting the parable of the tares.[41] When Duessa later comments on the invincibility bestowed by his 'charmed shield' (1.4.50), she combines the romance convention of magical arms with an equally magical conception of the cross as an apotropaic charm. As one student of such English charms explains, the user was investing himself with 'the power implicit in the theme of the cosmological cross', which is 'the power to fix and determine directions and to impose order'.[42] Without the glorification of comparing his hero to the cosmological tree, Spenser associates him with the *axis mundi*, all the while reminding us that although the individual justified by faith bears a shield that none can pierce, he must nevertheless regularly consult his moral compass.

Redcrosse needs this navigational assistance because he inhabits a disorienting world, and also because he overgoes earlier heroes by subsuming their many quests within his own as he journeys to an unprecedented number of traditional epic centres. Within Spenser's Platonic world of multiplicity 'infolding' into unity and unity 'unfolding' into multiplicity, Redcrosse is subject to unfolding romance repetition and at the same time overcomes it by the fact that his repeated journeys also infold, for they all are but types of the same ideal antitype.[43] When we close Book 1 and reflect upon its hero's past and future trajectory, we recall that after journeying to Cleopolis the knight entered his legend pricking his horse toward Eden, that after numerous misadventures he ascended the Mount of Contemplation and gazed upon the New Jerusalem, that after continuing on to his destination and completing his assigned task he began his return to Cleopolis, from which he will proceed to a crusade against the Paynim king, apparently return at some point to Eden, and eventually arrive at the same heavenly city that he earlier approached on the mount. Spenser, it appears, is conducting an allusive grand tour of epic centres available from the continent. In considering Redcrosse's destinations, it is difficult not to recall Dante's mount of askesis and its numerous Renaissance imitations, Tasso's Jerusalem delivered by the first crusade, the Eden of the burgeoning tradition of hexameral epic, even the contemplative paradise represented by Italy in Cristoforo Landino's allegorized *Aeneid*.[44] The unitary nature of Redcrosse's quest, however, becomes apparent only when we, to use the poet's words from the Letter to Raleigh, gather 'the whole intention of the conceit', and 'in a handfull gripe all the discourse'. In experiencing the 'discourse' itself, in immersing ourselves in the confusing world of diachronic process that we share with the hero within his own legend, we become trained in the establishment of similarities and differences upon which this synchronic vision depends. Indeed, without the application of typological comparison, which allows us to see his various journeys as types of the unitary Christian quest, Redcrosse's itinerary bears a suspicious resemblance to the to-and-fro series of wanderings that befalls him between Errour's den and the Cave of Despair.

Spenser follows Ariosto in linking epic to a morally positive linear teleology and romance to cyclical patterns of infernal error. But Spenser incorporates the romance chronotope much more finely into the texture of his work. The romance settings of the *Orlando Furioso*, although internally unmappable, can be located in relation to more orderly regions of epic historicity. Spenser locates his poem's action in a more fluid, indeterminate setting in which both readers and characters experience a continuous epistemological crisis of an intensity sustained by Ariosto only in the palimpsestic episode recounting Ruggiero's visit to Alcina's isle. Since St. George's ultimate success is not in doubt, Spenser can redirect our focus toward the very problematic process of living correctly in the time before the rewards of election are manifest. Ultimate success is perhaps the only thing not in doubt. Like Errour's den, which 'Breedes dreadfull doubts (1.12.4), the larger romance setting, for which this liminal setting serves — in the first of many doubt-breeding structural confusions — as both entrance and synecdoche, is designed to dramatize the new challenges of decentred Protestant existence. The hero's greatest challenges are no longer to defeat the enemy, but to recognize him (or her), and to orient himself in a world lacking reliable points of reference. Only by continually adding orienting faith unto his irresistible force can he live a life of holiness in a world thoroughly contaminated with multiplicity, infernal repetition, blurred distinctions. The Protestant hero's labour, in effect, is to distinguish between the *dritta via* and paths that lead nowhere, between epic and romance.

In the proem to Book 1, the poet awarded the title 'the Vergil of England' by Thomas Nashe asserts his poem's generic identity with painstaking thoroughness.[45] He announces that he is leaving behind the 'Oaten weeds' of pastoral for the epic 'trumpets sterne' (Proem 1.4), but in the new, mixed Renaissance manner, for like Ariosto he will 'sing of Knights and Ladies gentle deeds' (1.5). Nor will he fail to satisfy the various requirements attached to epic by theorists and practitioners in Ariosto's wake. It will be an elevated poem directed at the Muse's 'learned throng' (1.8), and 'moralised' (1.9) through the didactic play of interacting generic features. Even without the proem's preparation, the reader would have no trouble detecting epic tonalities in the opening scene of canto 1. The *in medias res* beginning reveals the knight pricking toward his goal with commendable rectilinearity upon the plain. Una's background economically introduces such familiar ideas as dynastic succession, universal empire, and vertical classification:[46]

> And by descent from Royall lynage came
> Of ancient Kings and Queenes, that had of yore
> Their scepters stretched from East to Western shore,
> And all the world in their subjection held. (1.1.5)

The tempest of 'angry Jove' promptly continues the idea of epic verticality and directs us allusively to Vergil's divinely initiated storms. Given this compact set of generic references, even the casually informed reader will not fail to suspect that within the nearby shady grove lies the labyrinth of romance error.

The reader can also only expect that in vanquishing the monster within the hero will free himself from the maze of infernal romance and resume the path of righteousness. Ariosto's series of scenes 'per mezzo il bosco' certainly supports this expectation. Closely following the Ariostan pattern, Redcrosse's combat with personified Errour 'amid the thickest woods' (1.11.7) ends with the knight apparently resuming his linear progress along the *dritta via*:

> Then mounted he upon his Steede againe,
> And with the Lady backward sought to wend;
> That path he kept, which beaten was most plaine,
> Ne ever would to any by-way bend,
> But still did follow one unto the end,
> He which at last out of the wood them brought.
> So forward on his way (with God to frend)
> He passed forth, and new adventure sought.
> Long way he travelled, before he heard of ought. (1.1.28)

The stanza's last two lines, however, should give us pause. Has Redcrosse forgotten the 'great adventure' (1.3.1) assigned him by Gloriana and wandered off in search of a new one? Has he given up the unitary epic quest to become a romance knight errant? Does he travel long before he hears not merely of aught, but of 'ought', the moral obligation he assumed at the court of the Faerie Queene? The preceding stanza contains an answer:

> His ladie seeing all, that chaunst, from farre
> Approcht in hast to greet his victorie,
> And said, Faire knight, borne under happy starre,
> Who see your vanquisht foes before you lye:
> Well worthy be you of that Armorie,
> Wherein ye have great glory wonne this day,
> And proov'd your strength on a strong enimie,
> Your first adventure: many such I pray,
> And henceforth ever wish, that like succeed it may.

Exploiting what Martha Craig calls the 'secret wit' of his archaic diction and syntax, Spenser has made the meaning of Una's wish dangerously obscure.[47] The theologically soundest reading would have Una wishing that many such knights succeed in the way hers has, that the success of this Christian soldier be repeated by all who put on the armour of Christ. The stanza as a whole lends considerable support to this reading. Since no less than eight pronouns or possessive adjectives preceding Una's wish refer to Redcrosse, emphasizing, as Hamilton explains, this 'Knight's worthiness to wear the armour of Christ', he is a likely referent for 'such' in line 8. A more natural way of reading, which assigns priority to the nearest logical antecedent — and which, significantly, reflects the tendency of natural language to inscribe within its syntactical patterns our dependence on temporal sequence — would understand 'such' to refer to 'adventure', and would have Una wishing either that Redcrosse succeed in the many adventures that he will face, or that many adventures 'succeed' — i.e., follow, echoing the pun on 'successi' in *Orlando Furioso* 1.9.5 — his first. The first of the two more natural readings is morally unexceptionable, for it simply assumes that life in our fallen world can be represented, accurately if unfortunately, as a series of adventures. The second, however, has the maiden whose name signifies unity in a variety of contexts, including epic's Aristotelian unity of action, actually advocating a form of fallen multiplicity that conflicts with her theological and generic significance. Redcrosse's desire for 'new adventure' suggests that this last possibility, unfortunately, is the one he hears.

Accordingly, Redcrosse asks the first inhabitant of Faerie Land he meets, Archimago disguised as a devout hermit, where he might find the 'straunge adventures' (1.1.30) that form the knight errant's vocation. Ironically, despite his wicked intentions (or is the clever enchanter supporting his facade of holiness by giving the knight precisely the advice he needs?), Archimago directs him away from plural adventures and toward the 'straunge man . . . That wasteth all this countrey far and neare' (1.1.31), the goal of his assigned 'great adventure'. But despite correct advice, despite the presence of unified Una, despite his defeat of Errour, Redcrosse seems condemned to err. The problem, I propose, is that the knight inhabits a new kind of narrative designed to dramatize the post-Reformation challenges of living without the comforting certainties of priestly authority. Beneath Ariosto's irony there remains a coherent universe ordered by stable categories that facilitate moral judgement, at least a good part of the time. The pervasiveness of the Hercules *in bivio* theme in *Orlando Furioso* confirms that alternatives can be defined and prudent choices can be made. The central forest scenes on which the Errour episode is modelled occur within story lines ordered by a familiar causality; they are scenes of anagnorisis and peripety in a comprehensible tragicomic plot. Hercules is no less prominent in the *Faerie Queene*, as we shall consider in the next chapter, but the bivium is conspicuously absent. As an emblem of prudential choice between seductive evil and a good requiring repression for eventual reward, it is far too logical to describe the dilemmas confronting the new Protestant hero. In retrospect, we see that the straight way out of Errour's wood was not really the true way, but the multitude's proverbial erring 'broad high way that led, / All bare through people's feet, which thither traveiled' (1.4.2) to the House of Pride. The ostensibly 'forward' (1.1.28) motion resumed on returning to the plain, therefore, remained in fact the 'backward' (1.28.2) motion of the knight's departure. Redcrosse has entered a world of apparently hopeless directional paradox best described by Despair himself: 'For he, that once hath missed the right way, / The further he doth goe, the further he doth stray' (1.9.43).

Spenser sustains the fall of the patron of 'wholeness' into perplexing multiplicity by making the relation of both part to part and part to whole a problem requiring 'endlesse worke'.[48] Pushing Ariosto's method of disposition to a new extreme, he overlays his epic to an unprecedented degree with romance chronotopic effects. Diachronic principles of progress and causality remain at work in the narrative, but they are systematically countered and confused by the synchronic operation of establishing similarities and differences between scenes linked extensively by repetition. The Errour episode, predictably, launches us efficiently into these treacherous narrative cross-currents. By locating the episode at the poem's beginning rather than imitating Ariosto's use of similar scenes as central turning-points, and by undercutting the sense of causality that might explain the characters' progress into the subsequent episodes,

Spenser is creating a radically new kind of narrative organization. The Errour episode serves as the first step in the hero's progress toward Eden, but it does so ironically, since it actually leads him in the other direction. It also serves as a type of the scenes to follow, which are connected to it and to one another by a figural principle of narrative succession coexisting with, but frequently eclipsing, causal-progressive succession.

Our ability to read this new kind of narrative is challenged and exercised as the knight and lady proceed from the wandering wood into a setting at once very similar and dissimilar, where they encounter another familiar instrument of romance intrusion into Renaissance epic: the magician. Spenser revises tradition by demystifying the magician's mysteries, using the epic device of crossing cosmic planes to expose ludicrously complex machinery of sprights and infernal powers. This adherence to a burlesquely rationalized causality characterizes the entire episode, as the wily deceiver first instils confidence in his victims, carrying his pretext of piety, as we have seen, even to the point of sagely diagnosing Redcrosse's condition and offering a genuine remedy, then moving the victims into place, activating the machinery, and assaulting the knight with a series of increasingly effective deceptions until his plans are accomplished. If, encouraged by the episode's atmosphere of cause and effect, we look back seeking to understand why, even after defeating Errour, the knight remains susceptible to error, grounds can be discovered for linking the two episodes causally. Perhaps the pride of victory makes him overconfident in his own judgement, moral superiority and self-sufficiency. But such diachronic connections remain more tenuous than the connections available through synchronic figural analysis. Most obviously, comparison suggests that Redcrosse, as he will continue to do, re-enacts his earlier experience by again battling error, although this time he loses. To succeed, he again needs but to follow Una's advice to 'add faith unto your force' (1.1.19), faith in his companion this time, who is nothing less than Truth and Fidelity itself. The pair has again entered a setting cut off from heaven's light, as the false Una implies when, invoking the epic problem of divine causality, she blames her lust on 'the hidden cruell fate / And mightie causes wrought in heaven above' (1.1.51). Noticing that the false Una suspiciously reverses direction from the earlier blocking of descending rays, we might expect that similar reversals will again undermine the knight's judgement, despite the episode's elaborate causality. Such proves to be the case when the false Una blatantly revises her history:

> Your owne deare sake forst me at first to leave
> My father's kingdome, There she stopt with teares;
> Her swollen hart her speech seemed to bereave,
> And then again begun, My weaker years
> Captiv'd to fortune and frayle worldly feares,
> Fly to your faith for succour and sure ayde. (1.1.52)

'In effect', A. C. Hamilton sagely observes in his annotated edition, 'she inverts his role as dragon killer and identifies him with the dragon'. Consistent with her new identity as a romance heroine afflicted with courtly love-sickness, she is also attempting to recast the epic 'great adventure' as a typical romance scenario by implying that Redcrosse is the reason for motion away from the centre whose power he would oppose and disrupt, and by invoking the unresolved conflict of familial and erotic allegiances that constitutes one of romance's defining features. Unfortunately, the situation is also so dissimilar to the combat with Errour that Una's advice can no longer be applied. Left with only force to apply (and from this he is restrained by Archimago), Redcrosse reverts to the dwarf's earlier advice (cf. 1.1.13) and flees from the scene of error.

The pattern continues as the legend proceeds. The Apollonian 'son of day' (1.5.25) encounters a series of characters related one to another primarily through their familial ties to and associations with Night and the underworld. Running counter to this emphatic opposition is Spenser's careful blurring of the distinction between the knight and his foes, a technique found by a number of critics to be a distinctive feature of this legend's combats. Individually and in combination, episode after episode leads us into an epistemological impasse and warns us against presuming that our categories are adequate to the job of making crucial distinctions. A nadir is finally reached at the cave of Despair. There Una rescues her knight through the simple expedient of reminding him that he is one of the elect: 'Why shoulds't thou then despair, that chosen art?' (1.9.53). Unlike Ariosto's heroes, who return to a familiar epic world after their encounters in the middle of the forest, Redcrosse now learns that he must in effect create his own generic alternative to the infernally repetitive world through which he has progressed without truly progressing. During his stay at the House of Holiness he receives ministrations from a host of moral agents. Among these it is Charissa who is given special prominence. Fidelia and Speranza, like faith and hope in the preceding cantos, help the knight to regain his perfect integrity, but after their cure he quickly lapses into an unheroic contempt of the world, and even reverts to despair:

> The faithfull knight now grew in litle space,
> By hearing her, and by her sisters lore,
> To such perfection of all heavenly grace,
> That wretched world he gan for to abhor,
> And mortall life gan loath, as thing forlore,
> Greev'd with remembrance of his wicked wayes,
> And prickt with anguish of his sinnes so sore,
> That he desirde to end his wretched dayes:
> So much the dart of sinfull guilt the soul dismayes. (1.10.21)

Mediating between harsh Penance and the gentler guidance of Mercy, Charity, it is now clear, is Spenser's solution to the Protestant dilemma of good works, and to the Protestant epic poet's challenge of reconciling undirected duties with the generic convention of directed labour. The whole process culminates in a definition of the holy and heroic life that echoes the earlier cure, but with an important difference:

> Shortly therin so perfect he became,
> That from the first unto the last degree,
> His mortal life he learned had to frame
> In holy righteousnesse, without rebuke or blame. (1.10.45)

Hamilton notes that here 'for the first and only time the Knight is linked directly with the virtue of Holiness, which is not an inner moral state but an active virtue displayed in acts of charity'. The scene also, together with its negative type in Despair's urging Redcrosse not to draw his days 'forth to their last degree', stands as the first and only time Spenser applies temporal modifiers to 'degree', a term he elsewhere reserves for vertical classification. Wording this crucial definition with careful attention to chronotopic implications, he fuses temporal and spatial distinctions to express the type of exemplary life that can replace the regressive progress of romance and the earned salvational progress of Catholic epic. Charity allows the knight to 'frame' — a term Spenser employs throughout the *Faerie Queene* to designate the architectonics of literal and figurative constructions — his mortal life in the sense that his invulnerable integrity is once again 'perfect'; in the sense that the full hierarchical range of his activities, from large to small and from high to low, is beyond reproach; and in the sense that each step along his life's pilgrimage, from first unto the last, (and, of course, from earthly life below to heavenly life above) is 'in' holy righteousness and 'without', or beyond, the reaches of sin, which would taint his exemplary status. In a new version of epic's folkloric threefold repetition, by adding Faith Redcrosse achieved the victories he has achieved so far; by adding Hope he returned to the true path; by adding Charity he can sustain the cure effected by Faith and Hope and frame for himself an epic itinerary of heroic action that is no less exemplary and no less consistently motivated than that of his predecessors.

The hero who proceeds from the House of Holiness to achieve earthly glory and, at the same time, to cooperate with the Providential plan, appears to have returned to the best of all possible epic worlds. The elaborate generic trappings of the combat with the dragon — invocation, similes, allusions linking classical epic to the Christian apocalypse, the defence of the Edenic omphalos, the apparent founding of a new dynastic line — reward the saint for and correspond to the inner achievement realized at the House of Holiness. And then suddenly, like the return of the repressed, paradox intrudes upon this splendid harmony. While he is rewriting Homer's plot to allow the hero to marry the utopian king's daughter, Spenser also gives Redcrosse the occasion to speak to his hosts 'of straunge adventures, and of perils sad, / Which in his travell him befallen had' (1.12.15). The hero, the narrator informs us, 'discourst his voyage long', proceeding with Odyssean diligence 'from point to point' (1.12.15). The Emperor of Eden duly replies with sympathy for 'the great evils, which ye bore / From first to last in your late enterprise' (1.12.17). But as Jacqueline Miller most recently points out, after Archimago suddenly appears with a letter claiming the knight is betrothed to Duessa, it is revealed that Redcrosse, strangely, has neglected to mention his encounters with Fidessa / Duessa during his allegedly comprehensive, 'point to point' account.[49] It appears that his ability to frame his epic itinerary 'from the first unto the last degree' is accompanied by a tendency to suppress those events of the past that do not lie neatly upon this newly and retrospectively constructed true path. If it were not unsettling enough to witness the patron of wholeness practising half-truth, substituting the part for the whole in the manner of Archimago, Duessa, and Despair, Redcrosse immediately follows his account with the surprising announcement that he must rush off to six years' service against the Paynim king. Even after its apparent reduction of romance to its own ends, epic, we now find, imitates its generic double by ending with its conflict of allegiances unresolved. Reaffirming the lessons that our recent vision of Edenic harmony might have allowed us to forget, the paradoxical ending of the Legend of Holiness sends us into the remaining books with a better understanding both of the need to 'grip the whole discourse as in a handful' and of the difficulties and dangers this process entails. Or to put the matter allegorically, Wholeness has been betrothed to Truth, but it will be some time before the marriage is consummated. We remain, with our attention heightened by anticipation, in the expectant yet anxious period in between.

Notes

1. For a detailed summary of the quarrel over the generic status and propriety of *Orlando Furioso*, see Weinberg (1961), vol. 2, pp. 954-1073.

2. Bloomfield's (1970) chapter on 'Episodic Motivation and Marvels in Epic and Romance' makes similar distinctions, although he does not consider classical epic. It is the romance forest's mystery, in large part evidenced through vague geography and missing causes and motivations, not infernal associations, that makes it a *périlleux* location in Chrétien and his medieval followers. Bringing to medieval romance the Dantean and Renaissance association of the dark forest with the infernal ignores an important ambiguity in medieval literature. See as correctives to such anachronistic assumptions Kohler (1956) and Ajam (1982). On the convention of the knight errant, see Menard (1976).

3. Larry Sklute (1953) relates the moral ambiguity of medieval romance to the new Aristotelian epistemology of the thirteenth century. Robert Hanning

(1977) offers explanations of late medieval individualism based on broader social developments, including the decline of the socially mobilizing barbarian
threat and a 'new grasp of Latin as a literary language capable of expressing
personal relations in all their ambiguity' (p. 2). Patricia Parker's (1979) is the
most developed argument about the inconclusiveness of romance endings,
and about the opposition of epic and romance modes. Parker's work strays
into error, in my view, from a failure to recognize epic's systematic assimilation of romance as a subordinate genre.

4. My description of pastoral here avoids a host of distinctions that would be
crucial to any consideration of its use in epic that goes beyond the existing
critical literature. Launched as an Alexandrian counter-genre to Homeric
epic, Theocritean pastoral effected a 'removal of agonistic strife from the battlefield to the everyday world of amorous and poetic competition' (Halperin,
p. 178). Halperin's book on the pre-history of pastoral, which he links to the
Sumerian quarrel-poem, covers the competitive aspect thoroughly. But pastoral also transfers the cooperative aspect of epic strife to the countryside and
develops a strong egalitarian impulse. Paul Alpers (1979) describes what I believe to be the product of Vergil's elaborate development of this impulse as the
'responsive human community' (p. 127) of his *Eclogues*. For the fullest discussion to date on pastoral's place in the epic tradition, see D. M. Rosenberg's
Oaten Reeds and Trumpets (1981), which discusses Vergil, Spenser and Milton.

5. Colie (1973) includes a suggestive chapter on 'uncanonical forms, mixed
kinds, and *nova reperta*'. Since her groundbreaking work, the theory of genres
has paid much attention to mixtures. See, for example, Alastair Fowler's
(1982) chapter entitled 'Transformations of Genre'.

6. Jakobson (1978), p. 82.

7. It might be objected that this claim could be made for Petrarch's *Africa*. In
this ambitious and unjustly disdained poem epic conventions do at times interplay with conventions of medieval hagiography, a genre that forms part of
the genealogy of medieval romance and a link between Greek romances and
later variants. But Petrarch is striving for a generic purity beyond that of his
Vergilian model, and he succeeds in avoiding opportunities for generic interplay. Margaret Hurley (1975) conveniently reviews discussions of romance's
link with hagiography.

8. Stinger (1985), pp. 222-6.

9. Stinger (1985), pp. 238-40. Stinger's 1981 article '*Roma triumphans*' covers
Renaissance triumphs in greater detail.

10. Stinger (1985), pp. 262-4.

11. In the introduction to his translation of Giraldi's discourse, Henry Snuggs
(1968, pp. xiv-xv) makes this point well: 'For Giraldi one of the basic genres
is the "epic" or "heroic," first defined by Aristotle. But since the *Orlando
Furioso* grew out of what were called *romanzi*, Giraldi retains that term both
in title and text using it synonymously with "heroic poem" to describe the
genre as it had developed in his time. As seems clear from the *Discourse*, the
Iliad, *Odyssey*, and the *Orlando Furioso* are all heroic poems; and if Giraldi
could have known the *Gerusalemme Liberata*, *The Faerie Queene*, and *Paradise
Lost*, he would have included these poems in the same genre'. The epic aspect
of the poem has been regularly minimized since the Cinquecento.

12. Passages from *Orlando Furioso* in the original Italian are taken from the edition of Lanfranco Caretti and cited by canto, stanza and line numbers. Since

neither Barbara Reynolds nor Guido Waldman remains close enough to the text for my purposes, I have provided my own literal-minded, if not always successfully literal, translations.

13. Murrin (1980), p. 226.

14. To my knowledge the question of Ariosto's knowledge of Homer has not been seriously investigated. Increased financial responsibilities following the death of his father in 1499 led him to abandon early plans to study Greek. As he writes in a poem from the time, 'My father dies, and I must need turn my thought from Mary to follow Martha, must change Homer for records of household expenses' (quoted in Gardner, 1968, p. 40). It is unknown if he ever turned back, though his life-long friend Pietro Bembo was passionate about the language and the literature. Ariosto's allusions to Homer are generally broad and situational, as in the example cited, and do not suggest to me closer familiarity than would be obtained by reading humanist Latin translations, which were freely available. For a detailed account of Homer's influence on Italian heroic poems, and especially Tasso's, see Baldassarri (1982). The reference to the Hesperides is conspicuously untrue and therefore even more likely to create a Vergilian connection. As far as we know, neither Orlando nor Angelica have been to 'la Esperia', the African realm of Soridano in both Boiardo (*O.I.*, 2.19.9) and Ariosto (*O.F*, 14.22.1).

15. Commentators since the poem's publication have discussed the problems of narrative succession it poses, and modern critics have followed their lead. Especially lucid on the subject are articles by Daniel Javitch on 'cantus interruptus' (1980) and 'narrative discontinuity' (1988). The weaving metaphor is of Homeric origin. In the earliest example, Antenor reports that Odysseus and Menelaos 'wove' ('huphainon', *Il.*, 3.212) their speech and counsel.

16. See, for example, Parker (1979), Carne-Ross (1966), Griffin (1974), Donato (1972).

17. Quotations from *Orlando Innamorato* are cited by book, canto and stanza from the edition by Aldo Scaglione. The history of Hector's armour is told in 3.1.25-30 and continues into *Orlando Furioso*.

18. Doroszlaï (1991), p. 33. Although he is accurate in describing movements inside Paris, I believe that Doroszlaï errs in his description of the Saracen deployment outside. Believing that Ariosto is using a map that places west at the top and that both Sobrino's location to the left ('a man manca', 14.108.1) and Rinaldo's left turn mean left on the map and therefore to the south, he locates Sobrino's forces to the southeast of Paris. After sending contingents into the city through the northern gates, Rinaldo is then seen to circle around Paris to the east and cross the Seine on the southeast side of the city. But it is much more logical to locate Sobrino at the northeast flank of Agramante's armies, along the Seine where it turns again to the northeast, where he would await any attack by expected reinforcements from the north. The deployment of forces is told from Agramante's point of view; just as Moslem territory lies 'to his rear' ('dietro'), so does he reasonably place Sobrino 'to his left' while other forces remain behind him 'in the countryside' ('alla campagna', 14.107.8). Guido Waldman's translation exhibits a similar confusion, rightly rendering Sobrino's location 'to his left', but then translating 'sopra' in 16.19.5 and 16.31.4 as 'upstream' rather than above Paris, a rendering that supports Doroszlaï's reading but contradicts the meaning of 'to his left'. Doroszlaï supports his reading with an engraving illustrating canto 16 in a

1556 Venetian edition. He also notes that this engraving inverts the standard orientation of contemporary maps of Paris, which place the east at the top. The mirror-reversal not uncommon in Renaissance prints is a better explanation for this engraving's orientation than is Ariosto's use of an orientation neither he nor his readers are likely to have seen. On the drawing of the north-south *cardo* and the east-west *decamanus*, and on Roman city design in general, see Joseph Rykwert's superb *The Idea of a Town* (1988).

19. Olschki (1913), p. 207.

20. Carne-Ross (1966), p. 223. See also Murtaugh (1980, p. 93), who suggests that 'the original Apollonian context of Medea's concern for Jason was also present to the poet when he developed the image of Orlando kept from sleep by the torment of his love and fear for Angelica'. This association would interact interestingly with Ariosto's interest in sexual cross-dressing. At the very least it adds a context for viewing Orlando's dismembering rage and the issue of Angelica's 'infidelity'.

21. Saccone (1974, p. 201) writes, 'l'Ercole del titolo genera due eroi, le cui traiettore sono insieme analoghe e opposte'.

22. Kirk (1974), p. 184. The major discussions of the Renaissance Hercules are by Panofsky (1930), Jung (1966) and Galinsky (1972). For Ariosto's use of Hercules, see also Ascoli (1987) and Shapiro (1988). Dante's (1893, p. 82) labelling of Hercules 'magnanimus' in Epistola 7 is the earliest post-classical instance of which I am aware.

23. David Quint (1979) argues convincingly that Atlante is a surrogate figure for Boiardo, whose endless and digressive romance Ariosto rejects, a rejection figured in the magician's defeat and death. Marianne Shapiro (1983) captures the sense of Atlante as a cosmic figure: he 'controls a world unto himself' (p. 327); his 'realm is the center of a domain whose circumference is nowhere, the focus of a centripetal movement rivalling that toward Christian and Saracen capitals alike' (p. 328). She finds Ovid and Petrarch's *Africa* to be shaping influences on Ariosto's conception.

24. Omphale is the grammatically feminine form of *omphalos*. Alcina's identification with her thus supports her role as counter-centre located at the antipodes, a new version of Calypso's role in her island at the navel of the sea.

25. Dante, *Inferno*, 26.109. Citations and translations of Dante are drawn from the edition by Charles Singleton (1970).

26. Freccero (1986, pp. 29-54) thoroughly explains Dante's use of the left foot as part of his poem's systematic spatiality.

27. The best account of the T-in-O map remains that by Raymond Beazely (1906). For a discussion of a later Renaissance poet's use of this cartographic form, see Anderson (1972). The tripartite division of the world in this type of map corresponds to Ariosto's tripartite Parisian 'terra'.

28. Greene (1963), p. 119.

29. Parker (1979), p. 52.

30. The liar's paradox, epitomized in Epimenides the Cretan's perfect contradiction, 'All Cretans are liars', has been studied in considerable detail for both its logical implications and its pervasive influence on Western thought. For a discussion of its uses in Renaissance literature and further bibliography, see Colie (1966), especially pp. 6-7, 119-22, 391-2.

31. Harvey remarks in a 1580 letter accompanying the return of a manuscript of the *Faerie Queene* that Spenser's 'Elvish Queene' seeks to 'overgo' *Orlando*

Furioso (Hamilton, p. 2). The *Faerie Queene* is cited by book, canto, and stanza numbers from the Variorum edition of Greenlaw (1932-66).

32. Rowse (1955), p. 1.
33. On the sacred spatiality of the Gothic cathedral, see Von Simson (1962); of the monastery's paradisal cloister, see Leclercq (1958); of Rome in both classical and Christian frameworks, see Müller (1961).
34. This passage comes from Hooker's influential 'A Learned Discourse of Justification', which is included in the Morris edition of *Of the Laws of Ecclesiastical Polity* (1925, vol. 1, p. 59).
35. Lewalski (1979), pp. 128-9.
36. Nelson (1963), pp. 174-5.
37. Berger (1966), p. 20. For a similar view, see Cheney (1966), p. 21.
38. Critics have long acknowledged Spenser's holiness / wholeness pun. For an interesting treatment in terms of Redcrosse's health and illness, see Nohrnberg (1976), pp. 279-80.
39. Brundage (1966) and Flori (1979).
40. On Jerusalem as omphalos, see Wensinck (1916), Müller (1961) and Terrien (1970). The Elizabethans found the crusade a useful model for their conflict with Catholic Spain. Redcrosse is being trained for a climactic campaign of the Faerie Queene 'Gainst that proud Paynim king, that works her teene' (1.12.18); George's traditional role as the Crusader's patron adds epic resonance to his struggles in Faery Land.
41. Langland (1978), Prologue, line 19.
42. Hill (1978), pp. 488-9.
43. On Platonic infolding and unfolding, see Wind (1958), pp. 204ff. and with reference to Spenser, Barkan (1975), chapter 5.
44. In Books 3 and 4 of Landino's *Camaldolese Disputations*, first printed in 1480, the interlocutor Alberti shows that in the *Aeneid*'s first six books Aeneas should be understood allegorically as the man who progresses from a Troy representing corrupt sensual pleasure, to Carthage representing the dangerous active life, to Italy representing the paradisal realm of perfect contemplation.
45. Nashe makes this statement in his 'Preface to Greene's *Menaphon*', reprinted in Smith (1904), vol. 1, p. 318.
46. The universal realm of Una's ancestors contrasts with Duessa's claimed descent from an Emperor 'that the wide West under his rule has / And high hath set his throne, where Tiberis doth pass' (1.2.22). As Kermode (1971, pp. 42-3) and others have noted, Una's is the true imperial church opposed to Duessa's imperial papacy.
47. Craig (1967).
48. I am appropriating Jonathan Goldberg's appropriation of this Spenserian phrase for the title of his book on the *Faerie Queene*. Although I am here approaching the poem from a different direction, I believe that Goldberg's description of the reader's endless re-writing is compatible with my own.
49. Miller (1986).

CHAPTER FOUR

The Copious Matter of
The Faerie Queene

The previous chapter observed Spenser, assisted by typological practices evolving from study of the Bible, infolding the multiple journeys of Redcrosse into the Christian pilgrimage as a subsuming form of the epic journey. In the *Faerie Queene* Platonic infolding and unfolding affect a remarkable abundance of other material as well. Rightly insisting that 'the process of the whole poem can be compared to this unfolding and reinfolding', Leonard Barkan provides cogent readings of the relations of several characters to the allegorical projections with whom they struggle or cooperate.[1] But since he is primarily interested in the image of the human body, Barkan devotes little attention in the poem's more complex mechanisms of infolding-unfolding, the rhetorical effects of these processes, or the relation of Spenser's innovations to his generic tradition. I wish to approach these neglected subjects by examining two related features of the poem that can help us understand its place in the evolution of the epic genre: its strangely systematic use of the Hercules myth, and its translation of epic's omphalic cosmology into 'allegorical cores' and synchronic textual structures. Hercules has been chosen because he is a central recurring figure in the epic tradition, but also because his limited role within the *Faerie Queene* can be treated comprehensively. The poem's myriad translations of epic cosmology, in contrast, inform every stanza, perhaps every line, but even a highly selective treatment can illuminate Spenser's adaptation of his genre to new cultural requirements.

Herculean Displacements

Ariosto's extensive allusions to Hercules, we saw in chapter 3, form an important part of his claim to overgo his predecessors and of his labour to establish epic as a viable Renaissance genre. As a patron of rational prudence, the pre-eminent classical hero was a natural choice to exemplify humanist ideology. His geographical inclusiveness, and most particularly his marking of the world's boundaries, served Ariosto's expansion of epic into the larger Renaissance world. And as a hero whose adventures were both unusually varied and unusually prominent in the common cultural memory upon which extended allusion relies, Hercules served as a convenient point of triangulation between characters. Ariosto's incorporation of Hercules into his epic machinery was so innovative and thorough, in fact, that later Renaissance poets would add only one significant device to his repertoire: a claim to artistic unity based on the unity of the individual life. Giraldi Cinthio, Ariosto's ablest advocate in the great Cinquecento quarrel over epic decorum, is the key figure in this development, in which the notion of artistic form adjusted to the values of an increasingly human-centred, self-fashioning age. Anxious to defend *Orlando Furioso* against rigid Aristotelians' complaint that the poem did not represent a single, unified action, Giraldi directly attacked Aristotle's notion of unity as overly restrictive. The *Poetics* was very clear about the issue:

> A plot does not have unity, as some people think, simply because it deals with a single hero. Many and indeed innumerable things happen to an individual, some of which do not make up any unity, and similarly an individual is concerned in many actions which do not combine into a single piece of action. It seems therefore that all those poets are wrong who have written a *Heracleid* or a *Theseid* or other such poems. They think that because Heracles was single individual the plot must for that reason have unity.[2]

Giraldi responded that, in the hands of a judicious poet, one who knows how 'to fill up the hollows and to equalise the size of the members' so that the poem's 'framework' attains the harmonious proportions of the human body, the story of a complete life need not exceed artistic bounds.[7] Assisted by the spatial analogy of the body, unity of character could in effect become temporal unity of action.

Giraldi's revival of the notion of a Heracleid in the 1554 *Discorso* participated in a mid-century revival of the hero's fortunes. Natale Conti's 1551 *Mythologiae* and Vincenzo Cartari's 1556 *Imagini de i Dei degli Antichi* carried the allegorized Hercules far beyond the limited circle of Italian humanists directly influenced by Salutati and provided writers throughout Europe with a common set of allegorical readings for the twelve labours and other episodes in the Alcidean biography. Giraldi himself soon followed theory with practice, publishing his epic *Dell'Ercole* in 1557. Farther north in 1555, Jacques Peletier du Mans, a charter member of the Pléiade and a Neoplatonist who advocated encyclopedic learning as the basis of moral development, proclaimed Hercules, whom the French proudly announced was of Gallic origin, the most noble possible subject for epic. But Peletier also feared that the subject, because it would require such wide-ranging erudition and heroic powers of synthesis (for the poem would have to include, he asserts in an interestingly untidy list, 'wars, wanderings, stars, the underworld, loves, all sects of philosophy, reconciliation of times and genealogies'), was beyond the capabilities of his century's poets.[3] When he began to write his own Heracleid, Spenser might be expected to benefit from this revival in a number of ways. The widely known and relatively consistent ethical allegorizations of the twelve labours could be useful in defining his own sequence of twelve virtues. Similarly, Hercules' long-standing characterization as a magnanimous hero uniting a variety of virtues of body and soul could prove useful in defining his own, highly revisionary version of *megalopsuchia*. Salutati's derivation of the name from 'glorious in strife' ('heris cleos' in Greek, which becomes 'gloria litis' in Latin), might have been suggestive to the etymologically sensitive Protestant poet who sent his patron not of spatially extensive Magnanimity, but of more active Magnificence (from *facere*, thus great in doing?), forward faring toward Gloriana in Cleopolis.[4] And certainly Hercules' association with the issue of epic's inclusive unity would have caught the attention of a poet seeking to overgo Ariosto with an epic that realized both a new kind of generative copia and a new kind of integral unity.

Spenser begins his Heracleid, we might say, *in medias res*. In the middle of the Legend of Holiness, he draws upon a labour from the middle of Hercules' career, usually the seventh of the twelve.[5] Arthur is pitted against a beast who combines features from the beasts of Revelation and the Lernean Hydra:

> Such one it was, as that renowmed Snake
> Which great Alcides in Stremona slew,
> Long fostred in the filth of Lerna lake,
> Whose many heads out budding ever new,
> Did breed him endlesse labour to subdew. (1.7.17)

The Hydra was an appropriate victim for the Protestant hero. While not as popular as such biblical notables as the apocalyptic Anti-Christ or Whore of Babylon as a figure of Catholic perfidy, the Hydra quite logically grew to be a commonplace of Reformation polemics. In humanist allegory the Hydra could represent tyranny.[6] With the Reformation the home of the multi-headed water snake moved from Lerna in the Peloponnesus to the Tiber, where Catholicism could be associated with history's favourite examples of tyranny. Spenser's wailing nymph in *A Theater for Worldlings* applies classical precedent to the current situation:

> Alas, suffisde it not that civile bate
> Made me the spoile and bootie of the world,
> But this new Hydra mete to be assailde
> Even by an hundred such as Hercules.
> With seven springing heds of monstrous crimes,
> So many Neroes and Caligulaes
> Must still bring forth to rule this croked shore.

Using Plato's conflict between the Socratic Hercules and the sophistic Hydra, Salutati distinguishes between the reasonable debate that seeks truth and the kind of disputation that could produce many heads of argument for each one cut off.[7] The latter was precisely the kind of expedient rhetoric and casuistic logic that Protestants found in the serpentine doctrines of Rome, and which was signified in the overflowing *copia* of Spenser's Errour. Henry VIII, the philosopher-king who fought papist tyranny by studying theology as well as arming God's kingdom, was thus appropriately celebrated for his 'moste famous subduyng of the Romayne monster Hydra'.[8] This kind of exegesis would be inescapable for the Elizabethan audience, who would use this and other details to connect Arthur's combat to the Errour episode and begin the experience of infolding Redcrosse as a soldier of God into Arthur.

The infolding process continues with the next allusion. We have observed in the previous chapter the conspicuous absence of Hercules *in bivio* in the directionally subversive opening canto. Hercules becomes conspicuously present as an analogue for Redcrosse at the other end of the story. Roused to fury by the knight's blows, the dragon of Eden attacks with his fiery breath, and Redcrosse suffers as did Hercules when poisoned by his jealous wife:

> Not that great Champion of the antique world,
> Whom famous Poetes verse so much doth vaunt,
> And hath for twelve huge labours high extold,
> So many furies and sharpe fits did haunt,
> When him the poysoned garment did enchaunt
> With Centaures bloud, and bloudie verses charm'd,
> As did this knight twelve thousand dolours daunt,
> Whom fyrie steele now burnt, that earst him arm'd,
> That erst him goodly arm'd, now most of all him harm'd. (1.11.27)

Redcrosse's situation provides an inviting field of inquiry for the typological imagination. Spenser inserts his young hero into Hercules' itinerary at the opposite end from the youthful crossroads episode favoured by writers of heroic poetry and humanist ethics. Repetitive closure on his armour, 'that earst him arm'd, that erst him goodly arm'd', keeps our attention directed toward beginnings and endings by asking us to recall the beginning of Redcrosse's story, his post-arming entry and the boon of heroic 'achievement' granted in the Letter to Raleigh. Predestined achievement rather than earned moral victory, we are reminded, characterizes Redcrosse's beginning. The allusion's presence near the end of the legend logically suggests that the twelve huge labours are now behind him, for the poisoned garment marks the initial stage of Hercules' apotheosis on Mount Oeta. Redcrosse, we are invited to infer, needs only to suffer through this final, painful purification before reaching his omphalic goal. The Oeta episode was long a favourite occasion for waxing eloquent on the theme of spiritual transformation at the sacred centre. Ovid

(*Metamorphoses*, 9.262ff.) portrays an elaborate transfiguration through fire, amplified, with an intertextual irony that has eluded explanation in the critical literature, by a skin-shedding snake simile borrowed from Vergil's Pyrrhus at Priam's threshold. In the other, the perhaps significantly un-Ariostan Hercules play of Seneca, *Hercules Oetaeus*, Oeta is the location from which, after subduing all of the horizontal world and the underworld, the deified hero rises to the only realm left. Early in the play he claims that in ridding both hemispheres of monsters he has outdone Apollo's cosmogonic killing of Python, for which the god received his Delphian shrine and a place in heaven (lines 92ff.). In his 'Hercule Chrestien' Ronsard equates Oeta and Calvary, likening Hercules to Christ 'burning' on the cross and then ascending above the clouds to his heavenly reward.[9] Spenser now adds Eden to the list of omphalic associations. The more specifically Reformation context of Arthur's combat facilitates interpretation of Redcrosse's rescue of Eden as a contemporary crusade against Catholicism, while the universality of this rescue adds apocalyptic resonance to any more specific applications.

As the Heracleid continues in the Legend of Temperance, several new obliquities and complexities challenge the reader who has benefited from the lessons of Book 1. After inviting us to compare the current legend to the previous by announcing Guyon's 'like race to runne' (2.1.32) and setting up extensive parallels, Spenser precisely reverses the Herculean pattern of the previous book, first associating Hercules with the legend's unfolded hero in canto 7 then with infolding Arthur in canto 11. As Guyon views the attractions of the underworld, Spenser introduces a labour commonly interpreted as the overcoming of avarice:

> Their fruit were golden apples glistring bright,
> That goodly was their glory to behold,
> On earth like never grew, ne living wight
> Like ever saw, but they from hence were sold;
> For those, which Hercules with conquest bold
> Got from great Atlas daughters, hence began.
> And planted there, did bring forth fruit of gold. (2.7.54)

Although positions have been reversed, as in Book 1 the most extensive Herculean labour is assigned to Arthur. Maleger, the 'Captain' of 'The enimies of Temperance' (2.11.arg.) and Arthur's primary foe, is a creature no less multiply allusive than Duessa's hydra-like beast, but his kinship with Antaeus, who sprang up stronger from the ground each time Hercules cast him down, is clear. In the Maleger episode, however, we are left to make the Herculean connection without the help of a simile. Antaeus' thematic relevance is also more challenging. For Salutati and the mythographers, Antaeus represents libido, and is therefore a most appropriate displaced opponent for temperate Guyon.[10] Deriving the monster's name from 'antheon', which he takes to suggest both 'contra', opposition, and 'simile', similarity, Salutati finds this labour to be a commentary upon the Aristotelian notion that vice lies in either the excess or defect of a passion, an idea very much at home in the legend where Elissa and Perissa are similar in being opposed to virtuous Medina, and where Guyon must navigate psychically between the extremes represented by Pyrochles and Cymochles. Nor, of course, is avarice resistant to analysis in terms of Aristotelian ethics. So, as we would expect from reading Book 1, Arthur's allegory comments meaningfully upon the titular hero's quest, but Maleger's pale and withered appearance works against the mythographic tradition, and additional readerly labour is required to make the connection through the ravages of libidinous sin.

What about Guyon's intemperate destruction of the Bower, we might ask? Is this simply a victory over libido? The hero's vehemence has long disturbed critics:

> But all those pleasant bowres and Pallace brave,
> Guyon broke down, with rigour pittilesse;
> Ne ought their goodly workmanship might save
> Them from the tempest of his wrathfulnesse,
> But that their blisse he turn'd to balefulnesse:
> Their groves he feld, their gardins did deface,
> Their arbers spoyle, their Cabinets suppresse,
> Their banket houses burne, their buildings race,
> And of the fairest late, now made the fowlest place. (2.12.83)

Connecting this action to Arthur's combat with Maleger-Antaeus produces little illumination. Rather than repeat the procedures of Book 1, Spenser offers a variation. In the previous legend the simile linking Arthur to Hercules occurred one canto before the actual combat. We are now asked to stretch even more for our interpretation, since the Herculean labour explaining Guyon's vehemence is separated from the act by seven cantos. Though Acrasia's bower is the site of Guyon's labour in the final canto, it is first described in canto 5 where, continuing the provocative interplay of beginnings and endings, Spenser refers to Hercules' very early labour:

> And on the other side a pleasaunt grove
> Was shot up high, full of the stately tree,
> That dedicated is t'Olympicke Iove,
> And to his sonne Alcides, whenas hee
> Gayned in Nemea goodly victoree.
> Therein the mery birds of every sort
> Chaunted alowd their cheareful harmonie:
> And made emongst themselves a sweet consort,
> That quickned the dull spright with musical comfort. (2.5.31)

Salutati again provides a useful gloss with his explanation of the conquest of the Nemean lion as the youthful conquest of irascibility, one of the

extreme vices opposed to Guyon, most clearly in Pyrocles, the logical opposite and complement to the equally intemperate Cymocles.[11] (The
brothers' traits unite in the simultaneously irascible and concupiscible
Maleger, who thereby forms a fitting foe to the similarly infolding
Arthur.) The Herculean matrix allows us to see not only the allegorical
labour in which Guyon succeeds when he resists the bower's appeals, but
also the one in which he subsequently fails in the tempest of his wrathful-
ness. It is probably no accident that the unstable co-presence of the
positive and negative Hercules occurs in the section of the *Faerie Queene*
densest with allusions to the epic tradition. As he navigates the treacherous sea of allegorized epic landmarks and penetrates to the centre, Guyon
imitates the various heroes who have worn the Herculean lionskin, the
fruit of the very labour that we must apply to Guyon's destructive wrath.
Once his mission is accomplished his actions more closely resemble the
treachery of Odysseus' inhospitable Hercules and mad Orlando's destruction of the countryside, as Spenser returns to a subject that the genre has
brooded over since its very founding: the collapse of difference between
the hero and his foe.

With the Legend of Chastity the pattern of mutually illuminating
Herculean labours distributed between Arthur and his local counterpart
breaks down. The bivium, conspicuously removed from Book 1, now
makes its appearance as Arthur and Guyon chase the fleeing Florimel:

> At last they came unto a double way,
> Where, doubtful which to take, her to reskew,
> Themselves they did dispart, each to assay,
> Whether more happie were, to win so goodly pray. (3.4.46)

Most noteworthy here is the depth of ambiguity surrounding a traditional
emblem of clear choice. The two paths are equivalent, each taken with the
hope that it will lead to the same object of desire. The choice of undiffer-
entiated paths is also motivated by a hopelessly ambiguous mixture of vice
and virtue. From the onset, the pursuit of Florimell has combined implications of noble rescue and the lustful hunt; only constant Britomart, who
refrains from the pursuit, keeps moving unambiguously 'forward' (3.4.18)
along 'her right course' (3.4.44), despite travelling 'withouten compasse,
or withouten card' (3.2.7). For the formerly Herculean Arthur, in contrast, we are informed that love 'to his first pursuit him forward still doth
call' (3.5.2), but the prince who encounters Florimell when he is 'seeking
adventures' (3.1.14) bears a suspicious resemblance to Redcrosse as he
moved deeper into romance multiplicity, as the 'unfolding' pun on 'themselves dispart' might suggest. Accordingly, we soon witness a reversal of
this ostensibly forward motion: 'So with the dwarf he bak return'd againe,
/ To seeke his Lady, where he mote her find' (3.5.12). As the pattern of

Herculean allusions breaks down, Satyrane finds that the Squire of Dames' world-encompassing (he must 'walke the world around', 3.7.56) series of seductions 'may emongst Alcides labours stand' (3.7.61). This ironic evaluation, where Ariosto's epic assimilation of circumnavigation is reversed, is applicable as well to the widely wandering Arthur and to Artegall, who 'restlesse walketh all the world around' (3.2.14) as Book 3 opens. At the end of the book in her struggle with Busirane, Britomart combines the roles played by Arthur and the titular heroes of the earlier legends. Like Guyon and Redcrosse, she takes on a Herculean aspect as she labours through the legend's climactic combat. She also replaces Arthur, for now she is assigned the book's principal labour. On Busirane, Thomas Warton writes in his 1762 *Observations on the Fairy Queene* that Spenser 'seems to have drawn this Name from Busiris, the king of Aegypt, famous for his cruelty and inhospitality'.[12] The mythographic tradition interpreted Hercules' defeat of Busirus, who sacrificed strangers on an altar to propitiate the gods, simply as the defeat of the prototypical 'cruel tyrant', without additional moral allegorization.[13] The allusion invites us to reflect upon the tyrannies of love, which in its improper forms cruelly and inhospitably subjugates the other to the needs of the self, and vice versa. It sharpens the contrast between the quests of Arthur and Britomart, the disoriented pursuit of Florimell and the constant search for Artegall, and it clarifies Spenser's conception of chastity as an epic virtue requiring a kind of psychic hospitality, a tactful assertion of the self that is simultaneously solicitude for the other: 'Be bold', she reads in the House of Busirane, 'Be not too bold' (3.11.54).

If the rearrangements of Herculean identifications in Book 3 can be described and interpreted after some heroic grasping of the discourse for which the clearer patterns of Books 1 and 2 have prepared us, Book 4 appears to continue Spenser's accelerating demands. The first and longest reference to Hercules occurs near the beginning when the dwelling of Ate provides the following sight:

> And there the relicks of the drunken fray,
> The which amongst the Lapithees befell,
> And of the bloody feast, which sent away
> So many Centaures drunken souls to hell,
> That under great Alcides furie fell;
> And of the dreadful discord, which did drive
> The noble Argonauts to outrage fell,
> That each of life sought others to deprive,
> All mindless of the Golden fleece, which made them strive. (4.1.23)

The reference is provocative both in what it suppresses from the well-known mythology and what it adds. Missing is precisely the detail that makes the episode thematically relevant: Hercules' accidental slaying of his old friend Chiron with an arrow tipped with the Hydra's venom. Moreover, as Hamilton notes, to the Argonauts' quarrel Spenser adds an uncanonical cause, apparently 'to link the classical stories of discord with the contest over the golden girdle'. In the very home of Homer's goddess of Discord, whose greatest achievement was to delude Zeus into unwitting subjection of Hercules to Eurystheus, and whose story is told in the *Iliad* in a context requiring that Achilles and the Homeric audience put together the discourse in a very demanding way, a process that includes linking Ate and Hera's deception to an earlier deception in which Hera used Venus' seductive girdle or Cestus, the origin of Florimell's girdle, Spenser provocatively overloads his Heracleid with interpretive challenges. In addition, just as the quarrel over the Golden Fleece links Hercules to the contest over the girdle, the poet's 'slip' in the book's title, which announces 'the legend of Cambel and Telamond', hints at a Herculean context for the combat between Cambel and Triamond, whom Telamond has mysteriously replaced. Hercules, a reader might recall, also won a girdle in combat: the Balteus of Hippolyta, queen of the Amazons, whom Hercules defeated in the company of his friend Telamon, or, in alternative versions, with his friend Theseus.[14] In the Thesean versions, Hercules re-establishes harmony by joining Hippolyta in marriage to his companion, a renowned act of friendship that finds an echo, though the parallels are not close enough to make us sure we are not overreading, in the reconciliation of Cambell and Triamond through marriage after their combat.

The juxtaposition of two combats so obliquely linked to Hercules represents the very limit of what Spenser can demand. Once we recognize the connections to which the text points so elusively, the interpretive process can begin. The Balteus is a girdle of Mars and a symbol of martial prowess, Florimell's golden girdle, like the Homeric Cestus, a girdle of Venus and a symbol of chastity. The two strands of Herculean allusion thus come together in a way echoed and confirmed by other instances of the Venusian-Martian *discordia concors*, and some such reconciliation must be suggested as the basis of the friendship which Hercules has accidentally betrayed. If the Amazons enter the text allusively through the irruption of a Herculean subtext, then their allegorical significance might also. Spenser of course reserves his major treatment of the Amazons for the Legend of Justice, but their allusive presence is equally appropriate in the Legend of Friendship, where as traditional symbols of sensuality they stand opposed to the chaste love that underlies true friendship between the genders. But as Hercules references continue Spenser confronts us with a carefully contrived aporia. The devotion of 'great Hercules, and Hylas deare' (4.11.27) is as obviously connected to the theme of friend-

ship as it is irrelevant to any interpretive process. The reader is likely to
expect that Arthur's restoration to heroic status through his defeat of the
giant Corflambo in canto 8 would be accompanied by a successful labour.
The giant himself very tenuously suggests Albion, a giant slain by
Hercules in English lore but not a product of the classical heritage or a
subject of continental allegorical speculation. When a stanza-length depiction of the slaying of Albion (4.11.15) confirms the suggestion, and we
attempt to follow it up in the manner the early books have encouraged,
there is nowhere to go. Hercules here adds conspicuous irrelevance to his
repertoire of textual functions.

In an astonishing reversal, following this descent into incoherence
Spenser in the second stanza of the Legend of Justice pronounces
Hercules the patron of justice in the half of the world of greatest interest
to Spenser and his readers:

> Such first was Bacchus, that with furious might
> All th'East before untamed did overrone,
> And wrong repressed, and established right,
> Which lawlesse men had formerly fordonne.
> There Iustice first her princely rule begonne.
> Next Hercules his like ensample shewed,
> Who all the West with equall conquest wonne,
> And monstrous tyrants with his club subdewed;
> The club of Iustice dread, with kingly powre endewed.

Responding to this uncharacteristically clear pronouncement, Spenser
criticism begins with the Legend of Justice to recognize the importance of
Herculean reference to the *Faerie Queene*. William Nelson (1963), Jean
MacIntyre (1966), Jane Aptekar (1969) and most recently James
Nohrnberg (1976) have amply demonstrated that, in Aptekar's words, 'the
myth of Hercules is as much the base motif of Book V as the legend of St.
George is of Book I'.[15] Artegall's subjugation to Radigund, readers now
generally understand, is modelled on Hercules' subjugation to the Lydian
queen Omphale, the defeat of Souldan on the defeat of the Thracian
tyrant Diomedes, Arthur's defence of Belge against Geryoneo on the slaying of the monstrous Iberian monarch Geryon. The similes and open
allusions linking these episodes to Hercules, the parallels of action and situation, the elevation of Artegall and Arthur through association with the
archetypal hero of civilization have all been grist for the critical mill.

To advance beyond the existing criticism it is necessary to consider how
this newly pervasive Herculean presence contributes to Spenser's analysis
of justice. The deployment of self-other relations in the workings of justice is no less problematic than in the workings of the other virtues.
Simple justice, as embodied most clearly in Talus (with connotations of
Latin *talis*, 'of such a kind') is enforced through the *lex talionis*, which

restores equilibrium by precisely fitting punishment to the offence. Thus must the cruel perpetrators of injustice be opposed by the enforcer's 'cruel' methods, an epithet applied repeatedly to both the unjust monsters and Artegall's hand and sword. The *lex talionis*, which underlies primitive, vengeance-based justice, carries with it the inevitable problem of the just agent's identification with the criminal, an identification softened but not eliminated in Christian ethics through the idea of clemency. The para-doxical nature of the justice-clemency opposition is manifest throughout Book 5, receiving its most emblematic expression perhaps in Britomart's dream in the Temple of Isis. Osiris, the representative of stern authority, takes on the nature of the storm and fire that he quells and is in turn coun-tered by Isis, the embodiment of clemency, who in fact subjugates Osiris by the strict authority of her rod, an object meant to recall the legend's formidable set of justice-dispensing instruments introduced with Hercules' 'club of justice Dread'. The problems inherent in applying a system so prone to the collapse of difference are the focus of the book's ethical argument.

The Heracleid participates in this argument in ways ranging from the relatively straightforward to the kind of challenging displacements that we have observed developing and then disappearing in the early books. The Souldan-Diomedes story falls into the first category:

> Like to the Thracian Tyrant, who they say
> Unto his horses gave his guests for meat,
> Till he himself was made their greedie pray,
> And torn in pieces by Alcides great.
> So thought the Souldan in his follies threat,
> Either the prince in peeces to have torne
> With his sharpe wheeles, in his first rages heat,
> Or under his fierce horses feet have borne
> And trampled downe in dust his thoughts disdained scorne. (5.8.31)

The inherited story presents a clear example of natural hierarchy reversed and then restored through retribution in kind; one allegorizer, at least, in-terprets the episode as virtue defeating vice with vice's own weapons.[16] Spenser adds only the detail that Hercules tore the tyrant in pieces him-self, rather than simply killing him and allowing the horses to devour the corpse. This addition entails emphases that, as we have seen beginning with the figurative dismemberment of Patroclus and the attempted muti-lation of Hector, are typical of epic: the integral body is reduced to the kind of chaotic multiplicity that Diomedes' injustice implies. Spenser's version also contrasts Hercules' direct revenge with Arthur's removal from responsibility. Arthur, after all, simply turns his uncovered shield upon the team pressing upon him. The result is a precise reversal of direction:

> Like lightening flash, that hath the gazer burned,
> So did the sight thereof their sense dismay,
> That backe again upon themselves they turned,
> And with their ryder ranne perforce away:
> Ne could the Souldan them from flying stay,
> With raynes, or wonted rule, as well he knew. (5.8.38)

The lightning bolt reminds us of the divine source of the shield's radiance. We can also detect aspects of the two Italian shields from which Spenser fashioned his own. The magic shield of Ariosto's Atlante (introduced in *OF.*, 4.17), of unspecified material, flashed forth to induce disorienting syncope. Tasso's shield, the source of Spenser's adamantine construction, was a polished mirror allowing Rinaldo to recognize his condition as Hercules effeminized, reverse his course, and reunite the allegorical body of Crusaders. Ariosto's shield converts epic warriors into romance wanderers, while Tasso's reverses the process. Spenser's radiant shield bewilders, but also reorients Souldan's team into a mirror-like reversal of itself: ruler and ruled exchange roles as the direction of motion reverses. The agents of injustice may not see their reflection in the shield, but in turning back upon themselves they unwittingly become agents of justice, restore natural order, and preclude Arthur's identification with the criminal. The entire procedure seems designed to avoid the kind of corrosive identification whereby Vergil's Hercules and Cacus met as *superbi*.

The critical literature on the Radigund episode generally assumes that we evaluate Artegall's misapplied clemency, the pity that leads him to spare the conquered Amazon when he sees her fair visage, by observing the inversion of the normal Renaissance hierarchies. The flesh has usurped reason and the woman is unnaturally on top. To this we should add another important inversion. The periphery usurps the centre as subjugation to a descendant of Omphale replaces the hero's proper submission to his 'great adventure' beginning and ending in Cleopolis. That the Amazons, whom Spenser has grafted onto the Omphale story following Sidney's example in the *Arcadia*, marked Hercules' easternmost labour, a counterpart to the famous western pillars, emphasizes how far this western-oriented (cf. 5.1.2) hero has wandered astray. All of this belaboured overdetermination of Artegall's sorry state helps us to appreciate the accumulating ironies of Britomart's rescue. In the poem's densely woven mythic substrate the woman hero, having usurped Arthur's role as the poem's leading Hercules figure by vanquishing Busiris in Book 3 and winning the girdle of Hippolyta in Book 4, now at once conquers Hippolyta and rescues the fallen Hercules from Omphale. But at the same time that her heroic standing continues its apparently irresistible rise, Britomart entangles herself in the thankless logic of justice.

Spenser layers another identification onto Radigund with what is usually thought to be a common, insignificant confusion:

> Who had him seene, imagine mote thereby,
> That whylome hath of Hercules bene told,
> How for Iolas sake he did apply
> His mightie hands, the distaff vile to hold,
> For his huge club, which had subdew'd of old
> So many monsters, which the world annoyed. (5.5.24)

Aptekar is surely correct in suggesting that Iole should remind us that Hercules' 'heroic virtue seems at times to be shaded with dubiousness, depravity'.[17] If the Iole story, understandably, did not appeal to Renaissance authors of allegorical emblem books or mythological dictionaries, who were humanists primarily interested in encouraging human potential through positive exemplars, it could certainly serve the purposes of a poet willing to confront the cruel paradoxes of justice. Having won Iole in an archery contest, Hercules was enraged by her father's refusal to give her up. In a vengeful fury he then sacked Iole's city and murdered her entire family before her eyes. After defeating the levelling giant in canto 2, Artegall, refusing to violate the just hierarchy that places commoners above the revenge of knights, and acting, in fact, rather like an Erasmian pacifist, sends Talus to inquire of the giant's follower's 'the cause of their array, and truce for to desire' (5.2.52). When the mob fails to respond to moderate overtures, the scene turns into a comic rout as Talus simply frightens them into acting 'like a swarme of flies' (5.2.53). The carefully contrasted scene in which the Amazons flee into the city following Britomart's beheading of Radigund reveals Talus taking on Britomart's vengeful frenzy:

> But yet so fast they could not home retrate,
> But that swift Talus did the formost win;
> And pressing through the preace unto the gate.
> Pelmell with them attonce did enter in.
> There then a piteous slaughter did begin:
> For all that ever came within his reach,
> He with his yron flail did thresh so thin,
> That he no work at all left for the leach:
> Like to an hideous storme, which nothing may impeach. (5.7.35)

Britomart follows Talus into the city 'her glory to partake' (36.2), but her Herculean fury lasts only until she view 'the heapes, which he did make, / Of slaughtred carkasses' (5.7.36). No Rodomonte finally yielding to the endless supply of potential victims, Britomart halts the slaughter out of 'ruth' (36.6), but the parallels with the Iole story remain to contaminate her with the just enforcer's cruelty. She has in effect become her cruel Amazonian victim, even if she immediately relents, and even if she afterwards declines to play Omphale, allowing Artegall to proceed manfully on his own Herculean itinerary.

It should not surprise us that Arthur's infolding of an individual legend's hero reaches a new level of subtlety in the book devoted to his double, Artegall. In the next Herculean labour, while the monstrous nature of his opponent allows Arthur to avoid taint, the subtle web of character identifications contaminates his nominal double even after the two knights have separated and Artegall 'on his first adventure forward forth did ride' (5.10.17). Arthur rescues Belge by first slaying the monster who has murdered her children. Geryon, Spenser recalls for us, was a Spanish giant who like Diomedes fed strangers to his beasts with the assistance of the 'cruell carle' Eurytion and 'his two headed dogge, that Orthrus hight', until 'Hercules them all did overcome in fight' (5.10.9-10). Arthur's labour pits him against Geryon's son Geryoneo, Spenser's invention, who infolds the now-deceased team of three oppressors within his own giant triple-body, his cruelty, and his mastiff-like bite. Good Fortune and the giant's own raging excess are at least as responsible for his defeat as Arthur's actions, which are made to appear almost self-defensive:

> Nought fear'd the childe his lookes, ne yet his threats,
> But onely wexed more the now aware,
> To save him self from those his furious heats,
> And watch advantage, how to work his care:
> The which good Fortune to him offred faire.
> For as he in his rage him overstrooke,
> He ere he could his weapon backe repaire,
> His side all bare and naked overtooke,
> And with his mortel steel quite through the body strooke. (5.11.13)

As in the conflation of Omphale and Iole, the small details of Spenser's treatment of mythological materials here carry large connotations. Lines of association, some very tenuous, others less so, link the episode to others. Geryon feeds strangers to his kine — a detail not in the source — and thereby claims kinship with Diomedes. Orthrus looks rather like Cerberus, another Herculean foe and, strangely enough, for Spenser both the father and brother of the Blatant Beast. Orthrus is also traditionally the father of the Nemean lion, whom Spenser recalled when Artegall-Hercules 'His Lyon's skin chaunged to a pall of gold' (5.5.24) in Amazonia. The versatile villain also fathered Hydra, whose Lernean lair reappears in 5.11.32 at the demise of the monster who guards the Idol consecrated by Geryoneo in 'the image of his monstrous parent Geryone' (5.10.13).

In a parody of the dynastic conflicts of epic, the filial ties proliferating from the Geryon episode, and especially the very noticeable addition of a generation to the brood of monsters, draw the two opposed sides into a relation of similarity. Given the legend's meditation upon the subtle like-

nesses that accompany justice and revenge, we are invited to view the conflict as a feud between families. The relationships are not logical and
direct: we cannot say that the clan of Geryoneo is paying back the clan of
Belge in kind for some past violence which Arthur then requites in turn.
We can say that the son of Geryon is combating an avatar of the hero who
killed his father. Furthermore, while Geryoneo is sacrificing Belge's people to the image of his dead parent, Arthur's equal is enforcing justice with
the cruelty that repeatedly invokes this father's name. The cruelty associated with the evil forces of Book 5 contaminates Artegall precisely
through the 'cruell hand' (5.2.18; and cf. 5.3.22, 5.5.13) that holds the
bright sword Chrysaor. Chrysaor in the classical tradition is Geryon's father. Skelton's translation of Diodorus Siculus, a likely source for Spenser,
brings him a generation closer to Geryoneo, making him King Geryon of
Spain himself.[18] 'Mightie Chrysaor' (4.11.14) also appears in the previous
book's catalogue of sea-gods descending (like Albion, who also was conquered by Hercules, Spenser notes two stanzas later) from Neptune. For
Renaissance mythographers, Spanish Geryon manifests this Neptunian
inheritance by ruling over the three islands of the Balearics, represented
by his three bodies, and by retaining the services of Orthrus, whose two
heads represent domination of both land and sea.[19] Thus, paradoxically,
can the abject cruelty of an infamous family of tyrannical monsters come
forth when Artegall unsheathes his sword. We can follow Spenser's generative process of typological linkages even farther, as the metal of
Artegall's 'steely brand' (5.1.9) is echoed in the legend's other instruments
of cruel justice: in the iron flail of iron Talus, who has metamorphosed
from the bronze man of antiquity to show how far humankind has re-
gressed; in Hercules' club of justice dread, which Skelton similarly
transforms from bronze to iron, and probably for the same reason; and of
course in the 'mortal steel' with which Arthur slays Geryoneo, as the text
labours and succeeds only partially in holding the epic's infolding hero 'in
holy righteousnesse, without rebuke or blame'.

Continuing his method of achieving emphasis through rhythms of
variation and contrast, after his fullest development of Herculean material, Spenser ends the six-book *Faerie Queene* of 1596 with a legend that,
until its closing canto, develops it the least. When Calidore finally returns
to his assignment and captures the Blatant Beast, Spenser compares his
achievement to, as Hamilton rightly notes, 'the most difficult of the
labours', the drawing of Cerberus into the upper world:[20]

> Like as whylome that strong Tirynthian swaine,
> Brought forth with him the dreadful dog of hell,
> Against his will fast bound in yron chaine,
> And roring horribly, did him compel

To see the fateful sunne, that he might tell
To griesly Pluto, what on earth was donne.
And to the other damned ghosts, which dwell
For aye in darkness, which day light doth shonne.
So led this Knight his captyve with like conquest wonne. (6.12.35)

In an age well trained in the poetics of the gaze and the semiotics of light, Hercules' drawing the hell-hound forth into the light was an image of inevitable appeal. It is unusual among the labours in more generally suggesting the height of achievement and recognition for the magnanimous hero. As Conti explains, 'Hercules, whose strength is greatness of soul, drew Cerberus into the light, and provided himself eternal glory'.[21] The hell-hound's three heads add to the labour's generalizing potential by symbolizing the components of a larger whole: the three ages of man, the three elements of the human body (fire, air, water).[22] The people of Faery Land, apparently agreeing with the mythographers' evaluations, 'much admyr'd the Beast, but more admyr'd the Knight' (6.12.37). This reaction linking the conquered and the conqueror, however, points to the complex ethics of the legend's virtue, and Renaissance mythography provides insight into the conceptual difficulties. In addition to the heroic celebration signified by Cerberus' forced emergence into the light, the labour was also subjected to more specific ethical allegorization. Salutati and Conti treat Cerberus as cupidity and avarice, following Isidore's etymology: 'creos beros', devouring flesh.[23] The details of Calidore's truancy amidst the pastoral life's 'perfect pleasures' (6.10.3) — especially his 'courteous' wooing of Pastorella and the Acidalian vision, which begins as indulgence of the skeptophile's secret pleasure and ends in a too grasping attempt to 'know' this pleasure's source — suggest the relevance of these ethical concepts to the problematics of courtesy. To what extent can courtesy be disinterested, the book inquires; can it remain free from the taint of avarice and cupidity? Also accompanying the defeat of the Blatant Beast is reference to 'the hell-borne Hydra, which they faine / That great Alcides whilome overthrew' (6.12.32). If avarice and cupidity are the hidden ends of false courtesy, is not shameless eloquence its means? The Legend of Courtesy, Isabel MacCaffrey wisely observes, is in large part about 'the power of words'.[24] We might recall Spenser's reported remark that 'by the Blating Beast the Puritans were understood'.[25] If this is an example of anti-Puritan satire, the beast's sacking of the monasteries (6.12.23) suggests the avaricious self-interest that underlay the Puritan's rhetorical fervor. As it continues the association with Catholicism evoked in the previous book and in the very first Herculean allusion of the *Faerie Queene* — a fine instance of Homeric ring-composition — the Hydra allusion by identifying the Puritans with their opponents also continues the epic genre's meditation on the problem of the subjector and the subjected. But of course the analysis cannot be comfortably limited to such easy targets. Calidore's truancy in the pastoral cantos of the legend is rationalized as a rejection of the hunt for 'shadows vaine / Of courtly favour, fed with light report' (6.10.2). How can we be sure that Hercules' most difficult labour is not similarly motivated, that the 'eternal glory' thereby earned is not part of a project compromised through self-interest?

Once we have gripped the poem's Herculean discourse as in a handful, the labours reveal themselves to be one of the most important mythological subtexts of the *Faerie Queene*, but the unity Hercules lends is countered by the burgeoning variety and multiplicity of interpretive demands that follow in his wake. As the Hydra allusion might suggest, there is an important sense in which the Legend of Courtesy returns to the play of beginnings and endings that the Herculean material evoked in the Legend of Holiness. Calidore's climactic achievement might again suggest that the poem is negotiating a kind of closure, even that the original plan of twelve books has been abandoned. But forces are also at work to problematize or forestall closure: the poet's warning that the beast would remain 'supprest' only until 'he broke his yron chaine, / And got into the world at liberty againe' (6.12.38); the addition of a generation to the Herculean monsters of Books 5 and 6, which may suggest that the labours are handed down to the heroes of Faerie Land, and to us, through a link that is more ineluctable and direct than mere typological succession; the implied possibility, which I believe we are prepared to perceive as our progress through the six books increases the number and types of segments we are prompted to organize into meaningful successions, that this closure of the Heracleid at the midpoint of the projected epic punctuates a six-book unit meant to be juxtaposed with a second six-book unit. Even as he completes his labours in the *Faerie Queene*, Hercules finds new ways to continue ours.

The Endless Argument of *The Faerie Queene*

Despite its richly generative presence, the Heracleid remains but a secondary feature in the *Faerie Queene*'s apparatus of meaning. The same cannot be said of Spenser's technique of allegorical cores, which forms a major component of the epic's 'argument'. It is necessary briefly to examine the idea of a poem's argument, a subject of considerable interest and confusion in Renaissance poetics. The most common definition equates the term with plot (*favola*, among the Italian theorists), the sequence of events that is the fictional work's counterpart to a logical argument's unfolding series of propositions. This appears to be the term's meaning as it is applied, for example, to a long night's storytelling in the Legend of Chastity:

> So long these knights discoursed diversly,
> Of straunge affaires, and noble hardiment,
> Which they had past with mickle ieopardy,
> That now the humid night was farforth spent,
> And heavenly lampes were halfendeale ybrent:
> Which th'old man seeing well, who too long thought
> Every discourse and every argument. (3.9.53)

The use of 'argument' for plot coexisted uneasily with Aristotle's distinction between plot and thought (*dianoia*). In the *Poetics* the latter concept, though one of the essential components of a poem, also 'is the function of the statesman's or the rhetorician's art', for it refers to the element of persuasion that fulfils the poem's didactic purpose.[26] The term 'argument' tends to appear in Renaissance discussions that define the literary object's ontology by comparison with oratory. Tasso, for example, compares the method of the logician, who uses induction and the syllogism, to the method of the orator and poet, who both use enthymeme and example. He concludes that the poet argues more effectively than the orator because his argument is concealed in fictional form.[27] Thus in addition to its primary literary use as 'plot', 'argument' retained for the Renaissance poet a range of potential connotations: the general subject matter of a discourse, a process of persuasive reasoning, the middle term of a syllogism (cf. the OED's citation of Watt's 1724 *Logic*: 'The middle term is often called the Argument, because the force of the syllogisms depends upon it'). To this list we might also add the related mathematical definition as 'the angle, arc, or other mathematical quantity, from which another required quantity may be deduced, or on which its calculation depends' (OED 2).

After announcing his epic theme and invoking the muse, Spenser closes the proem to Book 1 with a declaration of his argument:

> And with them eke, O Goddesse heavenly bright,
> Mirrour of grace and Maiestie divine,
> Great Lady of the greatest Isle, whose light
> Like Phebus lampe throughout the world doth shine,
> Shed thy faire beames into my feeble eyne,
> And raise my thoughts too humble and too vile,
> To think of that true glorious type of thine,
> The argument of mine afflicted stile:
> The which to heare, vouchsafe, O dearest dred a-while. (1.Pr.4)

With his usual mastery of ambiguity, Spenser allows 'argument' to be defined here as both an object, the queen's 'glorious type', and a process, the action that includes both the queen's raising of the poet's thoughts and, what is the same thing simply transferred to another agent, the poet's thinking of her glorious type. Gloriana, the poem's argument-as-object, cannot be separated from the poem's argument-as-process, for she functions as a kind of logical operator bearing some resemblance to the syllogism's middle term and the mathematical quantity from which another may be deduced.

The *Faerie Queene* argues, Spenser implies, by repeatedly re-enacting the poet's gesture of turning his thoughts, and therefore our thoughts, toward the being for whom it is named, the embodiment and spur of all virtue who stands as a still point of comparison for negative and positive antitypes throughout the poem. As the proem's vertical imagery indicates, this turn is an elevation in terms of value. As soon as the narrative begins, the turn also becomes a horizontal flection toward the centre, toward Gloriana's court at Cleopolis, the origin or goal of every quest and the *point de repère* orienting the distinction between the epic *dritta via* and romance error. Both Gloriana and Cleopolis are minimally characterized absolutes. Beyond the fact that her light shines with imperial universality, of Gloriana we are told only that she is superlatively great, glorious, fair, and virtuous. Cleopolis is reduced to three emblematic features: the crystal (with a pun on 'Christall', 2.10.73) tower Panthea, whose brightness signifies transcendence and whose name implies infolding inclusiveness; a golden wall marking off sacred from profane space; and a bridge of brass reaching over a glassy sea, which suggests both the city's imperial dominion over its surroundings and the ontological decline measured by distance from the centre.[28] As a result of the poem's argument, however, the minimally featured centre steadily infolds implied attributes. Errour's den, the first of many antitypes, characterizes Cleopolis negatively, suggesting by simple reversal a number of the traits of ideal earthly existence, including the absence of disorienting directional paradox. It also shares with Cleopolis, in precisely those features leading us to make the comparison, details requiring more subtle interpretation. What is implied, for example, by Errour's female hermaphroditic self-sufficiency? Is not, according to the poem's frame of reference, the only thing lacking at Cleopolis the prince who is journeying there erratically and whose presence is required to assure that generation works according to epic's teleological abundance rather than romance's self-defeating, cyclical multiplicity? As a negative antitype, Errour participates in an argument for the queen's marriage and against the androgyne ideal used by Elizabeth to assert her self-sufficiency.

Of course, there would be no need to lift our thoughts repeatedly toward the glorious type if the narrative did not also 'afflict' us with a countervailing tendency. Once past Errour's den, we proceed through the poem's continuum of varying allegorical intensities according to a rhythm of error and revelation, as adventures unfolding the romance features by which Errour's lair differs from Cleopolis alternate with allegorical cores offering conceptual tools for interpretation.[29] Soon after Redcrosse comes under Duessa's erring influence, the House of Pride appears on the scene as a prototype for cores to come. Its stylized, medieval conventionality, complete with convenient allegorical labels and tidy schemata, must have lent this episode an air of comforting certainty, perhaps even of nostalgia, for an audience experiencing the epistemological turbulence of Reform; the poet's unusual combination of radically decentred Protestant and retrograde, even medieval poetics is essential to the effect. Spenser enhances this effect here and in later allegorical houses by contrasting the problematic diachrony of the erring adventures with the cores' much simpler temporality. In the cores narratives are often reduced to visual representations, as the momentum of the knight's journey is transferred to the motions of figures who comment upon it. Processional pageants move before our eyes as the most elementary, most frameable form of diachrony. In the House of Pride temporal occurrence in the parade of sins translates effortlessly into conceptual prominence. Pride's appearance at the parade's head bespeaks her pre-eminence as a sin, which in turn prompts our understanding of pride as a cause of error. Pride of place at the other end goes to 'Slowth', reinforcing with effortless clarity the need to 'forward fare'.

Despite its base in simple binary opposition, the *Faerie Queene*'s argument quickly burgeons into copious complexity. At the same time that the allegorical cores point centripetally toward Cleopolis and centrifugally toward the surrounding territory, they also point toward each other. Book 1 promotes this form of comparison most energetically through the abundance and variety of parallels connecting the two prominent 'houses' of Pride and Holiness that neatly frame the pride-despair sequence. In a mirror-symmetry, the hermit Archimago precedes his allied house and directs the knight to it, while the hermit Contemplation follows his allied house and directs the knight from it. The easy, well-trodden path of error contrasts with the seldom travelled, 'streight and narrow' (1.10.5) way of virtue. The welcome by 'a gentle Husher, Vanitie by name' (1.4.13) is answered by the porter Humiltà. The seven deadly sins meet their match in the seven holy beadsmen. Most importantly, both houses create a hierarchy of value reflecting their personifications' order of appearance. The only temporarily effective lessons of Fidessa and Speranza are lumped together. The two subordinate sisters even enter 'ylinked arme in arme' with 'even steps and equall pace' (1.10.12) to emphasize the climactic pre-eminence of Charissa, the integrative virtue, opposed to both Sloth and Pride, that enables Redcrosse humbly to submit to his laborious itinerary.

Allegorical cores also direct their interpretive force toward their counterparts beyond the boundaries of their own legends. Two examples from the first two books must suffice to illustrate this function, though a similar analysis could be made and is made, to some degree and at some level of recognition by readers who profit from Spenser's didactic conditioning, of the relations between an ever-increasing number of episodes as the poem proceeds. At the same time that it is setting up internal parallels with the House of Temperance of canto 9, Medina's castle in 2.2 recalls both of the major framing houses of Book 1. Like the House of Pride, this is a discordant house ruled by a female whose allegorical significance comments directly on the virtue in question, and at which the hero arrives early in the action after a long journey with his companion. But now, as the poem rearranges its repeated elements according to the new logic of temperance, the contrast between the earlier houses is internalized; the virtuous Medina recalls Coelia and Charissa, while her two sisters would certainly feel more at home in House of Pride. In Book 1 the sequence of daughters ended in an integrative climax. Now the middle daughter, introduced first, mediates between extremes. Recognizing the significant patterns of Book 1 helps us to perceive both the importance of the next book's patterns, and vice versa. Recalling how a pattern from Book 1 was repeated and manipulated prompts us to apply the pattern of virtuous mediation between vicious extremes to episodes where its significance is less blatantly propounded: to the 'halfe dead, half quicke' (2.1.39) Amavia's virtuous moment between life and death; to Phaedria's island 'in the midst' (2.6.11) of the Idle Lake; to a host of inviting details in the House of Alma.

The final stage of Redcrosse's recuperative visit in 1.10, his vision of heavenly Jerusalem, also exchanges implications with Book 2. By advice and example, Contemplation advocates the 'Pilgrim's poor estate' (1.10.64), continuing the charitable lessons of Coelia's beadsmen, who represent a life of selfless service that includes renunciation of wealth (1.10.36ff.). Declining to make the commonplace association of worldly wealth and glory, he also insists that to pursue glory, to 'covet in th'immortal book of fame / To be eternized' (1.10.59), can be an important part of service in the world. This episode is echoed in the cave of Mammon. The two aspects of Contemplation's teaching re-enter the poem together when the god of wealth offers Guyon his daughter Philotime, 'love of honor', 'that she may thee advance for workes and merites just' (2.7.49). Guyon of course rejects the offer, and the overt reference to a doctrine of salvation by works clarifies the moral lesson. Contemplation's placing of the love of glory in a context of service helps us to understand how Guyon can continue his own service to Gloriana despite his rejection of Philotime. And the episode from Book 2 can help us to appreciate how carefully Spenser has removed from the Contemplation vision any implications of salvation by merit. The woman being offered Guyon embraces the *axis mundi*:

> There as in glistring glory she did sit,
> She held a great gold chain ylincked well,
> Whose upper end to highest heaven was knit,
> And lower part did reach to lowest Hell;
> And all that preace did round about her swell,
> To catchen hold of that long chaine, thereby
> To clime aloft, and others to excell:
> That was Ambition, rash desire to sty,
> And every linke therof a step of dignity. (2.7.46)

Since temperance implies a mean between extremes, Ambition is intemperate because it seeks to move from a rightful place on the cosmic hierarchy to attain a desired extreme. Redcrosse's vision of the *axis mundi* is carefully drawn to avoid conflict with the lessons of Book 2, at once elevating those who aspire to glory and maintaining a temperate hierarchy:

> As he thereon stood gazing, he might see
> The blessed Angels to and fro descend
> From highest heaven, in gladsome companee,
> And with great joy into that Citie wend,
> As commonly as friend does with his frend.
> Whereat he wondred much, and gan enquere,
> What stately building durst so high extend
> Her loftie towres unto the starry sphere,
> And what unknowen nation there empeopled were. (1.10.56)

'And lo, the Angels of God went up and down by it', Genesis 28.12 observes of Jacob's ladder. Spenser's formula is less logical, and an extension of the epic genre's meditation on the paradoxes of vertical classification; the angels 'to and fro descend', indicating two-way motion as well as keeping the motion one-way. Spenser is furthering his Protestant message of salvation by grace alone by agreeing with Calvin's assertion that even in heaven there will remain a 'wide distance between Him and ourselves'.[30] Although the 'unknowen nation' are the elect, and therefore patrons of Holiness who have appropriately sought glory on earth, they cannot be accused of Ambition. Their golden chain reaches to 'highest heaven', but they do not seek to climb there, to advance for works and merits just. They do not, in fact, ever arrive there. Spenser has retained a common Renaissance feature of heaven, a hierarchical differentiation between a lower and higher level, but he has again adapted convention to Protestant requirements by making the lower level not the usual temporary anteroom, but the saints' permanent abode.[31] Redcrosse through his question reveals his imperfect perspective, reading a Babel-like Ambition into those whose construction 'durst so high extend', but he is immediately corrected when the hermit names the most un-Nimrod-like builder and the means by which the city was populated:

Faire knight (quoth he) Hierusalem that is,
The new Hierusalem, that God has built
For those to dwell in, that are chosen his,
His chosen people purg'd from sinfull guilt,
With pretious bloud, which cruelly was spilt
On cursed tree, of that unspotted lam,
That for the sinnes of all the world was kilt:
Now are they Saints all in that Citie sam,
More deare unto their God, then younglings to their dam. (1.10.57)

The integrative aspect of Holiness-Wholeness, which allowed charitable service to be translated into a glorious epic itinerary, helps to remove a potential logical anomaly of Book 2. In turn, the mediating differentiation of Temperance underscores the Protestant theology that distinguishes the new quest for glory from the old.

In its descent into the cave of Mammon, the text demands that we make several additional acts of juxtaposition and mutual commentary across legend boundaries. The lowpoint of Guyon's trajectory is also, not coincidentally, the textual midpoint. In their 1969 article, 'Placement "In the Middest" in *The Faerie Queene*', Michael Bayback, Paul Delany, and A. Kent Hieatt call attention to a salient Spenserian repetition: in the 1590 poem, 'all three books . . . turn upon passages that are central by both arithmetic and significance. In addition, all three passages are signaled by the phrase "in the middest" or a variant'.[32] Although I remain sceptical about arithmetical critics' assumption that line counts underlie a major portion of the *Faerie Queene*'s signification, the larger and vaguer experience of textual symmetries (and asymmetries) in reading cannot be denied, in fact is almost universally assumed in discussions of literary organization at least since Plato and Aristotle. The highlighting of textual centres noticed by Hieatt and company no doubt is meant, as they claim, to plug the *Faerie Queene* into the mystic currents of Renaissance Platonism, which, as it 'valued circles, so it valued centers'. More importantly, I believe, what Spenser achieves by pointing to his symmetries with such noticeable verbal repetition and thematic compression is to dramatize a new Protestant problematics of the centre. By unfolding his overall epic into a series of smaller epics of imperfectly isomorphic structure, Spenser can allow these epics' centres, both in represented space (the various manifestations or types of the cosmic omphalos) and in textual space (the legends' midpoints) to engage in dialogue. In the instance in question, the axial cave of Mammon converses not only with the axial Mount of Contemplation, but also with Redcrosse's defeat at the textual centre of the Legend of Holiness.

When we follow the text's request to compare backwards from Guyon's epic *descensus* to the nadir of Redcrosse's fortunes, the first legend's spatial logic comes more clearly into focus. In contrast to his infernal foes, who twice visit the underworld, Redcrosse has until this point pursued his misadventures consistently along the horizontal plane, even if his quartered shield has not provided sufficient orientation. Errour's cavernous lair, the first of many a 'darksome hole' (1.1.14) in the poem, displays no vertical dimension, despite the conspicuously observed trees that surround it. At the House of Pride the solar knight metaphorically declines with the sun, but the dwarf's visit to Lucifera's dungeon prevents the hero's literal descent. The only important vertical movement in the first half is Redcrosse's ironic bending of 'humble knee' to Pride below her 'high throne' (1.4.12-13), a parody of ascent through lowering. It is not until he escapes to the textual centre of his legend, and imitates Diana's nymph who 'sat downe to reste in middest of the race' (1.7.5), that he loses his ability to remain upright and we find him, imitating the nymph as well in his newfound liquidity, 'pourd out in looseness on the grassy ground' (1.7.7). Redcrosse now experiences a series of literal descents: dismounting his steed, reclining, being knocked 'full low' (1.7.12) by towering Orgoglio at the precise 1590 midpoint and then cast into the dungeon from which he will be rescued by hell-harrowing Arthur. He then descends yet once more into the cave of Despair, a setting that restores the vertical aspect of caves suppressed in the cave of Errour. After his elevation in canto 10 and his downward gaze of genuine submission, he returns to a horizontal plane devoid, at least for a heroic moment, of disorienting paradox. Like the Legend of Temperance, the Legend of Holiness breaks neatly into two equal halves. But instead of descent becoming reascent, the first legend's midpoint is defined by a transfer of vertical motion from the forces of evil to the knight as his metaphorical descent becomes literal. Guyon's faint upon resurfacing signifies that he is no less dependent, ultimately, upon divine mercy. But negotiating his 'middest' episode is an appropriate specialty for the knight of mediating Temperance, whose quest, though arduous, lacks the intense demands for self-definition, for framing from first to last in a shape-shifting world without adequate coordinates, imposed upon the knight of integral Holiness.

Book 3 continues the interplay of 'middest' episodes. In their central episodes the heroes of Books 1 and 2 face a personal crisis expressed in vertical terms. Redcrosse's fall implies an erring assumption of self-sufficiency, the pride to which, paradoxically, he earlier bowed. Guyon can reascend because he rejects an inappropriate ascent upon the Jacob's ladder of ambition. Book 3 defines its difference in large part by suppressing the vertical dimension. Witnessing no epic ascents or descents, we follow the characters through a horizontal world. But we do not follow them to the midpoint, for the Garden of Adonis remains sealed off from the human world. The book's hero, in fact, grows even more conspicuously absent from the 'far away' (3.6.28) centre by remaining the only major female character of the middle books not mentioned in canto 6. The garden nevertheless manages to apply the vertical spatiality of its counterpart centres to its hero. Britomart's combination of love and heroism engages the venerable tradition of epic imagery springing from Vergil's use of the mountain, volcano, earthquake and storm as symbols of repression and release. After telling Britomart, 'Thou in dull corners doest thy selfe inclose . . . ne doest spred / Abroad thy fresh youthes fairest flower' (3.2.31.), the nurse Glauce shifts from a lyric model to the vocabulary of Vergilian psychoanalysis:

> Like an huge Aetn' of deepe engulfed griefe,
> Sorrow is heaped in thy hollow chest,
> Whence forth it breakes in sighes and anguish rife,
> As smoke and sulphure mingled with confused strife. (3.2.32)

Britomart's prayer to Aeolus for calm within her stormy soul (3.4.10), the long simile describing Paridell's pent-up winds of rage bursting forth (3.9.15), and the storm and earthquake that shake the House of Busirane (3.12.2), to cite only the most developed examples, also participate in this book-long network of Vergilian imagery. Though the Garden of Adonis is immune from 'Aeolus' sharp blast' (3.6.44), this network enters the garden in a new guise at the precise centre. 'Right at the middest of that Paradise, / There stood a stately Mount' (3.6.43) that represses another natural force:

> For that wilde Bore, the which him once annoyd,
> She firmely hath emprisoned for ay,
> That her sweet love his malice mote avoyd,
> In a strong rocky Cave, which is they say,
> Hewen underneath that Mount, that none him losen may. (3.6.48)

Spenser subjects the ethical allegory to his usual process of complicating reversals and rearrangements. Multiple ironies blossom from the fact that Love's perpetual satisfaction comes from repressing a sexual force, which then remains a permanent phallic presence raging within the *mons veneris*. But the allegory remains coherent, the episode a coherent part of the series of vertically evaluated midpoints. Just as Redcrosse learned true submission to his epic labour, and as Guyon evidenced a Christian-heroic willingness not to climb, Britomart must attain the self-mastery that sublimates the erotic into the heroic, a category that for her includes the production of the dynastic womb.

Redcrosse's successfully framed life of active holiness will culminate in the contemplative paradise of 1.10. The poem does not envision Guyon's end, but we understand that through successful temperance he will avoid

Ambition's hopeless ladder and the delusive pleasures of Proserpina and Acrasia. Similarly, Britomart's self-mastering repression and sublimation will allow her existence to approach the condition of the Garden of Adonis, to define a positive version of the phrase 'eterne in mutability' (3.6.47), which Spenser uses in Book 3 to describe Adonis, who 'liveth in eternall bliss' (3.6.48), but which can also be applied *in malo* to such unhappy figures as Tantalus and Despair. For life before the blissful rewards of election are manifest, I have argued in the previous chapter and adumbrated in this one, the *Faerie Queene* represents the ideal encapsulated in the phrase as the genre-associated subordination of the cyclical to the linea , the despairingly repetitive to the hopefully purposive. As the garden canto projects its image of ideal existence outward to the surrounding adventures, we are asked to make a subtle logical adjustment. It is important to remember that the garden pointedly lacks the divinity's utter perfection beyond space and time. It is located 'on earth' (3.6.29) in a horizontally oriented legend; the boar has only been imprisoned, not killed; and 'wicked time' (3.6.39) remains as the beast's implicit ally. The garden's two walls of iron and gold reflect its intermediate position between our iron age and the age of eternal spring, both of which contribute features to Venus' domicile. The endless cycle of regenerating souls, though a positive version of romance's infernal cycles, is not an emblem of fully ideal existence, but a translation of the human realm's unfortunate but inevitable error into a partially idealized setting where cyclicality sheds its normally negative significance. Behind the ideological scenes stands an assumed atemporal *kairos* to which the cyclical machinery of souls is subordinated as a temporary, and temporal, expedient. The patron of chastity, whose womb forms a part of this machinery, succeeds by subordinating the cyclical reality in which she is necessarily enmeshed to the forward faring that leads to eternal life. It was not her 'wandering eye' that initiated her quest for Artegall, Merlin informs her, 'But the streight course of heavenly destiny', and she is told, 'therefore submit thy wayes until his will' (3.3.24). Drawing another variant from the cultural reservoir of cosmic symbols, Spenser allows Britomart to transform the destructive natural cycles evoked to describe her love-sickness into the epic, teleological Tree of Jesse:[33]

> For so must al things excellent begin,
> And eke enrooted deepe must be that Tree,
> Whose big embodied braunches shall not lin,
> Till they to heavens hight forth stretched be.
> For from thy wombe a famous Progenie
> Shall spring, out of the ancient Troian blood,
> Which shall revive the sleeping memorie
> Of those same antique Peres, the heavens brood,
> Which Greeke and Asian rivers stained with their blood. (3.3.23)

The passage portrays a providentially sanctioned upward striving and, at the same time, signals the way her horizontal progress imitates that of the axial Aeneas as he turns successfully toward the Roman centre.

The Legend of Chastity's central allegorical core unfolds centrifugally into the surrounding narrative. The unchaste boar wreaks havoc early in the book, contributing to the atmosphere of romance reversal. Wounded by the forster's 'bore-spere' (3.5.20), Timias becomes identified as both Adonis and the beast (cf. 28). Ironically, of course, since they are trying to enforce an unchaste allegiance, Malecasta's six henchmen attack Redcrosse like curs attacking a 'salvage beast' (3.1.22). The latter incident begins the legend's opposition of line and circle, as Malecasta's men form a 'compacted gyre' (23) around the knight, besetting him unchivalrously 'all attonce' 'on every side around' (21) until Britomart rescues him and turns the battle into a more proper sequential combat:

> She mightily aventred towards one,
> And down him smot, erre well aware he weare,
> Then to the next she rode, and downe the next did beare.

> Ne did she stay, till three on ground she layd,
> That none of them could reare againe. (3.1.28-9)

She possesses the correct spatio-temporal instincts, it seems, but she proceeds only halfway through the opposition. Inside the castle, the henchmen's synchronic attack in circular array unrolls even more systematically into the diachronic sequence of the *gradus amoris* begun by Gardante. Since, as Hamilton notes, the six stages of love are then acted out in Malecasta's courtship of Britomart, we see that in helping Britomart escape from the Castle Joyous, Redcrosse is returning the favour with meaningful precision. It is interesting that Britomart's intervention transforms synchrony into diachrony, while Redcrosse's works in the opposite direction, helping to prevent the ascent upon the *gradus* and to dispatch the henchmen 'in short space' with pell-mell strokes 'here, there, and everywhere' (3.1.66).

By calling our attention to this crucial chronotopic opposition in Britomart's first combat, Spenser allows us to measure his heroine's progress toward the garden's (qualified) ideal. In the House of Busirane, a studiously parallel core at the legend's opposite end, Britomart evinces a fuller mastery over both herself and the opposition. There, in what is on one level of allegory a projection of her own mental processes, she witnesses a complex interaction of diachronic and synchronic phenomena. The ecphrasis of Ovidian tapestries enumerates a repetitive series of variations on the theme of divine rape. Among its other functions, the sequence serves to remind us of the similarities and differences between Ovid's method of narrative organization and Spenser's. Ovid's method of narrative progress through repeated variations on a theme parallels Spenser's principle of typological progression, and is of course one of its contributing sources, but for Spenser the world's Ovidian aspect is what the virtues are enlisted to counter; heroic chastity is the answer not only to lust and rape, but also to the hopeless repetition that accompanies a failure to repress and sublimate. This spatial array is followed by the 'enraunged orderly' (3.12.5) procession of Cupid's masque, whose six couples recall the six henchmen of the *gradus*. Spenser informs us that Britomart 'saw both first and last' (27) of this procession. That is, in contrast to her partial and temporary victory at Malecasta's castle, she encounters all of its elements in proper sequence; she also sees its endpoints for what they are and so is able to frame it as a meaningful progression. Her new mastery even includes an ability to use spatio-temporal reversal to her own ends. Glauce's attempts to cure her charge's love-sickness included a quaint ritual of magical undoing through reversal:

> That say'd, her round about she from her turnd,
> She turned her contrarie to the Sunne,
> Thrise she her turnd contrary, and returnd,
> All contrary, for she the right did shunne,
> And ever what she did, was streight undonne.
> So thought she to undoe her daughter's love. (3.2.51)

With better results than those obtained by Glauce, who after all turns her ward in the direction epic defines as unpropitious, Britomart forces Busirane to reverse his magic:

> And rising up, gan streight to overlooke
> Those cursed leaves, his charmes back to reverse;
> Full dreadfull things out of that balefull book
> He read, and measur'd many a sad verse,
> And all the while he red, she did extend
> Her sword high over him, if ought he did offend. (3.12.37-8)

At this point, the earthquake (3.12.2) that opened the canto recurs, but Britomart is again unfazed, in contrast to her situation evaluated earlier through Vergilian repression imagery. And if the canto's opening quake threatened catastrophe of cosmic dimensions, 'as if it streight would lose / The worlds foundation from his centre fixt', in the microcosmic allegory being played out by Britomart's rescue of Amoret this loosening is now the desired effect. As 'that great brasen pillour broke in peeces small' (37), Amoret and therefore Britomart who enfolds her becomes 'perfect hole' (38). The lines of association this node connects are of course rich and multiple. If we gather in only a few most pertinent to my argument, we will see Britomart incorporating within herself the Wholeness with whom she earlier was only allied in the form of Redcrosse, controlling the force threatening destruction at the centre, channelling the recurring throes of passion toward a charitable end — in short, growing into a likeness of the Garden of Adonis, which represents the closest approach to eternity possible in a world of mutability.

Focusing the vertical component of each legend's ethical argument within a highlighted textual centre contributes to the three 1590 legends' isomorphism. Using such means, Spenser lays a systematic base of similarity that allows for the perception of significant differences. He organizes methodically enough to encourage the reader's typological sense, but he is also disruptive enough to force us continually to refine our techniques of perceiving similarity and difference. Between boldness and too much boldness we hone our own critical chastity. The textual centres that we have been examining are a case in point. In addition to the vertical consistencies and variations, they are also linked by the *locus amoenus* topos, the first two containing false loci, the third helping us to understand the appeal of both prideful stasis and intemperate progress with its own genuinely happy reworking of these terms. Readers can also be expected to notice, at some point on the continuum between critically conscious and subliminal awareness, that isomorphism is strengthened by the appearance in each book of a climactic struggle and two allegorical cores that rather neatly frame the central action and develop extensive parallels. The climactic struggles themselves take place at variants of the epic omphalos. Eden is a positive centre needing restoration. The Bower of Bliss is a negative antitype, a false centre threatening the true with its own universe of perverted values. Spenser fills this episode with details underscoring the Bower's omphalic aspect: allusion to Delos 'amid the Aegean' (2.12.13); extensive Edenic parallels; the presence of the palmer, who would normally be trekking toward Jerusalem; the Odyssean analogue, by which Guyon's quest parallels the voyage toward the rising hearthsmoke of Ithaca rather than toward Calypso's isle. The House of Busirane too is a negative antitype duly destroyed. Yet, this episode differs from its counterparts in Books 1 and 2 in that it includes, rather than follows, the hero's triumphant regaining of *integritas*. Even after the house's destruction the 'centre fixt' remains, for Britomart's newly acquired 'perfect wholeness' represents the notion of cosmic unity transferred to the microcosm, a transfer that I earlier suggested as one signification of the patron of Wholeness' polysemic cross. The effects of this transfer become evident as Britomart rides into the later books armed with a newly confident mastery, and freed from the encumbering reversals and symptoms of unsuccessful sublimation that proclaimed her imperfection in Book 3. As with the textual centres, carefully unpacking similarities and differences assists our interpretation of the crucial omphalic episodes.

In the second half of the *Faerie Queene*, in the legends added after 1590, the major allegorical cores continue to radiate outward across legend boundaries. The Temple of Venus is packed with details evoking other cores. Especially noteworthy are those reaching out to the Garden of Adonis, which seems to function as a privileged node connecting the poem's two halves: Venus at the centre of concentric enclosures (4.10.39); the 'subdewing' of strife by Venus' agent Concord, under whose influence Hatred gnashes his 'yron tuskes' (33). Aided by the shield of Love, which assists 'the man who well can use his blis' (8), Scudamor's rescue mission forms another variation on the theme of heroic repression and sublimation. At Isis Church, Britomart's humble entry, the Egyptian deities' astronomical cycles, the volcanic imagery, and both the crocodile's tail spiralling around Isis' statue and his position under her foot should provoke our typological sensibilities. The repression model, the episode suggests, affords insight into the relation of Justice to Mercy.

Calidore's vision on Acidale demands comparison with the Garden of Adonis perhaps even more insistently. Venus, her mount's utopian isolation, the concentric circles of the sitting and dancing maidens, even the Graces' delicate evocation of Neoplatonic procession and return, all forge correspondences with the earlier core. Since we were left to deduce from the pervasive unchastity of Faerie Land that the boar was a difficult beast to keep enchained, the poignant fragility of Calidore's vision speaks what the earlier scene left unsaid. In turn, the model of chaste repression can help unravel the mysteries of Calidore's discourtesy. 'I rashly sought that, which I mote not see' (6.10.29), the knight of Courtesy cryptically confesses after being told that the vision he sought was centred by Gloriana in her aspect of 'Firme Chastity' (27). The root of unchastity in Book 3 is the wish to own, to coerce the other's affections, as is evidenced most powerfully in Busirane's abduction and torture of Amoret. Calidore's approach to the Graces on Venus' mount, like his failure to pursue the boar-like Blatant Beast, implies an irruption of Adonis' boar and a violation of Firme Chastity that is reflected in his discourteous appropriation of Pastorella and the soft, undemanding pastoral realm she personifies. True courtesy, we conclude, requires a very difficult navigation of confusing self-other distinctions. Calidore errs in making the related assumptions that he can appropriatively 'know' the Graces and that Colin exercises some control over them. These assumptions, though they suggest no malevolence, reveal an insensitivity to the other's integrity. Together they lead to unhappiness for both Calidore and Colin, who might be seen to represent the innocent third party who suffers because of one party's discourteous act toward another. Failure to repress the boar leads to abandonment of the heroic quest as Calidore falls into eroticized reversal. He pursues Gloriana on the *mons veneris* when he should be pursuing the quest she assigned him. Logically, the forward faring hero 'mote not see' her until he has captured the Blatant Beast and returned. Nor can Gloriana's own agent pursue her without most unchastely collapsing the distinction between subject and object.

At the same time that this continuing series of connected allegorical cores helps unify the *Faerie Queene*, the suppression of familiar isomorphic structures helps divide the poem in two. The reader trained by the first three books looks in vain for several familiar patterns in the last three. Determined arithmetical critics might continue to locate textual centres, but the poet no longer labels them for us or uses them to mark spatialized peripeties. The frames of allegorical houses give way to an apparently meaningless disposition of locales engaging in relatively little mutual commentary. The Temple of Venus, for example, has more to do with other legends' cores than with the House of Care in 4.5. Isis Church in 5.7 and the Court of Mercilla two cantos later stand as two contrasting applications of the justice-mercy relation, but their contrast is uncomplicated and unchallenging and their positioning defines no discernible frame. The combats ending the later legends are less than climactic. Scudamor's is told in retrospective narration and is followed by the long and unrelated section recounting the wedding of the Thames and Medway and the reunion of Marinell and Florimell. Artegall's concluding liberation of Irena is but one of a series of military interventions. Calidore's final combats are a little more climactic, but we are bound to notice that there are two of them, that these two form no real sequence but rather a meaningless repitition, and that the hero's mountaintop revelation, unlike Redcrosse's, can hardly be said to prepare either him or the reader for the coming struggle.

We should not allow familiarity to obscure the utter strangeness of the *Faerie Queene*'s organization. It is neither difficult nor surprising to notice that the poem divides neatly into two halves and that the isomorphism of these large units allows their differences to be discerned. Precedent abounds in the western epic tradition, and most clearly in Spenser's two most important generic models: the *Aeneid*, with its opposed Odyssean and Iliadic halves, and *Orlando Furioso*, with its tragicomic reversal following Orlando's central descent into madness. But to recognize that this large instance of isomorphism and comparative difference is but one instance of an operation that takes place on every level of the poem's organization is to recognize, I believe, the astonishing originality that allowed Spenser to adapt a genre to an ideology with which it was fundamentally incompatible. All discourse, and of course especially verse, consists of unitary components that unite into larger wholes. Spenser develops this elementary fact into a extraordinarily complex generator of meaning, or at least of heuristic challenges that can be turned into meaning. From the smallest components to the largest, he displays a propensity for at once enhancing the autonomy of units and subordinating them to larger wholes. At a very small level, Spenser assigns various degrees of unity to individual words, often elevating them above their syntactical function within a statement that would otherwise refer unproblematically to a consistent reality, by the extensive use of such devices as shifting levels of personification (capitalizing an abstraction is only the most obvious method of heightening its level of personification, and of course all capitalized personifications are not created ontologically equal), etymological secret wit, punning, and phonemic echo. Unitizing, it should be stressed, is not a matter of removing an element from its primary matrix, but of assigning it a supplementary referential function that distinguishes it from its neighbours at the same time that it continues to function within the primary matrix these neighbours define. Earlier critics have noticed such phenomena. Paul Alpers, for example, who has given us the most thorough and illuminating discussion of Spenser's smaller units, refers to 'the trick of making us apprehend the names of personifications as abstract nouns'. He also examines 'Spenser's treatment of the line as an independent unit', the stanza as a multiple unity, and the canto as what he believes is 'the basic large unit of the *Faerie Queene*'. While Alpers' claim that 'we observe and remember the canto we are reading in much more detail than we retain other cantos and books' is undoubtedly true, a similar claim could be made, *mutatis mutandis*, for any unit of any size, from the line to the multibook unit, that we define as the unit we are reading.[34]

The process of experiencing simultaneously the autonomy of the unit at hand and its place within a larger signifying whole, I would insist, continues up the scale of units. Just as we do not fail to compare the current line or stanza or canto to preceding ones — indeed, in part because Spenser trains us so rigorously in the typological principle of narrative succession on these smaller scales — we do not as we read Book 3 fail to notice both its significant similarities and differences with the earlier two books. As we proceed into Book 4, we are led to group some of its similarities with Book 3 — e.g., their 'Ariostan' interlaced narrative styles, to cite a familiar if somewhat misleading description — into a set of differences with Books 1 and 2 that prompts most readers, whether consciously or subliminally, to experience the two middle books as a unit opposed to the unit comprising the first two. The process continues, growing ever more challenging as components regroup and unit boundaries conflict. The three-book units are incompatible with the two-book units. Books 5 and 6 resist being as easily grouped together as the previous sets of two; is this a prompt to seek out new forms of common ground, or simply a symptom of the exhaustion or disillusionment often read into the later books? More large-scale patterns form as the number of units increases. These patterns are not simply devout reflections of the creation's divine order, as they generally appear to be in medieval literature, but indispensable parts of the poem's argument that stimulate and direct our interpretive energies.

Consider, for example, the oft-noted alternation of odd-numbered and even-numbered books championed respectively by Briton and Faery knights. If it is noticed that this alternation recapitulates the poem's more finely textured oppositions of epic and romance chronotopes, important nuances can be applied to the natures of the knights' missions and virtues. For the Briton knights, who enter from the time-bound world of epic, which Spenser scrupulously restricts to sixth-century Arthurian material and characterizes as the scene of large-scale warfare and dynastic concerns, Faery Land proves to be a liminal training ground that teaches the skills needed for epic achievement. Accordingly, Gloriana allows the Britons who enter her service to complete their ritual crossing of the liminal space by sending them on missions beyond the border of her realm: Redcrosse to rescue Eden land and Artegall to liberate the realm of Irena. For such internal affairs as destroying the Bower of Bliss and capturing the Blatant Beast, Gloriana picks the native Faeries Guyon and Calidore, for whom romance is not a liminal training ground, and who need to maintain their virtue with constancy rather than learn its nature before succeeding.[43] In addition to such patterns founded on opposition and alternation, the *Faerie Queene* may be seen to fall into more complex orders, such as the mirror symmetry proposed by James Norhnberg, wherein the private virtues of Books 1, 2, 3 are reflected in the public virtues of 6, 5, 4.[35] As complex as the poem is now, consider the overwhelming argumentative possibilities had Spenser achieved the 'whole intention' of a twelve-book poem announced in the Letter to Raleigh. Or was it in fact a twenty-four book plan, 'these first twelve books' referring to the first half of an epic consisting of two twelve-book units, two six, three four, six two, with multiplex alternations and overlaps and mirrorings?

Looking at the *Faerie Queene* against the background of its Italian models, C. S. Lewis concludes that 'Spenser has allegorized the romantic epic', and he adds parenthetically, 'that is the only formal novelty of his work'.[36] If 'allegorized' were changed to 'typologized', the sweeping statement would approximate truth more closely. One of the principal burdens of my argument has been to propose, even as I acknowledge the impossibility of demonstrating, that Spenser set out to produce a poem posing inexhaustible interpretive challenges. Like an apparently endless brood of brothers modelled on the Legend of Friendship's Priamond, Diamond and Triamond, the poem challenges, and then challenges again with the redoubled force arising from the continuing presence of the elements we have mastered. Thus do we remain, to pick another of the poem's many models for our activity as readers, 'in doubtfull ballance hong' (4.3.37). *Orlando Furioso* proliferated confusions upon a solid base of optimism, humanist in origin but also compatible with Renaissance Catholicism and epic, about the human potential for measuring and mastering experience. Spenser's optimism is quite different. By adding to proliferating confusions a matching bounty of means for comprehension, he teaches us both to frame wholes and to recognize their inevitable inadequacy. The essential tension of the *Faerie Queene* is embodied in the ambiguity of that favourite Spenserian term, the 'middest'. We and the knightly exemplars remain *in medias res*, faring forward toward the stable centre which also remains the liminal in-between. This new problematics of the centre is imaged in the poem's structural symmetries, for the isomorphisms that frame the various units into cosmic forms also serve as the basis for dissolving these forms. Spenser's optimism is grounded in a faith that we can continue functioning within this endlessly perplexing environment.

Notes

1. Barkan (1975), chapter 5: 'The *Faerie Queene*: Allegory, Iconography, and the Human Body'.
2. Aristotle (1982), p. 33. *Poetics*, VIII.2-3. There is no surviving Heracleid from antiquity.
3. Peletier du Mans (1930), pp. 86-7.
4. Salutati (1951), 3.9.5. Salutati is cited by page in the Ullman edition, as well as by book, chapter and section number, which are the original Renaissance divisions.
5. The number and order of labours varied from author to author, especially as encyclopedic compilations like Salutati's began accumulating earlier lore. The list that comes closest to a standard for the twelve is contained in the Book 4, seventh verse section of Boethius' *Consolation of Philosophy*: Centaurs, lion, Stymphalian birds, apples of the Hesperides, Cerberus, Diomedes, Hydra, Achelous, Antaeus, Cacus, Erymanthian boar, Atlas (Boethius, 1962, pp. 361-3). As Carl Van de Velde (1965, p. 118) observes, Fulgentius in the fifth century and Albericus in the twelfth use Boethius' list but substitute Geryon for the Stymphalian birds. Chaucer in his translation of the *Consolation* follows his original faithfully. Salutati includes a total of thirty-one labours and a host of other incidents.
6. Salutati offers three chapters of relevant materials: 3.8-10. Dante (1893, p. 470. Epistola 7) seems to have initiated the association of the Hydra with tyranny. Shakespeare's Coriolanus appears to have this association in mind when he speaks of the Hydra's 'peremptory shall' (3.1.93).
7. Salutati, p. 196. 3.9.14-15.

8. Anthony Coke, *The History*, Preface. Cited by Merritt Hughes (1953), p. 205. As Hughes observes, the reference could work both ways. When waxing Reformist, Giordano Bruno pronounced Luther 'the new Alcides'. Later, in a repentant mood, he found him 'worse than the Lernean monster'.

9. Ronsard (1950), vol. 2, pp. 206ff.

10. Salutati, p. 322. 3.27.9.

11. Salutati, pp. 188-9. 3.8.12.

12. Warton (1762), vol. 2, p. 173. Facsimile edition of 1969.

13. Salutati, pp. 280-1. 3.20.8.

14. For a listing of this labour's principal sources, see Graves (1961), vol. 2, pp. 129-30. Spenser probably used Skelton's translation of Diodorus Siculus' *Bibliotheca Historica*, which contains a Thesean version, but also imported Telamon from another source to add cosmological resonances. Hardie (1986, p. 341) discusses Eustathius' allegorization of the *telamon* or shield-strap of Achilles' shield as the *axis mundi*. Popular features of Renaissance architecture, telamones were supporting statue-columns also known as Atlantes, after the Titan who held up the earth. On the use of telamones in Vitruvian theory and Renaissance architecture, see Hersey (1988, pp. 125-9). In Spenser Triamond-Telamond is the brother who stabilizes the narrative order by subordinating repetition to closure, and is thus appropriately given these associations (reversing, we should note, Ariosto's Atlante as described by Quint). In addition to Telamon's connotations available through architecture and the allegorized Homer, Hercules' friend was also associated with the oak tree (cf. Graves, vol. 2, p. 30) and with the construction of the walls of Troy (Graves, vol. 1, p. 214).

15. Aptekar (1969), p. 244.

16. Albericus of London, as quoted by Van de Velde (1965), p. 118.

17. Aptekar (1969), p. 164. It is also interesting to note that Iole (from *ioleis*, 'moon flock') shares lunar associations with the Amazons.

18. Diodorus Siculus (1956-57), pp. 383-4.

19. Conti, as noted by MacIntyre (1966), p. 11.

20. Hamilton edition, p. 708. Note to 6.12.35.

21. Conti (1567), p. 63b. Book 3, chap. 5. 'At Hercules, quae virtus est animi magnitudo, Cerberem in lucem extravit, sibique perpetuam gloriam comparavit'.

22. Isidore of Seville offers the former triad (11.3.33). Salutati seconds Isidore and adds the latter (pp. 525-6. 4.1.3-4).

23. Salutati, p. 525. 4.1.2.

24. MacCaffrey (1976), p. 381.

25. Spenser's remark is reported in *Ben Jonson's Conversations with Drummond of Hawthornden*, as noted in the Variorum, vol. 6, p. 232.

26 Aristotle (1982), pp. 28-9. *Poetics*, VI.22.

27. Tasso, *La Cavaletta, overo dell poesia toscana* (1587), as noted by Weinberg (1961, p. 1152; cf. pp. 984, 994). In Lionardo Salviati's *Riposta all'Aplogia di Torquato Tasso* (1585; cf. Weinberg, pp. 1016ff.), *argomento* has to do with the logical inevitabilites created by plot-events. Adding to the confusion deriving ultimately from Aristotle's distinction between plot and thought was the use, deriving from Latin rhetoric, of *argumentum* to refer to a kind of fiction characterized by both untruth and versimilitude; for a discussion of these uses see Steadman (1974), esp. pp. 140-1.

28. Such superlative characterizations of Gloriana are pervasive. Panthea is described in 1.10.58 and 2.10.73. The latter passage includes the poem's only description of the brass bridge and is preceded by the only mention of the golden wall built by Elfiline. I take the metals to be part of the poem's larger classification of ages by metals deriving ultimately from Hesiod. Brass is compared negatively to gold in 4.9.2 and 6.Pr.5.

29. The phrase 'allegorical cores' comes originally from C. S. Lewis (1958), p. 335. The fullest exploration of the poem's alternation between such cores and the realms outside them is Angus Fletcher's *The Prophetic Moment* (1971), which interprets the poem as a 'dialectic of the temple and the labyrinth'.

30. Calvin, as quoted in McDannell and Lang (1988), p. 148.

31. McDannell and Lang devote a fascinating chapter to Renaissance attempts to reconcile the idea of hierarchy and equality in representations of the afterlife. The most common solution was to turn the lower heaven into a pastoral stage preceding full incorporation into 'highest heaven'. Spenser's solution (not noticed by McDannell and Lang) appears to be unique, and suggests to me that the opposition between epic progression and romance cyclicality gives way for the elect in the hereafter to an existence in which the cyclical, to-and-fro motion is reconciled to the linear.

32. Baybak, Delany, and Hieatt (1969), p. 227.

33. On the Tree of Jesse and the cosmic tree in general, see Greenhill (1954) and Butterworth (1970). Spenser is also conflating the Tree of Jesse with the *arbor amoris*, a popular image from the thirteenth century on. Marriage, widowhood, and virginity were its three fruits; we note that Britomart is destined to taste all three. For a masterful discussion of the tradition, see Dronke (1981).

34 Alpers (1967), chapter 2, 'Narrative Materials and Stanzas of Poetry'.

35. Nohrnberg (1976), pp. x-xii.

36. Lewis (1958), p. 310.

CHAPTER FIVE

The Endless Work of
Paradise Lost

In *Paradise Lost* Milton makes use of the epic tradition in a variety of ways. As both early and modern scholarship demonstrate, the poem abounds in elaborately constructed allusions rewarding detailed intimacy with classical texts. These are not passages that this chapter can survey, much less explicate, but before turning to Milton's systematic reworking of the epic chronotope, it is worth observing that our understanding of allusions is invariably enriched by adding to consideration of specific contexts a more general awareness of epic's generic features. An instance that has been explicated apparently independently by Wolfgang Rudat and Charles Martindale concerns the multiple references to Vergil's question about the cause of the Trojans' persecution: 'can such great wrath dwell in heavenly breasts?' ('tantaene animis caelestibus irae?', *Aen.* 1.11).[1] Both critics find the phrase echoed in 6.788 as Raphael marvels that the devils could take up arms against God, in 9.729-30 as Satan tempts Eve with the suggestion that God could not be so envious as to deny her the knowledge to be obtained through eating the forbidden fruit, and in 3.216 as the Father asks rhetorically whether there dwells in heaven charity so dear as to redeem humankind. As the alignment of all three passages by both critics suggests, this kind of allusion is carefully crafted so as to be perceived and interpreted. Knowing that it is part of Vergil's opening question about the 'cause' ('causas', 1.8) allows us to connect these passages to Milton's own opening question about the 'cause' (1.28) of the Fall, a connection encouraged by awareness that causality is an issue perennially addressed by epic and addressed moreover through the vertical dimension. The result is a provocative parallel between two poems similarly concerned about issues of human autonomy and divine power but markedly different in how these issues are resolved. Or consider another allusion analysed by Rudat.[2] Adam announces before eating the fruit that he is 'certain to undergo like doom' (9.953), a phrase long recognized as a translation of Aeneas' announcement that he is 'resolved to go' ('certus eundi', 4.554) from Carthage but also, as Rudat points out, an echo of Dido being 'resolved to die' ('certa mori', 4.564). Knowledge of the Vergilian text allows us to connect the three passages meaningfully, and the presence of both a Latinate meaning of 'certain' as 'resolved' (supported by 'resolved . . . to undergo' conspicuously separated in 9.968-71) and a more familiar vernacular meaning keeps issues of free will and determinism in play. Awareness of the generic omnipresence of vertical classification helps us to appreciate the choice of 'undergo', which perhaps not accidentally translates the sound of 'eundi' into the vertical implication of 'mori', an effect that would not be lost on a readership more accustomed than we are to memorizing poetry and reading aloud. It will be recalled that the paths of Aeneas and Dido are here diverging vertically as well as horizontally, a point emphasized by the imagery surrounding this passage in the *Aeneid*. Milton invariably evokes the spatial aspect of 'undergo', and the shared descent of Adam and Eve, even if it is not the exact kind of descent they now expect, contrasts with the diverging paths of their predecessors.[3]

More frequent and important than precise allusion to specific texts, however, are the elaborate re-deployments of generic concepts. These can be subtle, as when the concept of epic unanimity, a battlefield ideal in the fallen world, finds its originary moment in the evening worship of Adam and Eve. 'Both stood, / both turned', we are told with evocative economy, and out of their mouths comes a single prayer 'said unanimous' (4.720-36), a feat repeated the following morning, when Milton adds the detail that these prayers are extemporaneous, 'each morning duly paid / In various style', 'unmeditated' (5.145-9) according to the Protestant ideal. Later the couple will have to confront the problem of the one and the many, deciding whether they will work independently or together. In doing so they define their place among the other animals, who are divided into solitary or gregarious species: the fish 'part single or with mate' (7.403) graze the sea; the birds 'part loosely wing the region, part more wise / In common' (425-6); mammals range 'those rare and solitary, these in flocks' (461). Other generic allusions are far less subtle, as in the association of epic's drive for vertical one-upmanship with hell. It is not accidental that Milton imitates not only Homer's description of Hephaestos' fall in Mulciber's headlong tumble from the crystal battlements (1.740ff.), but its placement at the end of the first book, where in both epics vertical classification is established as a norm and as a problem. The specific allusion supports a host of more generic allusions in the first two books and asks us to extend our ongoing reconsideration of epic values back to the very well-head of European literature. At the end of a conceptually rich and well known tradition, Milton can also create meaning through conspicuous absence. A notable instance is the figure of Hercules. This quintessential epic character appears in the prose works as frequently as any other figure from Greek mythology, and Milton refers to a variety of his labours and other traditional incidents and attributes.[4]

The only extended reference in the epic occurs when some of the fallen angels vent their rage by rending up the rocks and hills of hell:

> As when Alcides from Oechalia crowned
> With conquest, felt the envenomed robe, and tore
> Through pain up by the roots Thessalian pines,
> And Lichas from the top of Oeta threw
> Into the Euboic sea. (2.542-6)

Hercules as usual demands considerable meaning assembly. To the immediate parallel of characters uprooting as they burn and rage the simile adds the idea of a Hercules-like aspiration to ascend to heaven, an understandable aspiration now, but also an explanation of why the devils' resemblance to Hercules turns into a resemblance to Lichas, who is thrown from a height. Even as it continues the epic genre's creatively oblique use of the hero and its meditation on the collapse of difference, the simile effectively removes him as a possible heroic exemplar, and he will make but one more meagre and degrading appearance as 'Herculean Samson' (9.1060) rising from the harlot-lap of Dalilah in a quick linkage of the human and angelic Falls. An understanding of the hero's prominence in epic tradition helps us to perceive that his figural presence in hell and his subsequent absence in the poem are part of a revaluation of magnanimity.

The Epic of Heaven and Hell

If, as readers have long discerned, so much of epic's traditional material ends up in hell, we can best appreciate Milton's revision of the genre by examining the locale the fallen heroes have self-destructively abandoned. Milton's heaven reconciles epic methods of vertical classification and the Protestant rejection of hierarchical order through a familiar device: spatial paradox. In the grand chronological reprogramming whereby his epic, while concluding and summarizing a generic tradition, also establishes the norms followed in degraded or less developed fashion by earlier poets recounting post-Edenic events, Milton prefigures Aeneas' attempts to rise by lowering and Redcrosse's vision of angels descending to and fro by creating a heaven whose basic governing principle is the paradoxical yet harmonious attenuation of binary oppositions. As we will consider later, paradox characterizes the relationship between the divine order and the chaos it in one sense contains, for all is made of 'one first matter' in Milton's radically monistic universe. But in another sense the Creator's order opposes an external chaos where starkly opposed qualities — 'hot, cold, moist, and dry' (2.898) — lead their no less starkly opposed 'embryon Atoms' (2.900) — 'light-arm'd or heavy, sharp, smooth, swift or slow' (2.902) — in perpetual conflict. Within the walls forming the prototype for epic's cosmic spaces, 'light and darkness in perpetual round /

Lodge and dislodge by turns' (6.6-7), but these seeming opposites are in fact parts of a subtle continuum, for 'darkness there might well seem twilight here' (6.11-12), and the diurnal round provides but a 'grateful vicissitude' (6.8).

Binarism is similarly attenuated in heavenly society. The angels enjoy ludic flirtations with a disorder that is not really disorder, dancing their 'mazes intricate' around the heavenly throne, 'eccentric, intervolved, yet regular / Then most, when most irregular they seem' (5.621-3). The angels, in other words, prefigure both the concerted warcraft and the pondering assemblage of epic heroes by seeing through the part's apparent irregularity to the regularity of the subsuming whole. But the 'eccentric' can remain merely apparent only if it retains its orientation, if it avoids the full realization of opposition, to the centre's centripetal pull. The vertical axis is defined by God's central 'high mount' (5.643), the first in a long tradition of sacred mountains and high places to be considered the navel of the world. Yet it is worth reflecting upon the subtle illogicality of this tradition's originary type. In a self-cancelling phrase, we learn that God is 'high Throne'd above all highth' (3.58). From one point of view, the divine order is tied to God's high point, but from another it can be seen to avoid vertical classification altogether, to be above all height. Unfallen angels do not aspire or orient themselves vertically, except through elevation by submission, as when 'lowly reverent / Towards either throne they bow' (3.349-50). Even this prefiguration of epic submission comes after the Father announces to the son, 'thy humiliation shall exalt / With thee thy Manhood also to this Throne' (3.313-14), a basic Christian lesson that lends meaning to the gesture accompanying the angels' bow: they joyfully cast off their own 'Crowns enwove with amarant and gold' (3.352) and then re-crown themselves to take up their celebratory song, enacting the pattern set by the ultimate exemplar. The poem's first true plot-event is the Son's elevation, at which the Father decrees, 'to him shall bow all knees in heaven' (5.607). We should not assume that the downward direction implied at this point really exists as an 'irregular' direction truly opposed to the divine upward. Rather, until the first Fall any such downward motion also includes a reciprocal elevation; the very denial of this opposition-defying reciprocation constitutes the first sin. As Abdiel argues, the Father's action is not meant 'to make us less', but 'rather to exalt / Our happy state under one Head more near united' (5.829-31). In the ordinary course of heavenly life, the angels simply dispose themselves effortlessly about God's throne without any indication of vertical hierarchy or ascent. Nor does Milton allow centring in heaven to authorize centralized Catholicism's earthly hierarchies. A complex of familiar forms clusters around God's throne in heaven's centre, including the river of bliss (3.357), the fount of life (3.356), and an abundance of precious materials which in human history will be used to evoke this original transcendent splendour. But to prevent such details from adding up to a Catholic heaven, Milton also includes the original type of Protestant de-centring. In the nightly dispersal following their dance about the throne:

> . . . the angelic throng
> Dispersed in bands and files their camp extend
> By living streams among the trees of life,
> Pavilions numberless, and sudden reared,
> Celestial tabernacles, where they slept
> Fanned with cool winds. (5.650-5)

'Numberless' and 'sudden reared', the manifestations of sacred space are not tied to fixed sacramental locations in the Catholic manner, but appear to rise automatically, responding to the original type of Luther's 'priest-hood of all believers'. In ways such as these Milton subtly accommodates heavenly to human reality and founds in heaven the paradoxical axis of ascent and descent that will function as a moral index throughout the poem, but he does this without manifesting true oppositions among heaven's unfallen population.

Horizontal aspects of omphalic spatiality grow complex as soon as we are permitted to view the empyreal realm. Our first vision presents it 'extended wide / In circuit, undetermined square or round' (2.1047-8). This indeterminacy has positive implications, for it suggests that in Milton's monistic universe the traditional use of round and square to contrast spirit and matter does not apply.[5] Similarly, 'undetermined' could mean unbounded, indicating that God rules over a heavenly empire without end no matter what its shape. When we consider that this vision comes to us through the eyes of Satan, who is 'at leisure to behold / Far off the empyreal Heaven' (1046-7), negative possibilities come to the fore. It could be Satan who cannot decide whether heaven is spiritual or material. Or it could in fact be Satan who in another sense once had to decide, since the shape is undetermined and he was therefore 'undetermined' or free to realize its square potential by sinning. Although matter and spirit are not truly opposed, they are distinguishable by degree, as is suggested by the emphatic (and yet ultimately unreal) materiality of hell, where angelic dancing is replaced by vast engineering projects. Satan's confusion is logically bound up with his free choice to sin, an act which has the effect of temporarily increasing the materiality of heaven, as armoured spirits collide with projectiles, much to the chagrin of many readers. A square heaven also implies a quartered heaven, and it is consistent with the descent into materiality that Satan's strategic retreat to 'the quarters of the North' (5.689), where he sits 'high in the midst exalted as a god' (6.99), introduces yet another traditional set of horizontal distinctions. Heaven acquires compass points only when it is affected by the fallen angels' sinful presence. Like the other oppositions Satan disattenuates, this one too has sinister implications to which he remains oblivious. Although he attempts to avoid submission to the Son and to raise himself to equal the Father on high, in going north he travels in the direction defined by Thomas Aquinas as down. Suddenly failing to participate in the heavenly paradox by which submission elevates, Satan creates and suffers the infernal antitype to this paradox by which the climbing aspirer plummets into damnation.

Related effects accompany the introduction of epic's left / right distinction. The Father presents the Son 'at my right hand' (5.605), and the fallen angels fear the offended deity's 'red right hand' (2.174) no less naturally than Sin wishes to rule at her preferred sovereign's 'right hand voluptuous' (2.869) over a Satanic *imperium* 'without end' (2.870). But just as heaven's blazing day lacks a truly opposed darkness, and the downward direction remains only a regularized potential before Satan falls, the right does not acquire a fully realized opposite until Sin springs forth from the left side of Satan's head (2.755). Following the chronology of events, after the introduction of the left, right and left first occur together as an explicit opposition in the military manoeuvres accompanying the introduction of artillery (6.555 and 569), and they occur together once more as Satan, initiating epic's to-and-fro form of motion, 'scours the right hand coast, sometimes the left' (2.633), now more knowingly and literally seeking the gates of hell.[5] The origin of their fallen, rigid opposition is further suggested in Satan's illogically two first experiences of pain: when he felt the 'miserable pain' (2.752) accompanying the birth of Sin from his left side, and when he later — according at least to how we understand chronology — 'first knew pain, / and writhed him to and fro convolved' as Michael's sword 'deep entering shared / All his right side' (6.326-8). Satan aspires to the sovereignty of the Father's right hand, but in travelling to his quarters to the north he moves in a direction defined by St. Jerome as the left.[6]

Although composed of individuals navigating as only angels can, the heavenly dances are also collective exercises of intersubjectivity, perfect examples of epic unanimity made possible by the angels' easy attenuation of self-boundaries. The fallen angels retain some degree of this ability, as we can see in their sometimes disciplined performance in the war in heaven and in their superhuman cooperation in transforming hell into a facsimile of heaven, focused upon its own 'high capital' (1.756). Their progress is neither real nor continuous, however, for in hell intersubjectivity can suddenly invert into a means of heightening conflict and punishment, as an epic virtue redounds to the detriment of its owner. An ironic climax occurs in Book 10 when, in parody of the angels' harmonious turnings about the throne of God, a 'dismal universal hiss' (10.508) of serpents answers Satan's oration. Pandemonium, their new counter-centre, is now graced by

> A grove hard by, sprung up with this their change,
> His will who reigns above, to aggravate
> Their penance, laden with fair fruit, like that
> Which grew in Paradise, the bait of Eve
> Used by the tempter: on that prospect strange
> Their earnest eyes they fixed, imagining
> For one forbidden tree a multitude
> Now risen, to work them further woe or shame. (548-55)

If we are not alert to the intricate spatial component of the poem's argument, we can easily miss this passage's splendid ironies. The grove parodies the central tree of Eden, and the proliferation of Tantaluses comments upon the recent fall into multiplicity and frustrating separation on earth. The grove also parodies the original multiple centring embodied in heaven's numberless Trees of Life, a memory that must redouble the devils' pain. It prefigures future phenomena that will indeed work them further woe and shame: the Redeemer's rood tree, conventionally viewed as an antitype of Eden's tree, and here multiplied to form a devil's nightmare; and the 'paradise within', the earthly shadow of the angels' multiple centring and the means by which humankind will resist the devils' work.

For Satan and his followers, the non-oppositional angelic self is replaced by a confining and painfully paradoxical interiority. 'The mind is its own place', Satan infamously declares, 'and in itself / Can make a heaven of hell, a hell of heaven' (1.254-5). Although this pronouncement has elicited a great deal of commentary, the full measure of its irony has not been sounded. What I wish to point out is its easy sliding between internal and external referents, a movement that Satan will soon learn to exploit. Externally, as Satan begins his revenge against God, he here anticipates both the feverish building program of Book 1 and the infernal council of Book 2. Ground will soon be broken to begin the attempted transformation of hell into heaven, and he believes that if the fallen angels remain steadfast, maintaining the 'union, and firm faith, and firm accord' (1.36) of a collective will that is causally sufficient 'in itself', hell's take-over of heaven too will occur. Unfortunately for Satan, in the external realm both parts of his statement are false. Using internal referents and taking 'in itself' as spatial containment rather than causal sufficiency, Satan is also claiming self-sufficient sovereignty over his integral self. This reckless claim, at once a recognizable epic boast and an infernal parody of Protestant individualism inherent in the priesthood of all believers, generates even crueller ironies. Only the second half of his statement is true,

and only in a limited sense. Satan has fallen away from attenuated binarism into a dynamically polarized world. He is so caught up in a relentless
system of punishment that converts all positives to negatives that even
success in conquering heaven would intensify his internal hell. Eventually
attaining greater insight, he later revises his claim to self-sovereignty, explaining more clearly the limited way he can make a hell of heaven:

> . . . and the more I see
> Pleasures about me, so much the more I feel
> Torment within me, as from the hateful siege
> Of contraries; all good to me becomes
> Bane, and in heaven much worse would be my state. (9.119-23)

Nevertheless, Satan achieves the success Providence allows him by
finding a way to become, like his Maker, an emanational centre externalizing his internal state. His pivotal moment of insight occurs atop Mount
Niphates. A typical Vergilian hero 'much revolving' (4.31) in his mind
how to regain forward progress along his heroic itinerary toward the centre, Satan shrewdly analyses his error:

> What could be less than to afford him praise,
> The easiest recompense, and pay him thanks,
> How due! Yet all his good proved ill in me,
> And wrought but malice; lifted up so high
> I sdeigned subjection, and thought one step higher
> Would set me highest, and in a moment quit
> The debt immense of endless gratitude,
> So burdensome still paying, still to owe;
> Forgetful what from him I still received,
> And understood not that a grateful mind
> By owing owes not, but still pays, at once
> Indebted and discharged; what burden then?
> O had his powerful destiny ordained
> Me some inferior angel, I had stood
> Then happy; no unbounded hope had raised
> Ambition. (4.46-61)

Tempted by proximity to the central deity, Satan believed that by rising
one step higher he would become an independent omphalos. As the logical incongruity of the relative 'immense' and the absolute 'endless'
suggests, his fall resulted from a breakdown of the calculus needed to reconcile the moment to eternity.[7] But Satan is now coming to terms with his
error, for the means of quitting the debt of gratitude occurs precisely 'in
a moment', though not in the climactic moment of an epic conflict. One
can avoid incurring and accumulating a debt of creaturely gratitude only
by continuously returning thanks, by converting what Satan here describes as an incremental, diachronic process into a synchronic, spatialized
stance affording reciprocation 'at once', immediately at each moment. His

failure to understand that the infinite distance between himself and a Creator who 'sits high throned above all highth' (3.58) could not be crossed by incremental steps corresponds to his failure to understand the lesson contained in the Father's description of humankind:

> . . . a creature who not prone
> And brute as other creatures, but endued
> With sanctity of reason, might erect
> His stature, and upright with front serene
> Govern the rest, self-knowing, and from thence
> Magnanimous to correspond with heaven,
> But grateful to acknowledge whence his good
> Descends, thither with heart and voice and eyes
> Directed in devotion, to adore
> And worship God supreme, who made him chief
> Of all his works. (7.506-16)

Since the 'good' the Creator distributes is a constant, form-giving, onto-logical energy proceeding down the vertical axis and outward from the centre, a creature's only proper response is continuously to maintain the grateful 'upright heart and pure' preferred by the Spirit 'before all tem-ples' (1.18). The only 'moment' in which one can quit, or rather avoid, the accumulating Satanic debt is always now. By remaining directed in devo-tion, continuously sustaining the moment of gratitude and corresponding to heaven in the sense of 'communicating with', unfallen humanity would itself also correspond to the heavenly centre in the sense of 'being analo-gous to'. Epic magnanimity does not combine vertical superiority and territorial aggression in the Homeric manner now assumed by the devils. Rather, it converts humble submission to the Creator into a centrifugal beneficence toward all creatures, who imitate the magnanimous hero's de-votional return.

In Milton's unprecedented synthesis of Christian *figura*, epic conven-tions, Neoplatonic emanations, and a variety of cosmological models — all of which are subsumed into an omphalic spatiality that ties his poem perhaps line-by-line to the epic tradition — the Creator oversees a vari-ety of emanations from the centre: goodness, grace, light, bounty, love, the fountain's waters, even Adam and Eve's projected unfallen offspring, those 'generations' foreseen spreading outward and then returning 'from all the ends of the earth' to celebrate their solemn days at their Edenic 'capital seat' (11.343-5).[8] All participating in a process of ontological sus-tenance, these emanations are characterized by both positive value and overflowing abundance, a combination economically expressed by 'bounty' (from Latin *bonitas*, 'goodness'), one of the poem's key terms, which finds its clearest opposite in 'misery'. Satan fully realizes his imita-tive genius when he learns to replace naive ambition with a subtle, complexly imitative antitype of the Creator's bounteous system. Realizing that his only efficacious course lies in exploiting his own painful paradoxes, he sets out to propagate his own internal hell, in effect to focus a kind of negative cosmic order around himself. He begins his imitation unwittingly, when the very act of conceiving rebellion produces a grotesque parody of creation and instantaneously introduces precisely the diminishment he mistakenly fears the Son's ascension entails. As Sin recalls:

> In bold conspiracy against heaven's king,
> All on a sudden miserable pain
> Surprised thee, dim thine eyes, and dizzy swum
> In darkness, while thy head flames thick and fast
> Threw forth, till on the left side opening wide
> Likest to thee in shape and countenance bright,
> Then shining heavenly fair, a goddess armed
> Out of thy head I sprung. (2.751-8)

Creating Sin in his own image, Satan at the same time introduces into creation a set of emanations that stand as a true opposite to God's — pain, misery, evil, hate — all symptomizing ontological diminishment. When Michael first encounters the fallen archangel, he marvels at Satan's parody:

> Author of evil, unknown till thy revolt,
> Unnamed in heaven, now plenteous, as thou seest
> These acts of hateful strife, hateful to all,
> Though heaviest by just measure on thy self
> And thy adherents: how hast thou disturbed
> Heaven's blessed peace, and into nature brought
> Misery, uncreated until the crime
> Of thy rebellion? (6.262-9)

Finding themselves in hell, where 'misery hath joined / In equal ruin' (1.90) all of Satan's cohorts, the fallen angels' instinctive reaction is to 'raise Magnificence' (2.273), to found an imperial 'metropolis' (10.439). The insufficiency of this citadel is seen in the bee simile placed strategically at the end of Book 1:

> . . . As bees
> In spring time, when the sun with Taurus rides,.
> Pour forth their populous youth about the hive
> In clusters; they among fresh dews and flowers
> Fly to and fro, or on the smoothed plank,
> The suburb of thir straw-built citadel,
> New rubbed with balm, expatiate and confer
> Thir state affairs. (1.768-75)

Drawing on both Homer's description of the assembling Greek forces (*Il.*, 2.87-90) and the view of Aeneas as he stands on a height above Carthage observing the construction of the citadel (*Aen.*, 1.430-6), Milton's bee-simile uses Homer's to-and-fro motion to explicate the error behind Aeneas' attraction to Carthage. The illusory satisfaction the cowardly party of Mammon takes in their new metropolis strengthens Satan's claim to foremost epic stature when, in his great moment of insight atop Mt. Niphates, he proclaims his preference for a new form of epic centring. He at once despairingly and triumphantly exclaims, indeed in a moment when despair turns into triumph, 'Me miserable!' (4.73), punningly announcing his newly recognized 'ability', which will allow him to progress beyond the naive strategies of decisive warfare and static spatial imitation to a more effective approach of emanational activity sustained moment by moment. From this point on, he will not futilely seek to regain the lost condition of ontological fullness available only through orientation to the Creator, but will turn his efforts to the only activity that allows him to imitate the divine economy. As he later explains to himself:

> But neither here seek I, no nor in heaven
> To dwell, unless by mastering heaven's supreme;
> Nor hope to be my self less miserable
> By what I seek, but others to make such
> As I, though thereby worse to me redound:
> For only in destroying I find ease
> To my relentless thoughts. (9.124-30)

What Satan can do is propagate his internal hell, continuing the creation of 'miserable' creatures in his own image begun with the birth of Sin. And in doing so he will, in a real if paradoxical sense, suffer no diminution. Extending his parody even to the return grateful creatures direct to their Maker, he notes (whether unwittingly or not, it is hard to tell) that his own miserable essence will be enhanced rather than diminished, for 'thereby worse to me redound'. A more thorough and creative imitation-through-inversion of God's system could scarcely be conceived.

The Human Epic

Eden is an ideal space constructed in imitation of the heavenly model. But as many readers have noticed, the Garden and its inhabitants also include a number of features, from the 'mazy error' (4.239) of the paradisal streams to Eve's 'wanton ringlets' (4.306), that allow us to experience the Fall as the transformation of potential into actual evil. Of course, to see even potential evil in such adumbrations evidences our own fallenness, a state lacking the resources to represent prelapsarian perfection faithfully. Nevertheless, Milton takes great care to portray the Fall of humankind, in strong contrast to the Fall of the rebel angels, as a typological process in which fallen antitypes recapitulate unfallen types. The directional quartering manifest in heaven with the first Fall exists from the very beginning on earth. Wielding his celestial compasses, the Son initiates creation by establishing centre and circumference, the basic horizontal distinctions of omphalic space, but the creation of the material universe apparently requires a more elaborate differentiation of parts than the undescribed creation of heaven. Preparing the ground for humanity's nearly universal practice of quartering the cosmos, the Creator assigns the elements to 'their several quarters' (3.715) and sets the winds blowing from their respective 'quarters' (5.192). Even the waters issuing from the garden's central fountain do not simply emanate centrifugally in imitation of the divine model, but are 'divided into four main streams' (4.233). The potential polysemy of the cross thus inscribed by the Son from this central point to the world's end will unfold in the course of history.

The typological 'argument' created by the poem's spatial configurations contributes to our experience of the Fall as a gradual process. The innocent cosmic separation of the world's elements, for example, finds a subtle echo in Eve's more ominous separation from Adam on the fatal day. Satan's glee at finding 'Eve separate' (9.422 and 444), emphasized by the phrase's repetition, comments ironically on his own painful exile and on Eve's moral position somehow already somewhere between unfallen innocence and his own state. A parody of the epic warrior's seeking out his chosen foe on the battlefield, the scene situates itself suggestively on a continuum that includes the grotesqueries of Sin and Death, who participate in their own ungrateful vicissitude of separation and union and whom 'no power can separate' (10.251), as well as the Son's vision of heavenly union restored, when the saints, 'from the impure far separate' (6.743), will join the heavenly dance of regularized wandering away from the centre. The poem's internal typology can also exploit more elusive parallels. Consider, for example, that upon descending to earth Satan lands on 'the mount that lies from Eden north' (4.569). Our typological imagination should alert us to the fact that Satan is about to requite his earlier failure to usurp God's throne through an antitype of his action in heaven. He now successfully proceeds from his northern station to the centre, ascends 'the middle tree and highest there that grew' (4.194), and successfully attacks God's newest minions. The pattern is then repeated on a smaller scale, without the directional detail but with equivalent moral commentary added through a familiar emblematic allusion, when Satan enters the serpent's 'labyrinth of many a round self rolled, / his head the midst' (9.184-5). Ironies arise from the hero's entering the 'labyrinth of many' that his prototypes-successors seek to escape, and ultimately his manoeuvres about the earthly centre will prove no more advantageous than his earlier heavenly campaign. But to reverse his short-term gain Providence will have to work through the full paradoxical itinerary of the Fortunate Fall.

The Jacob's Ladder 'ascending by degrees magnificent' (3.500) from Eden to heaven's gate stands as an emblem of upward aspiration for the first parents and signifies the macrocosmic sanction for humanity's vertical instincts, although 'magnificent' is a word that easily occasions such Satanic connotations as prideful pomp and earned salvation (cf. 2.273 and the fact that it is Satan who 'descries' this in 501). Raphael foresees a future in which humankind will freely rise upon this ladder:

> . . . time may come when men
> With angels may participate, and find
> No inconvenient diet, nor too light fare:
> And from these corporal nutriments perhaps
> Your bodies may at last turn all to spirit,
> Improved by tract of time, and winged ascend
> Ethereal, as we, or may at choice
> Here or in heavenly paradises dwell;
> If ye be found obedient . . . (5.493-501)

Adam's response confirms the vision's inescapable appeal to earthbound but instinctively rising mortals:

> Well hast thou taught the way that might direct
> Our knowledge, and the scale of nature set
> From centre to circumference, whereon
> In contemplation of created things
> By steps we may ascend to God.   (508-12)

Adam's translation of the angel's discourse might appear unexceptionable. His reference to knowledge and contemplation contrasts favourably with Satan's cruder ambition and suggests a perhaps unexpected theological sophistication. But we have not sufficiently understood Milton's complex spatiality if we do not notice a potential problem in Adam's directional reasoning. Adam's recent guided journey from circumference to centre following his creation outside the garden, Satan's analogous but morally reversed entry into the garden, and Eve's soon-to-be-attempted ascent to godhead at the central tree, which will lead to expulsion in the other direction, all should remind us that the direction of travel in omphalic space is of crucial importance. Though this is not the only possible reading, Adam's sentence strongly implies that we might direct our knowledge and ascend to God along a path from centre to circumference. *Paradise Lost* includes frames of reference in which Adam's sense of direction is entirely reasonable. In the poem's studiously ambiguous, Copernican-Ptolemaic astronomy, for example, there is probably nothing ominous about geocentrism. But if modern criticism has taught us anything, it is that Milton's is an art of multiple, superimposed, indeed often conflicting perspectives. In seventeenth century discussions of the Creation God creates 'heaven and earth, centre and periphery' ('coelum et terram, centrum et peripheriam'), with the distinction abundantly clear.⁹ On the fundamental question of humanity's relation to the central Creator, arguably the poem's crucial issue, Adam commits a Satanic slip of the tongue.

If Milton allows Adam's discourse to include a potential for ominous homocentrism, he incorporates this potential much more elaborately into the psychology of Eve. One of the most important ways Adam's account of his own origin differs from Eve's is that it is carefully motivated within the drama of character interaction. Adam's account fits into the narrative as at once an act of self-interest and a gracious gesture of reciprocation, an appropriately pastoral response to the visiting angel's long epic discourse. 'Now hear me relate / My story, which perhaps thou hast not heard', he proposes, 'How subtly to detain thee I devise' (8.204-7). In contrast, Eve's account is directed toward herself, as if she is trying to find within her own experience reasons for accepting Adam's counsel. As we progress from Adam's sermon on the need to submit to God's 'One easy prohibition' (4.433) and to 'extol / His bounty' (435-6), to Eve's recollection of her birth, to the poem's most sensual moment, we are really witnessing a drama within Eve's mind. She responds to Adam's preaching by first recollecting her own earliest experience of fulfilment and subsequent repression, and then with a sexual proposition that manages to combine both aspects of her earliest experience. Following her discourse, in a subtle but highly significant spatial contradiction, the naked Eve

> . . . half embracing leaned
> On our first father, half her swelling breast
> Naked met his under the flowing gold
> Of her loose tresses hid: he in delight
> Both of her beauty and submissive charms
> Smiled with superior love, as Jupiter
> On Juno smiles, when he impregns the clouds
> That shed May flowers. (494-501)

Modern readers, often missing the glancing use of the 'woman on top' topos that so fascinated the Renaissance, often interpret the scene as a simple emblem of Eve's submission to Milton's alleged principle of male authority. But as Joseph Addison more accurately notes in an essay on Milton in the *Spectator*, the passage signifies the 'mutual Subordination of the two sexes'.¹⁰ In a radically anti-hierarchical vision of prelapsarian gender relations, Milton portrays both of our first parents on top at the same time, a paradox beautifully rendered in the synchronic conflation of falling rain and growing flowers. This boldly physical and reciprocal enactment of elevation through submission, an earthly imitation of heaven's attenuated binarism, forms a type-scene of unfallen innocence to be contrasted with Eve's approaching ambitious ascent.

Adam and Eve at once gloriously and ominously yearn for ascent. Adam's birth scene supports the popular Renaissance derivation of 'man' from the Greek for 'upward' and 'leap':[11]

> Straight toward heaven my wondering eyes I turned,
> And gazed a while the ample sky, till raised
> By quick instinctive motion up I sprung,
> As thitherward endeavouring, and upright
> Stood on my feet. (8.207-11)

Unfallen humanity tempers this instinct with an instinct for gesturing humility. When Adam initiates epic's rituals of supplication and submission, he receives in return the appropriate elevation, proximity to the centre, and freedom from romance 'wandering':

> . . . here had new begun
> My wandering, had not he who was my guide
> Up hither, from among the trees appeared,
> Presence divine. Rejoicing, but with awe
> In adoration at his feet I fell
> Submiss: he reared me . . . (8.311-16)

Eve's combination of upward aspiration and humility is less straightforward. Unlike Adam, she notes that she 'oft remembers' her first day, a detail indicating that day's utility as a type she recalls during later acts of self-defining comparison:

> That day I oft remember, when from sleep
> I first awaked, and found myself reposed
> Under a shade of flowers, much wondering where
> And what I was, whence hither brought, and how.
> Not distant far from thence a murmuring sound
> Of waters issued from a cave and spread
> Into a liquid plain, then stopped unmoved
> Pure as the expanse of heaven; I thither went
> With unexperienced thought, and laid me down
> On the green bank, to look into the clear
> Smooth lake, that seemed to me another sky.
> As I bent down to look, just opposite,
> A shape within the watery gleam appeared
> Bending to look on me, I started back,
> It started back, but pleased I soon returned,
> Pleased it returned as soon with answering looks
> Of sympathy and love. (4.449-65)

Parallels with Adam's waking scene, placed symmetrically on the opposite side of the poem's midpoint to encourage comparison, underscore crucial differences. Both awaken in a horizontal posture of repose, but circumstances determine opposed reactions. Eve awakens in pastoral's innocent shade, but if the shade of flowers shelters her, it at the same time ominously cuts her off from heaven's light, functioning as did Spenser's trees in Errour's den, which 'Did spred so broad, that heaven's light did hide, / Nor perceable with power of any star'. Her setting combines the 'blissful bower' whose 'roof / Of thickest covert was inwoven shade / Laurel and myrtle' (4.690-4), the paradisal site from which Adam and Eve instinctively gaze upward and hear the celestial voices that 'lift our thoughts to heaven' (4.688), with the bower's negative antitype, the setting of fallen Adam's shame-induced fantasy:

> . . . O might I here
> In solitude live savage, in some glade
> Obscured, where highest woods impenetrable
> To star or sunlight, spread their umbrage broad
> And brown as evening: cover me ye pines,
> Ye cedars, with innumerable boughs
> Hide me, where I may never see them more. (9.1084-90)

The circumstances of her awakening lead Eve to seek a solitude with ominous similarities to Adam's fallen fantasy. Her instinctive motion toward the heavenly light is redirected into a horizontal and then downward quest. As Janet Adelman observes, Milton omits any description of Eve's rising, which would logically precede her stroll to the reflecting pool.[12] Only a downward motion is described as she in effect moves from one horizontal posture to another, from supine to prone. Yet her bending down toward the pool reflecting the sky condenses Adam's upward gaze into the more truly ample sky and his bowing submission to the divine presence. Adam's rise not only allows him to recognize a higher reality and submit to its representative. It at the same time manifests his godlike erectness and allows him to redirect his attention to the world 'about me round' (8.261). Upright and launched immediately into process of 'self-knowing', Adam 'peruses' himself as a comprehensible creature and 'surveys' himself as the sum of his parts and as one existence located among many:

> My self I then perused, and limb by limb
> Surveyed, and sometimes went, and sometimes ran
> With supple joints, and lively vigour led:
> But who I was, or where, or from what cause,
> Knew not. (8.267-71)

By the simple expedient of dividing Ovid's foliage-covered pool of Narcissus into two locations, the covered site of awakening and the uncovered pool reflecting the sky, Milton causes Eve to experience a fixity and self-sufficiency contrasting sharply with Adam's vigorous activity and outward direction.

As a result, Eve not merely loves, but implicitly worships herself. The pervasive omphalic spatiality of *Paradise Lost* allows Milton to superimpose upon the conventionally psychological reading of the Narcissus myth a reading drawing upon what he finds to be the no less fundamental terms of religious phenomenology, which are also generic terms of epic. The vertical axis defined by Eve's face and its reflected image functions as an *axis mundi*. Her own face against the sky, though in reality a sky-effacing 'shadow' (4.470), figures within her subjectivity as a theophanic irruption founding sacred space. Eve explains that she would have 'pined with vain desire, / Had not a voice thus warned me' (466-7), but it is important to observe that this retrospective assessment, the result of the divine voice's promising something better, does not describe the experience itself. In fact, the very 'pleased' Eve is not shown to feel the absence-driven desire that moves Ovid's Narcissus to beat his breast and bemoan his fate. On the contrary, her solipsistic stare creates the fulfilling sense of presence that Milton, following biblical precedent, associates with the beheld face of God.[13] Adam's greatest sorrow after the Fall, he tells Michael, is to be deprived of God's blessed 'countenance' (11.317). What Eve finds and founds at the limpid pool is a bounteous cosmos of divine presence.

If Eve oft remembers her awakening scene, so too should we as readers, once we have discerned its structure and implications. Milton validates Eve's experience, sustains its simultaneously psychological and religious meaning, and enhances its moral ambiguity by allowing others to observe Eve in ways resembling her original theophany. Adam approaches rather dangerously to an idolatrous view of Eve as a self-contained, alternative cosmos: 'so lovely fair, / That what seemed fair in all the world, seemed now / Mean, or in her summed up, in her contained / And in her looks' (8.471-4). Satan's 'gaze admiring' (9.524) and 'gaze / Insatiate' (535-6) are similarly inspired. 'Her every air / Of gesture or least action overawed / His malice' (9.459-61), and the seducer stands transfixed, seduced by the original type of epic's seductive counter-centre, who receives homage 'From every beast, more duteous at her call / Than at Circean call the herd disguised' (9.521-2). Even unfallen nature acts as if to confirm Eve's primal view of herself as a radiant sacred centre, providing a 'pomp of winning graces' who 'from about her shot darts of desire / Into all eyes to wish her still in sight' (8.61-6).[14]

But if her beauty makes Eve an irresistible cynosure of all eyes, including her own, there remains the implication that her awakening scene describes, and even causally explains, a dangerous predisposition toward egocentric self-sufficiency, the form of pride so contrary to the Protestant vision of human depravity and utter dependence upon the merciful deity. Satan, himself a devotee and victim of such thinking, knows precisely how to exploit Eve's predisposition. Whispering a dream into her ear, he first uses parallels of vocabulary ('face', 'shadow', even the retrospective 'in vain') and situation (the meeting of vertical gazes) to evoke the scene of awakening. He then implants a kind of cosmological curiosity most appealing to her mind-set:

> . . . now reigns
> Full-orbed the moon, and with more pleasing light
> Shadowy sets off the face of things; in vain,
> If none regard, heaven wakes with all his eyes,
> Whom to behold but thee, nature's desire,
> In whose sight all things joy, with ravishment
> Attracted by thy beauty still to gaze. (5.41-7)

Satan has understood and fulfilled the wish underlying Eve's earlier question: 'But wherefore all night long shine these, for whom / This glorious sight, when sleep hath shut all eyes?' (4.657-8). As others have noted, in the evening following Eve's dream Adam poses his own version of this question to the heavenly authority:[15]

> When I behold this goodly frame, this world
> Of heaven and earth consisting, and compute
> Their magnitudes, this earth a spot, a grain,
> An atom, with the firmament compared
> An all her numbered stars, that seem to roll
> Spaces incomprehensible (for such
> Their distance argues and their swift return
> Diurnal) merely to officiate light
> Round this opacous earth, this punctual spot,
> One day and night; in all their vast survey
> Useless besides, reasoning I oft admire,
> How nature wise and frugal could commit
> Such disproportions . . . . (8.15-27)

The contrasts with Eve's wish-fulfilling dream are pointed. Whereas a number of Adam's esteemed descendants, including Spenser's Redcrosse though not Ariosto's Astolfo, will understand earth's contemptible insignificance only after celestial journeys, Adam begins his rational 'computation' with earthly insignificance as a self-evident assumption.[16] Adam's instinctive rise to the heavenly perspective this assumption implies — the familiar direction-reversing paradox is never long absent — proclaims his humility, in contrast to Eve's self-flattering dream of herself as universal cynosure. Moreover, when Eve in her dream-vision is granted the to-be-traditional epic ascent that Adam does not need, rather than prefiguring later Christian heroes' attainment of *contemptus mundi*, she marvels at her own exaltation:

> . . . Forthwith up to the clouds
> With him I flew, and underneath beheld
> The earth outstretched immense, a prospect wide

And various; wondering at my flight and change
To this high exaltation.   (5.86-90)

As soon as Adam has questioned the angel about earth's central place,
Eve rises and departs, preferring her lessons intermixed with 'grateful di-
gressions' and 'conjugal caresses' (8.55-6). She leaves as well because she
already knows the answer to Adam's question, or at least the answer she
prefers. In a telling contrast to Adam's submission to the angel's superior
knowledge, she chooses not to hear a logical explanation devoid of narcis-
sistic pleasures, for she would rather walk among her adoring fruits and
flowers, accompanied by her graces, who shoot darts of desire into all surrounding eyes. Her separation thus recapitulates the type-scene planted in
her fancy by Satan. And of course it also links that scene to one both scenes
in turn prefigure: her later separation from Adam, when the tragic implications of her preferred answer will be realized.

The issue of Eve's freedom to choose and sufficiency to stand blurs
most critically when her conditioned vulnerability encounters Satan's
growing understanding of the divine, omphalic economy. Milton follows
biblical precedent in showing Eve succumbing to an offer to become god-
like, but he also portrays her as irresistibly pushed to accept the offer by
more powerful and even defensible appeals. In his address to the tree the
angel of Eve's dream introduces her to a previously unavailable perspective on God's emanational bounty. 'O fair plant, said he, with fruit
surcharged, / Deigns none to ease thy load and taste thy sweet' (5.58-9).
Until this moment, Eve has not connected the ideas of bounty and burden, of abundance and a painful 'surcharge' needing to be eased. Satan's
planting of this association is remarkably deft. He first appeals to Eve's
self-denying benevolence, to which she has been educated by the other
male figures in her life, whose first interactions with her consist of re-
pressive demands that she turn from the generation of 'answering looks of
sympathy and love' according to the economy of her own instinctive desire, toward the initially less winning company of Adam. The sympathy
Satan promotes between the 'fair creature' and the 'fair plant' implies her
identification with its plight, preparing Eve to feel the 'burden' that originally prompted Satan's sin. The tempter then directs his appeal to Eve's
more deeply ingrained desire: her urge to create in her own image and
emanate her own bounty. This is a desire pressed upon her by her oft-re-
membered experience at the pool, sanctioned by God's own example and
Raphael's preaching, even appealed to by the Creator Himself, who soft-
ens her resistance to repression with an offer simply to trade her situation
for its equally satisfying equivalent:

... but follow me,
And I will bring thee where no shadow stays
Thy coming, and thy soft embraces, he

> Whose image thou art, him thou shall enjoy
> Inseparably thine, to him shall bear
> Multitudes like thyself . . . (4.469-74)

Given everything she has experienced and learned, Satan's argument is enormously appealing and perhaps even morally right:

> And why not gods of men, since good, the more
> Communicated, more abundant grows,
> The author not impaired, but honored more? (71-3)

Ovid's Narcissus was not saved by divine intervention. Consequently, his story ends tragically, but from his fate he plucks the wisdom of his famous pronouncement on self-generated bounty: 'inopem me copia fecit', 'the very abundance of my riches impoverishes me'.[20] This is precisely the crucial information Eve is denied.

Urged on by an apparently innocent desire to recapture the lost paradise of the Narcissan pool, striving to ease both the tree's burden and her own, a weight of repression she feels but cannot recognize, Milton's Eve succumbs to her traditional temptation. Her seduction and Adam's remarkably less excusable and more calculated choice to fall result in their assimilation into Satan's inverted cosmic system, which now replaces God's emanations with its own. Declaring the couple 'despoiled / Of all our good, shamed, naked, miserable' (9.1138-9), Adam sees that humankind will turn its generative capacity in a new direction, straightforwardly imitating Satan's inverted imitation of God:

> . . . yet well, if here would end
> The misery, I deserved it, and would bear
> My own deservings; but this will not serve;
> All that I eat or drink, or shall beget,
> Is propagated curse. O voice once heard
> Delightfully, Increase and multiply,
> Now death to hear! For what can I increase
> Or multiply, but curses on my head? (10.725-32)

By the time God prevents a further slide toward Satan's extreme binarism by tempering justice with mercy, Eve's egocentric self-sufficiency, now shared by Adam, has evolved into the traditional image of the hardened heart. Lacking both sympathy toward each other and openness toward God's descending grace, Adam and Eve after the Fall indulge in fruitless mutual recriminations. Cruel ironies arise from conceptual references to Eve's awakening scene. Eve finds Adam to be lacking the centring fixity we must associate with her earlier 'fixed' gaze on both her reflected face (4.465) and the fatal fruit (9.735). 'Had thou been firm and fixed in thy dissent', she complains, 'Neither had I transgressed, nor thou with me' (9.1160-1). Ironically, Adam now develops a strong sense of self-centring as he invokes his creaturely status:

> . . . all from me
> Shall with a fierce reflux on me redound,
> On me as on their natural centre light
> Heavy, though in their place. O fleeting joys
> Of Paradise, dear bought with lasting woes!
> Did I request thee, Maker, from my clay
> To mould me man, did I solicit thee
> From darkness to promote me, or here place
> In this delicious garden? (10.738-46)

As he continues in this vein, his self-centring parodies as well the mazy dances of the intuitive angels:

> And reasonings, though through mazes, lead me still
> But to my own conviction: first and last
> On me, me only, as the source and spring
> Of all corruption, all the blame lights due. (830-3)

Eventually, as the first parents' self-centred isolation breaks down, like the devils joined by misery in equal ruin they achieve a shared state of 'commiseration' (10.940).

Dryden was only the first to observe that *Paradise Lost* ends where *The Faerie Queene* begins.[17] But in fact Adam and Eve are expelled onto an 'even ground' (11.348) lacking omphalic orientation, and even the more tenuous form of such orientation deriving from Spenser's intense contamination of epic with romance. Unlike Spenser's heroes, they have no origin to return to, no goal for their quest, no promise of refuge along the way. Nor do Adam and Eve enter the biblical terrain, where repeated theophanies and the promise of a temple offer hope to the exile. Desperate to remain in God's nourishing presence, Adam proposes to reform himself and his setting in line with the practice of the biblical patriarchs:

> . . . here I could frequent,
> With worship, place by place where he vouchsafed
> Presence divine, and to my sons relate;
> On this mount he appeared; under this tree
> Stood visible, among these pines his voice
> I heard, here with him at this fountain talked:
> So many grateful altars I would rear
> Of grassy turf, and pile every stone
> Of lustre from the brook, in memory,
> Or monument to ages, and thereon
> Offer sweet smelling gums and fruits and flowers. (11.317-27)

Michael responds with a limited assurance:

> Yet doubt not but in valley and in plain
> God is as here, and will be found alike
> Present, and of his presence many a sign
> Still following thee, still compassing thee round

With goodness and paternal love, his face
Express, and of his steps the track divine. (11.349-54)

It is in God's very nature to remain forever omnipresent, but in the fallen, lower world a copia of signs 'expressing' His presence, and indicating as much His absence, replaces the fulfilling abundance and centrality of high Eden. Since God 'attributes to place / No sanctity, if none be thither brought / By men who there frequent, or therein dwell' (11.836-8), there can be no use for altars of stone and grassy turf. Old Testament spatiality remains as a fact of history duly foretold to Adam, but we should notice that Michael emphasizes the portable ark of the covenant, not the fixed temple (12.244ff.). And the ark is superseded as a vehicle for hope by the figurative seed Eve carries within her, for the material trappings and local fixities of omphalic space have become as merely figurative as the 'local wounds / Of head or heel' (12.387-8) by which Satan will eventually be overcome.

It is only by means of the 'paradise within thee, happier far' (12.587), an interior cosmos sustained not through orientation toward a centre located outside the self in horizontal space, but through direct, vertical access to God, that Adam and Eve can navigate the fallen world's decentred plain and 'evil turn to good; more wonderful / Than that which by creation first brought forth / Light out of darkness' (12.471-2). The ending of Book 12 develops this concept with a series of container images: the Father will vertically 'dwell / His Spirit within them' (485-6) and, as the horizontal corollary to this indwelling, encase them in 'spiritual armour, ably to resist / Satan's assaults' (491-2); they will become 'living temples, built by faith to stand' (527). The most important of such images, and the one that locates Milton's poetry most clearly within English Reformation history, is the heart. Invoking a rich tradition begun in English with the penitential psalms of Wyatt, who sought to rebuild the walls of his own 'inward Zion', his 'hertes Jerusalem', Milton uses the image of the heart to complete his interiorization of epic's omphalic spatiality.[18] He first applies the model to himself as a poet dwelling on the fallen world's even ground. The poet in search of sacred song spiritually visits mount Sion (3.30), but he also remains in exile, no longer experiencing the presence of 'human face divine' (3.44). Through it all he is sustained by the descent of the Holy 'Spirit, that dost prefer / Before all temples the upright heart and pure' (1.17-18).

Satan's internal hell, unhappier far, develops as his 'heart / distends with pride, and hardening in his strength / Glories' (1.571-3), a description linking Homeric magnanimity with the common image of the hardened heart the Bible first applies to Pharaoh (Exodus 4:21), one of Satan's human representatives in the poem. Eve is subject also to a cruel paradox of the heart. The susceptibility she displayed at the pool is evidenced again when Satan's flattering words 'into her heart too easy entrance won' (9.845). Typically in satanically infected Eden, this excessive permeability and breach of cosmic walls leads to its conceptual opposite, the hardened hearts of both Adam and Eve in chaotic conflict. Then begins a process of contrition and atonement traced through the hearts of the principal parties. As soon as Adam and Eve fall into disharmony, Satan and his sinful consort form a pointed contrast. While the hardened hearts of Adam and Eve close them off both vertically from God's descending bounty and horizontally from each other's sympathetic 'cordial spirits', Sin gushes rapturously to Satan about 'My heart, which by a secret harmony / Still moves with thine, joined in connection sweet' (10.358-9). Then the mysterious operations of grace begin their work, and Adam and Eve move toward re-establishing their own harmony. As Adam's 'heart relented toward her' (10.940), Eve, 'recovering heart' (966), declares Adam's love 'the sole contentment of my heart' (973). As the first parents progress from renewed love for each other to renewed love for God, we learn that God 'removed the stony from their hearts' (11.4) and that Adam 'kneeled and before him humbled all my heart' (150). Milton calls upon additional varieties of inherited heart imagery to help represent the transition from satanic self-confinement to the paradise within. The image of the heart's freezing and thawing, of biblical origin but translated in the Renaissance into a Petrarchist commonplace employed in a secular, erotic context, conveys Adam's terror (11.264) at Michael's pronouncement of expulsion and his subsequent relief (293ff.) at the angel's suggestion that they may find 'native soil' elsewhere. Finally, the heart appears as a tablet for receiving the divine Word's inscription, another biblical idea reworked by Renaissance Petrarchism to describe a very different kind of 'faithfulness'. 'The Spirit within shall on the heart engrave' (12.524) the laws of proper conduct, Michael declares. The Mosaic ascent and theophany, we see, is really an internal affair.

Anticipating Peter's exhortation that the early Christian community 'be subject one to another' (I Peter 5:5), Eve initiates a return to attenuated binarism. If her conditioned narcissism precipitated the Fall, it also prefigured the internal paradise independent of external orientation. Her idolatrous descent at the pool, then, should be seen to be also a fortunate Fall preparing her for a privileged role in the fallen world. While God's messenger lectures to Adam, the allegedly weaker vessel receives her instruction in a manner growing more promising as the era of easy communication between heaven and earth draws to a close. Eve receives the Word directly from the source:

> Whence thou return'st, and whither went'st, I know;
> For God is also in sleep, and dreams advise,

Which he has sent propitious, some great good
Presaging, since with sorrow and heart's distress
Wearied I fell asleep: but now lead on;
In me is no delay; with thee to go,
Is to stay here; without thee here to stay,
Is to go hence unwilling; thou to me
Art all things under heaven; all places thou . . . (12.610-17)

This final speech of the poem reveals Eve's privileged understanding of what past events have meant, what the present requires, and what the future holds in store. 'With thee to go, / Is to stay here' precisely defines the paradise within and indicates Eve's new fluency in the language of paradox. 'Thou to me / Art all things under heaven, all places thou' introduces the crucial spatial qualification, 'under heaven', that uxorious Adam ignored when he chose to fall.

Into Adam's final silence some will read the resistance of a seventeenth century patriarchy to female self-assertion, masculinist relief perhaps that Eve has 'all her spirits composed / To meek submission' (12.596-7). But after following the poem's revision of an old misogynist tale, we should read into this smiling silence and the couple's 'hand in hand' (12.648) departure a return to a state of 'mutual subordination', as was represented most emblematically when the two were 'imparadised in one another's arms' (4.506) through Eve's ascendant-submissive initiative. Applying the structure of the Edenic 'society of the marriage bed' as the ideal model for human society, Milton makes the 'one faith unanimous' (12.603) of this relationship of equality the pattern for what in *On Christian Doctrine* he calls the elect's Invisible Church 'not confined to place or time' (*Works*, XVI.63) but uniting the paradisal souls of its individual members into an ever-larger paradise within.[19] As Milton tells us in *The Reason of Church Government*, the Creator 'by his own prescribed discipline cast his line and levell upon the soule of man which is his rationall temple, and by the divine square and compass thereof formed and regenerated in us the lovely shapes of vertues and graces, the sooner to edifie and accomplish that immortall stature of Christ's body which is his Church in all her glorious lineaments and proportions' (III.191). In the fulfilment of time, Adam and Eve's church of two will grow into a vast chorus of saints, humbly ascend from circumference to centre, and dance with regular irregularity about the throne of God. As the saints' first parents depart for the even ground of history, Eve intuitively begins preaching and practising the charitable discipline that this final return to the centre will require.

From the One to the Many: Milton and the Epic Body

Paradise Lost envisions human aspiration as a drive to approach the divine centre. This aspiration is also a drive for spiritual transformation, for ascent through refining the individual and the group. The remainder of this chapter will examine how Milton develops two interrelated aspects of epic tradition into means of representing and encouraging this ascent. We will first consider his reworking of the epic genre's preoccupation with the integral human body, which he carefully locates on the scale of nature and represents as the site of conflict between voluntary and involuntary forces. We will then turn to his equally innovative reworking of heroic pondering.

The perennial debate in western culture between dualistic and monistic views of the relation of body and soul, matter and spirit, reached a new intensity in the seventeenth century. If, as James Turner argues, Milton's divorce tracts of the 1640s reveal an author 'torn between materialist monism and hierarchical dualism', by the time of *On Christian Doctrine* and *Paradise Lost*, his position in this debate is unambiguous.[20] In the treatise as in the epic, the human being is 'not, as is commonly thought, produced from and composed of two different and distinct elements, soul and body. On the contrary, the whole man is the soul, and the soul the man: a body, in other words, an individual substance, animated, sensitive, and rational' (XV.40). When Raphael expounds this position in the epic, we find that the hierarchical scheme traditionally used to support dualistic theories has been reincorporated into this new materialistic monism as a vertical, infinitely divisible continuum of traversable 'degrees':

> O Adam, one almighty is, from whom
> All things proceed, and up to him return,
> If not depraved from good, created all
> Such to perfection, one first matter all,
> Indued with various forms, various degrees
> Of substance, and in things that live, of life;
> But more refined, more spiritous, and pure,
> As nearer to him placed or nearer tending
> Each in their several active spheres assigned,
> Till body up to spirit work, in bounds
> Proportioned to each kind. (5.469-79)

In his attempt to accommodate Adam's and our limited understanding, Raphael uses ambiguous vocabulary open to, indeed inviting, misinterpretation. It would be easy to infer that spirit and body are different in 'kind' and separated into clearly articulated spheres. They are not. Creatures are 'various' in the sense of 'different from one another, of different sorts or kinds' (OED III.8), but more importantly, they are various in the sense of 'variable, changeful' (OED I.1). The essential unity underlying their differences is seen in their potential to rise to the state of creatures above them. Our current sphere is an 'active' one, a place from which to rise through proper action. The pun in 'bounds', a Miltonic favourite (consider how Satan 'at one slight bound over leaped all bound',

4.181), continues the temptation to misinterpret even as it associates evolutionary ascent with epic action. These are boundaries delineating spheres, but they are also the boundary-crossing springs by which we can from 'body up to spirit work'. The spheres are 'several' in that they are marked off one from another, but to assume that they are divided in any rigid or quantifiable way is to make the mistake of Satan, who thought 'one step higher / Would set me highest'.

The angel's hearty consumption of earthly food while lecturing on monism and his amusing efficiency in expelling the waste products ('what redounds, transpires / Through Spirits with ease', 5.438-9) emphasize the continuity between degrees on the scale of being. What most clearly distinguishes angelic from human bodies is the complete homogeneity of the former, what Milton calls their 'uncompounded' nature (1.425). In the *Aeneid*'s climactic combat Turnus' sword shatters into shining fragments ('resplendent fragmina', *Aen.*, 12.741) on the god-wrought armour of Vulcan, and this fragmentation is echoed in Turnus' subsequent mad dashing 'now here now there turning wavering circles' ('nunc huc, inde huc incertos implicat orbis', *Aen.*, 12.743) over the plain. When Milton rearranges the scene in heaven, Michael's sword 'from the armoury of God' (6.321) slices through Satan's and continues on through his right side, so that Satan 'writhed him to and fro convolved' (6.328). The angelic body here experiences the first breakdown of its homogeneous unity, epic's to-and-fro motion finds its originary moment, and Satan's involuntary writhing continues the Miltonic project of internalizing epic structures. Satan's quick healing leads to an explanation that highlights the difference between heavenly warriors and human heroes, who understandably fear the fragmentation of the integral self:

> . . . Spirits that live throughout
> Vital in every part, not as frail man
> In entrails, heart or head, liver or reins,
> Cannot but by annihilating die;
> Nor in their liquid texture mortal wound
> Receive, no more than can fluid air:
> All heart they live, all head, all eye, all ear,
> All intellect, all sense, and as they please,
> They limb themselves, and color, shape or size
> Assume, as likes them best, condense or rare. (6.344-53)

Milton's uncompounded angelic body is one more remarkable synthesis in a poem suffused with remarkable syntheses. Galenic humoural physiology envisioned a body composed largely of fluids convertible one into another, and we might see here the idea carried to its logical conclusion. Seventeenth-century atomisms' conception of extremely fine particles as 'spiritous', as in the work of Robert Boyle, whose nephew Milton taught, undoubtedly played a role. Equally important is the Platonic notion that, as Milton puts it in *On Christian Doctrine*, 'the soul be equally diffused throughout any given whole, and throughout every part of that whole' (XV.47). Raphael's 'spirits that live throughout / Vital in every part' meaningfully confuses the life-giving 'all in all' soul and the Galenic 'vital spirit' believed to inhabit the heart and travel through the arteries, even as the rest of the passage denies the model's validity for the angels. Out of such materials Milton has created a body removed from the dangers that occasioned the epic genre's preoccupation with the integral self. It is significant that immediately following this explanation we hear an echo of epic's foremost example of bodily mutilation when furious Moloch threatens Gabriel, and perhaps the Father himself, 'at his chariot wheels to drag him bound' (6.358).[21]

Although the war in heaven purports to be epic combat, it is so really only for the angels who have sinned. God's forces possess 'high advantages' (6.401), most notably their ability to remain 'unobnoxious to be pained / By wound, though from their place by violence moved' (6.404-5). Moloch's threat is an idle one, for their innocence provides the equivalent of Zeus' protection of Hector's body from the attempted mutilation by Achilles. Individually they remain free from self-division, and they effortlessly maintain one-out-of-many discipline. 'The inviolable saints', we observe after the first day of combat, 'in cubic phalanx firm advanced entire, / Invulnerable, impenetrably armed' (6.398-400), a feat far beyond even the disciplined Myrmidons. Satan's cohorts in contrast fall into self-division. They begin the next day's battle arrayed 'in hollow cube' that hides their newly invented artillery, and their artillery barrage results in 'angel on archangel rolled' (594), but even at this point the unfallen angels remain in 'serried files' (599) and their gigantomachic hill-throwing destroys the hollow phalanx.

What the fallen angels feel most insistently from the beginning of combat until we last hear of them is sheer physical pain. *Paradise Lost* should be recognized as its century's deepest meditation on the phenomenology of pain. Of the sixty times Milton uses the word in his English verse, only four occur outside the epic. 'Pain is perfect miserie, the worst of evils' (6.462), Nisroc concludes after the first combat, and his colleagues' subsequent debate in hell reveals general agreement on the subject. Pain is so important as a primary symptom of sin that, as we have seen, Satan experiences it first twice. Suffering has of course always been a focus of epic. The topos of *agere et pati*, of doing and suffering, begins with Homer's two very different heroes. As Castiglione's Ottaviano conventionally observes, Homer 'fashioned two most excellent personages for example of mans life, the one in practices, which was Achilles, the other in passions and sufferances, which was Ulysses'.[22] This opposition would naturally appeal to

Milton, who sought to carry epic conventions to their logical conclusions and to elevate 'the better fortitude / Of Patience and Heroic Martyrdom' (9.31-2) over 'the wrath / Of stern Achilles' (9.14-15). But in their fall from the extreme of corporeal perfection to its opposite Milton's rebel angels elevate the epic discourse of suffering to a new level. Ellen Scarry's study of modern torture, *The Body in Pain*, helps to explain Milton's unprecedented insistence upon physical torment. 'Pain', she writes, 'is a pure physical experience of negation, an immediate sensory rendering of "against."... Even though it occurs within oneself, it is at once identified as "not oneself," "not me," something so alien it must be gotten rid of, something at once internal and external'.[23]

Experiencing this new and intense self-division and self-animosity leads the devils to frame their discussions in terms resembling those of such modern phenomenologists as Maurice Merleau-Ponty and Paul Ricoeur, who insist on the primacy of the body in all action and conceptualization. Ricouer's analysis of the developmental dialectic between the voluntary and involuntary as the body acts and is acted upon is especially helpful in understanding Milton's reworking of epic conventions. Confronting irresistible involuntary forces, the developing self can choose between excessive cherishing or abandoning of consciousness. 'On the one hand, Stoicism will represent the pole of detachment and scorn, on the other hand Orphism the loss of the self in necessity'.[24] Fierce Moloch might resent the label, but he initiates the debate in hell with Ricoeur's Orphic solution, yielding to the necessity of futile, self-destructive conflict. At worst, or perhaps at best, attacking God directly will 'incense his utmost ire' and 'we should be quite abolished and expire' (2.94-6). Moloch's delusion is evident in the way his heroic pose of self-assertion coincides with a clear desire for self-extinction. He even turns the difficulty of a route that 'seems difficult and steep to scale' (2.71) into physical necessity: 'in our proper motion we ascend / Up to our native seat: descent and fall / To us is adverse' (75-7). The cavalier Belial, who would perhaps appreciate the irony of being labelled Stoic while counselling 'ignoble ease, and peaceful sloth' (2.227), prefers withdrawal to preserve his cherished subjectivity:

> To be no more; sad cure; for who would lose,
> Though full of pain, this intellectual being,
> Those thoughts that wander through eternity,
> To perish rather, swallowed up and lost
> In the wide womb of uncreated night,
> Devoid of sense and motion. (2.146-51)

Recognizing the need for both 'labour and endurance' (2.262), Mammon proposes a wiser middle course of 'hard liberty' (2.256) between detachment and abandon, a devil's version of what Ricoeur calls the 'way of consent' to the human condition as inevitably both subject and object.

The foremost paradox of sin in the poem lies in the fact that it is a voluntary act that immediately reduces the scope of voluntary action. The birth of Sin is a forceful demonstration of the paradox, as free choice issues immediately in painful, unwilled self-division, a process continued as Sin hourly suffers her self-begotten depredations. Satan's first assertive motion, his initial rise from the burning lake only through 'the will / And high permission of all-ruling heaven' (2.211-12), is carefully framed to demonstrate that his autonomy is illusory. The poem's most concentrated play on this paradox occurs in the elaborately blurred agency of the expulsion from heaven. As the Son rolls toward his foes in the fierce chariot, 'they astonished all resistance lost, / All courage; down their idle weapons dropt' (6.838-9). 'Dropt' is here ambiguously transitive and intransitive; the fallen angels' bodies are reduced to the level of their inanimate weapons. 'O'er shields and helms, and helmed heads he rode / Of thrones and mighty seraphim prostrate' (6.840-1), but the Son, transcending the crude combat of epic, has not physically knocked them down. He has weakened them within with 'pernicious fire' 'that withered all their strength, / And of their wonted vigour left them drained, / Exhausted, spiritless, afflicted, fallen' (6.849-52). The last term reminds us that their defeat is self-afflicted through the choice of sin. The Son's observed direct action is actually restorative: overgoing the imperial *parcere subjectis*, 'the overthrown he raised' (6.856). In a final irony, this restoration allows the scene to conclude with a cruel parody of free choice and voluntary action. The walls of heaven have rolled inward,

> . . . and a spacious gap disclosed
> Into the wasteful deep; the monstrous sight
> Strook them with horror backward, but far worse
> Urged them behind; headlong themselves they threw
> Down from the verge of heaven. (6.861-5)

The carefully chosen 'strook' and 'urged' and the ambiguous location of 'sight' in the perceived object and the perceiving subject keep in play the distinctions between physical and moral force and voluntary and involuntary action. In the poem's series of five 'headlong' passages, four of which recount the Fall from the infernal viewpoint (1.45 and 750, 2.374 and 772), only now does Vergil's self-destructive *praeceps* hero find representation. The devils were not hurled and sent and driven headlong over the crystal battlements. Instead, they threw themselves toward the monstrous sight that they are becoming, that is being 'disclosed' to them and us. The density and ironic manipulation of chronotopic language here reveals the extent to which Milton has found the problem of agency to lie at the heart of the epic genre. In his revised epic, which intensifies and re-emphasizes features already present in his predecessors, real defeat occurs not through the superior strength of an adversary, but through sin, the choice by which the headlong of spirit throw themselves out of the citadel.

From the Many to the One: Discursive and Intuitive Reason

How does one avoid this fate? The answer lies in overcoming the partial vision figured in Satan's failure to see that one step higher could never allow him to surpass a deity high above all height. Milton develops the kind of heroic pondering needed for such a reconciliation of the one and the many through Raphael's distinction between angelic and human forms of reason: 'Discursive, or intuitive; discourse / Is oftest yours, the latter most is ours, / Differing but in degree, of kind the same' (5.488-90). Although the importance of Raphael's attenuated opposition has long been acknowledged, discussions of intuition and discourse in *Paradise Lost* are invariably brief and incidental. Editors duly note the 'traditional' nature of the opposition and cite precedents in Platonic and Christian thought. Occasionally a critic will point to a significant function of the opposition in the poem. Dennis Burden, for example, observes that human intuitive limitations are what allow the whole angelic discourse in the middle books to proceed.[25] Isabel MacCaffrey lays still greater weight on the opposition. Linking one of Raphael's terms to the divine viewpoint, she observes that Milton spatializes the temporality of his poem:

> Milton by a powerful releasing act of the imagination transposed the intuitive single glance of God into the poem's mythical structure. Our vision of history becomes, for the time being, that of the Creator 'whose eye Views all things at one view' (ii.189-90); like him, we are stationed on a 'prospect high Wherin past, present, future he beholds' (iii.77-78).[26]

MacCaffrey's remarks are illuminating as far as they go, but her own view then moves quickly away from Raphael's terms toward the larger structures Milton's own synoptic vision has created.

Despite the abundance of commentary Raphael's speech has occasioned, it appears to have gone unremarked that 'discursive' and 'intuitive' are Miltonic nonce-words. The noun 'discourse' appears frequently in the poetry and prose, unproblematically connoting such related ideas as reasoning, discussion, utterance (OED 2-6), what both seventeenth and twentieth-century readers would assume God means when he directs Raphael to 'such discourse bring on' with Adam 'as may advise him of his happy state' (5.233-4).[27] But discourse etymologically refers to a running to and fro, and Raphael highlights the spatio-temporal dis-cursiveness of discourse by opposing it to 'intuitive' reason, etymologically a word meaning gazing at or apprehending through vision. Milton used a version of this second term only one other time. At age twenty in the Latin 'Elegia

Quinta', he describes a 'sacred ecstasy' in which he sheds his body and ascends above the clouds: 'My spirit surveys all ('intuiturque animus toto') that is done on Olympus and the unseen infernal world is not impervious to my eyes' (I.194). Decades later, seeking a way to develop Vergilian 'cuncta videns' pondering, he returned to the idea of synoptic intuitive vision, this time making it an angelic attribute overtly opposed to earthbound discourse.

The distinction between intuitive and discursive cognition pervades and is identified with the writings of Thomas Aquinas and his followers (in epistemological matters, if not on many others) Duns Scotus and William of Ockham, who speculated extensively on the human, angelic, and divine cognitive orders, and on such questions as how human cognition would be altered in the afterlife.[28] It is, of course, true that much Reformation thought focused on the issue of humanity's knowledge of God and assumed that grace provided a direct and immediate apprehension of the divine that is unlike other, less immediate forms of knowing. Such concerns are especially central to Calvin, with whom Milton shares a wide range of views. Calvin's famous pronouncement in the *Institutes* that 'there is within the human mind, and indeed by natural instinct, an awareness of divinity' draws upon the language of perception ('sensus divinitatis') to suggest how like our sensation of physical objects is this immediate knowledge of God's presence, which registers with a directness that sets it in contrast to, for example, the ratiocinative knowledge or *notitia* of God's attributes derived from observing both microcosm and macrocosm, an activity that leads us back to their Source.[29] Ironically, however, because the Reformers were more interested in the factual certainty of directly revealed knowledge than its form or content (as Calvin observes, 'the knowledge of faith consists more in certainty than in comprehension'[30]), the intuitive-discursive opposition crucial to Milton's epic project is not systematically developed in such works as the *Institutes*, a situation which led this greatest of Reformation poets back to precisely those writers against whom Calvin and others defined their return to primitive Christian purity. In *Areopagitica* Milton declared Spenser 'a better teacher than Scotus or Aquinas' (IV.311), and he often heaped scorn upon Scholastic excesses. But as with Luther, Calvin and many learned Reformers, Milton's detailed familiarity with these authors is evident, his points of contention with them informed and selective, and there is no reason to assume that the strongly Scholastic pedigree of Raphael's distinction compromises the angel's analysis.

The Thomistic model of human understanding includes three operations: (1) abstractive apprehension; (2) judgement or 'composition and division'; and (3) reasoning proper, a category that includes both demonstration or deduction by syllogism, which proceeds from the universal to the particular, and induction, which proceeds from the particular to the universal. The third operation is often labelled 'discursive reasoning' because, as Aquinas likes to point out, it involves running from one thing to another: we must proceed from one thing which we know to something else which we don't.[31] Similarly, formal logic must move successively through its propositions to a conclusion. However, Aquinas insists that the imperfect human intellect requires time for each operation, and therefore each is, in an important sense, discursive or diachronic, as opposed to the synchronic beholding of intuition. Abstractive apprehension separates in several ways what exists together in reality. It grasps the substance of a thing separately from its accidents, the accidents of a thing separately from each other, and beings separately from their particular act of being. As Robert Schmidt paraphrases Aquinas, abstractive apprehension 'presents only partial views or aspects of the real thing which is known. . . . These views of the real, because they are many, must be obtained successively, one after the other; and thus the cognition of our human intellect falls under the vicissitudes of time'.[32] Because, according to Aquinas, many things cannot at the same time be known as many, judgement too is time-bound, for it must through successive comparisons construct an intelligible unity, a likeness or 'intelligible species' out of the separated data of abstractive apprehension.

Aquinas contrasts angelic understanding with human by arguing that all three of these operations are unnecessary in heaven. The first two derive from human inability to grasp the whole essence of a thing at once:

> If the intellect in apprehending the quiddity of the subject were at once to have knowledge of all that can be attributed to, or removed from, the subject, it would never understand by composing and dividing, but only by understanding the essence. Thus it is evident that for the self-same reason our intellect understands by discursion, and by composing and dividing, namely, that in the first apprehension of anything newly apprehended it cannot at once grasp all that is virtually contained in it.[33]

> Similarly in the realm of reasoning proper, humans obtain their perfection by advancing from one thing known to another. But if from the knowledge of a known principle they were straightway to perceive as known all its consequent conclusions, then there would be no place for discursiveness in human intellect. Such is the condition of the angels, because in the truths which they know naturally, they at once behold all things whatsoever that can be known in them.[34]

In this way the angels approach their maker's apprehension 'per simplicem intuitum': 'in God, there is a right judgment of truth, without any discursive process, by simple intuition'.[35] Aquinas is also careful to note that

angels 'can syllogize' and 'know composition and division', but they gain
no knowledge from these activities.[36] It remained for Duns Scotus to insist that angelic intellects do not differ in kind from our own, just as he
also anticipated and probably influenced Milton's universe composed of
homogeneous first matter, but Aquinas' remarks are sufficient to help us
understand why discourse is not exclusively but oftest ours, intuition not
exclusively but mostly the angels'.[37]

Christian epic is Milton's great oxymoron.[38] The Olympian deities of
Homer and Vergil make their entrances without subverting their poems'
assumptions of accessible representation. The omnipotent, omnipresent,
utterly intuitive God of *Paradise Lost* is something else entirely, and his author makes sure that we keep in mind the inadequacy of epic conventions
and our own discursive reason to comprehend him. *Paradise Lost* turns
Vergil's dramatic irony on its head by stressing the discrepancy between
our discursive powers and the Creator's perspective. This discrepancy occasions an especially dense texture of paradox in Book 3, which introduces
Father and Son amidst a developing problem of relating part and whole:

> Hail holy Light, offspring of heav'n first-born,
> Or of the eternal co-eternal beam
> May I express thee unblamed? since God is light
> And never but in unapproached light
> Dwelt from eternity, dwelt then in thee,
> Bright effluence of bright essence increate. (3.1-6)

'Or' may imply contrasting alternatives, a hesitation between the Arian
view that the Son is begotten in time and the Trinitarian view that he is
co-eternal with the Father.[39] 'Or' may also introduce additional formula-
tions more or less equivalent to the first: the Son, and / or the initial light
of creation may be first-born and eternal in the sense of infinite in future
duration (OED 3), an idea more appropriate for a directional 'beam'.
Shifting from temporal into spatial terms with the repeated 'in' of 4-5
seems to help, but only until we encounter 'increate', which carries potential spatial (within-created) and temporal (not created, and therefore
co-eternal) meanings. We might say that the answer to the poet's question
is doubly negative. Neither addresser nor addressee can remain unblamed
if the former can express the latter only in such logic-defying terms. The
'since-then' formula of what follows highlights the difficulties of applying
abstractive discourse to a reality available only through intuitive contemplation, as the part-whole problem concerning how the divine referents
are related finds reflection in the problem concerning how logical propositions are related to a larger truth.

This foregrounding of part-whole problems continues when the poet,
after an autobiographical passage to which we will return, inserts this in-
describable being into the action. God enters imitating the Jupiter of

Aeneid 1.223ff., whose synoptic vision allows him, immediately before Aeneas' first pondering scene, to announce the Roman *imperium sine fine*:

> Now had the almighty Father from above,
> From the pure empyrean where he sits
> High throned above all highth, bent down his eye,
> His own works and their works at once to view. (3.56-9)

Resplendent on his throne of glory, the Father is a presence who registers with great visual power but without making himself available for visual scrutiny. We catch glimpses of him in fragments, as if Milton wishes to recall and perhaps satirize the fragmentation inherent in human abstractive apprehension. Here it is the eye of God that particularizes within the cloud-obscured Shekinah. Later 'God's own ear' (5.626) will hear the harmony of the angels' celestial dance, whose movements are 'eccentric, intervolved, yet regular / Then most, when most irregular they seem' (623-4). Our fragmented perception contrasts starkly in both instances with God's intuitive grasp of a pattern beyond our ken. More surprisingly perhaps, the Creator's nostrils will break into visualizable representation in 9.196 as he inhales what the 'earth's great altar' sends up in silent praise. In our first apprehension of this fragmented deity the brilliantly referentless 'their' calls attention to the part-whole problem of separating Creator from creatures, who are all a part of Him. 'At once' means 'both', for all works are in some sense the works of the omnipotent and omnipresent deity. The Father's location in space is also a paradoxical variant of the part-whole problem. As we have noted, 'above all highth' is another oxymoron, and through it the distinction of relative vertical position that we need to understand God's gaze 'from above' and 'down' is denied and asserted at the same time. Temporally, 'Now had bent' manages to locate a point in the narrative sequence where the action seems to occur and to indicate that at this point the action has already occurred in the past. The long separation of auxiliary from main verb might at first obscure the problem, but on consideration reflects and confirms it. In case we miss the point, the paragraph ends with an explicit explanation: 'Him God beholding from his prospect high, / Wherein past, present, future he beholds'. We are shown in these lines the temporal aspect of what it means to view his own works and their works 'at once'. One should also notice that God does not behold all time *from* his prospect, as we might naively suppose, but *in* it. God is not a part that can be separated off from the whole, but is always the whole itself. 'About him all the sanctities of heaven / Stood thick as stars, and from his sight received / Beatitude past utterance' (60-2), the passage continues. Past utterance indeed! God's omnipresence within his creatures manifests both meanings of 'from his sight', from his looking at them and their looking at him, which from his incomprehensible perspective can amount to the same thing. Such is the divine parody of the fallen angels' subjective and objective 'monstrous sight'.

This dense presentation of God's unrepresentable nature transcending the space-time distinctions of discursive reason highlights the necessary unreality of the ploddingly sequential descriptions that follow. 'On earth he first beheld / Our two first parents' (64-5), and 'he then surveyed / Hell and the Gulf between' (69-70). The basic epic instinct to portray causality using diachronic sequences here jostles uneasily with the poem's various reminders that divine action is instantaneous. Next comes the infamous dialogue with the Son, which recalls and imitates most problematically Jupiter's dialogue with Venus, who is seeking permission to aid her demigod offspring. While the absence of an anthropomorphic parental bond enhances the Son's status as a universally benevolent god of love, contact with the Vergilian scene makes the Father's surprisingly defensive abjuration of responsibility more troublesome. If Jupiter's foresight is not simply a matter of knowledge, if the 'fates' blend suspiciously with what he said ('fata'), how are we to accept the Omnipotent's anticipatory dismissal of any potential excuses, 'as if predestination over ruled / Thir will, disposed by absolute decree / Or high foreknowledge' (3.114-16). The divine argument can be accepted by definition or on faith, but when a future-tense prophecy of human transgression culminates in name-calling — 'ingrate, he had of mee / All he could have' (3.96-7) — only an indifferent or inattentive reader can remain unprovoked. The Father responds to the Son's yea-saying response with 'All has thou spoken as my thoughts are' (171), a present-tense admission that should prompt further reflection on the conspicuous artificiality inherent in presenting two persons of the deity transforming what should be a much faster form of data transfer into the epic convention of drawn-out debate. After Milton has foregrounded so emphatically the difficulties of representing heavenly realities, we have no excuses if we later take as literal the even more absurd war in heaven as told to Adam by an angel who repeatedly professes his inability to get it right.

What is unique about *Paradise Lost* is the extent to which it sustains such powerful impressions of both regularity and irregularity. On the one hand, the announced impossibility of its theodicy ('can I express thee unblamed?') finds ample confirmation in the difficulties of representing God to support a reading like William Empson's in *Milton's God*, which describes a nefarious deity whose lies and schemes are redeemed only by the fact that He does it all for His Son. On the other hand, the poem also amply supports a reading like Dennis Burden's in *The Logical Epic*, which in its argument for the poem's logical consistency within Christian orthodoxy discursively confirms God's intuitive vision of regularity beneath apparent irregularity. The ultimate effect of Milton's unparalleled balancing act, and of his summation and founding of epic dialogism, is to force us fully to experience our fallen immersion in the vicissitudes of time and our partial vision of what we can only glimpse as a larger whole. We might say then that Raphael's crucial distinction between types of reason informs both the heavenly Author's plan for humanity and Milton's plan for his readers. In the early treatise *Of Education* Milton declared that 'the end of learning is to repair the ruins of our first parents by regaining to know God aright' (IV.277). By recognizing and labouring to remedy our partial view we begin this process of education and renew participation in the dynamic sublimation to which creatures in the epic aspire.

The paradoxes surrounding the deity are a crucial part of this educational process. They both obscure him, reminding us of our humble position, and reveal him as a presence available only through a kind of intuitive apprehension beyond our discursive faculty. To register the fertile ambiguities of such expressions as 'increate' and 'wherein beheld' is to intuit something of this presence. Milton's resources for pushing us toward intuitive apprehension are many. They include the rich lode of apparent illogicalities to which readers have long objected. Consider only one of the many 'errors' the hopelessly discursive Richard Bentley attributed to sloppy editing, whim, or the poet's blindness:

> His countenance, as the morning star that guides
> The starry flock, allured them, and with lies
> Drew after him the third part of heaven's host. (5.708-10)

Fowler notes that 'Bentley questioned the propriety of Satan's countenance telling lies' and offers a justification: 'But the point lies in the allusion to Rev. xxii 16, where Christ is the true morning star: 'the bright face of 'Lucifer, son of the morning' (Is. xiv 12) is itself a mendacious impersonation'.[40] Fowler's explanation is, as always, to the point. To it we should add that the passage furthers the elaborate interpenetration in Book 5 of beginnings and ends, of Genesis and Revelation, a merger which imitates God's trans-temporal vision. The suggestive discursiveness of 'lies' meaningfully interacts with the angel's 'countenance', for the poem, as we shall see, closely associates the face with intuitive vision. Immediately following the passage we are invited to read another countenance as it tells a kind of lie:

> And smiling to his only Son thus said,
> Son, thou in whom my glory I behold
> In full resplendence, heir of all my might,
> Nearly it now concerns us to be sure
> Of our omnipotence, and with what arms
> We mean to hold what anciently we claim

Of deity or empire, such a foe
Is rising, who intends to erect his throne
Equal to ours, throughout the spacious north;
Nor so content, hath in his thought to try
In battle, what our power is, or our right.
Let us advise, and to this hazard draw
With speed what force is left, and all employ
In our defence, lest unawares we lose
This our high place, our sanctuary, our hill. (5.718-32)

To which the Son replies, 'Mighty Father, thou thy foes / Justly hast in derision' (735-6), providing us with a privileged moment of (relative) interpretive certainty: the Father's tone, we understand in retrospect, is sarcastic. But even after we are forced to revise our reading of God's smile, the precise tonality is obscured by the fact that Milton is combining various types of epic expression. In Homer gods smile to each other out of affection, as when Hera smiles at Hephaestos' concern in *Iliad* 1.595, but smiling can also be a harsher expression of 'conscious superiority and feelings of victory', as Zeus smiles at his intimidated wife in *Iliad* 15.47 and Ajax smiles gruesomely while approaching Hector, terrifying the Trojans and encouraging the Greeks with his Gorgonian expression.[41] Jupiter's smiling ('olli subridens', with the *sub-* prefix suggesting smiling down) at his chastened spouse in *Aeneid* 12.829 combines both forms, signifying both his victory over Juno and the sympathy embodied in his concession to assimilate the Trojans into the Latin nation. The aggressive aspect of this smile is strengthened by the application of the 'subridens' formula to Turnus as he confidently attacks the Trojans inside their camp (9.740) and, in an even bolder association, to god-scorning Mezentius as he plants his foot on a fallen foe (10.742). The only other use of the formula links Jupiter's closing smile in one of the poem's longest ring compositions to his smile upon his daughter 'with that look by which he clears the sky and storms' ('olli subridens . . . voltu, quo caelum tempestatesque serenat', 1.254-5). Jupiter is here revealing his control over the Aeneadae's fate, and his confident prediction of Roman *imperium* closely, and as we have seen troublesomely, prefigures the Miltonic Father's trans-temporal view. The smile at the opening of Vergil's epic is thus already provocatively complex, and Milton's allusion further complicates rather than clarifies. It reminds us that we cannot confidently read God's face, but it also encourages us to aspire to this quintessential intuitive act.

In the most poignant autobiographical passage of *Paradise Lost* the blind poet laments what he has lost:

. . . Thus with the year
Seasons return, but not to me returns
Day, or the sweet approach of even or morn,

> Or sight of vernal bloom, or summer's rose,
> Or flocks, or herds, or human face divine. (3.41-4)

The sequence of pleasures denied moves from the sheer fact of daylight, to specific sights of natural beauty and pastoral joy, to a climactic image conspicuously framed with modifiers linking the human and divine realms. We should not assume that the poet is simply regretting the lost pleasures of Petrarchan contemplation, for the linkage of the human and divine through the face has a long history. The Hebrew Bible associates the face of God with the fulfilling sense of divine presence, which He can turn away when displeased. Patristic writers interpret Biblical references to God's face as figures of providential oversight, and identify it as well with Christ and the Holy Spirit.[42] Calvin believes that we can contemplate the divine countenance directly, perceiving the divine presence with the immediacy of sense perception.[43] Milton yokes such ideas to the expressive epic body.

The epic's action begins in hell with a series of expressive faces, as Satan 'with head uplift above the wave, and eyes / That sparkling blazed' (1.193-4) addresses Beelzebub, now a monstrous sight almost beyond recognition. Satan's rise imitates that of Vergil's Neptune, who 'raised his serene head above the wave' ('summa placidum caput extulit unda', *Aen.*, 1.127), but the comparison highlights the two figures' opposed functions. The procession of devils who arise from the burning lake is also an exchange of communicating glances between the defeated leader and troops, a development of the type of scene where Aeneas represses his cares and 'feigns hope on his face' ('spem voltu simulat', 1.209) to preserve morale:

> All these and more came flocking; but with looks
> Down cast and damp, yet such wherein appeared
> Obscure some glimpse of joy, to have found their chief
> Not in despair, to have found themselves not lost
> In loss itself; which on his countenance cast
> Like doubtful hue. (1.522-7)

Ending the infernal debate over continuing the fallen angels' revolt, Beelzebub convinces as much through facial expression as through specious reasoning:

> . . . with grave
> Aspect he rose, and in his rising seemed
> A pillar of state; deep on his front engraven
> Deliberation sat and public care;
> And princely counsel in his face yet shone,
> Majestic though in ruin. (2.300-5)

The passage continues the allusion to the sea-calming of Neptune, which is compared to the calming effect of a mob's setting eyes upon a 'grave'

('gravem', 1.151) statesman honoured for service. Aeneas' positive deception adds to the effect of 'seemed' to remind us of the contrast between
Satan's initial, accurate reading of Beelzebub's disfigured countenance as a
sign of fallenness and the mob's reading of wise statesmanship, an indication that angelic intuition has not survived the fall from heaven intact.
Irony at the devils' expense intensifies as they attempt to apply the lower
mode of cognition. Aquinas' angels have no problem with sequential
logic; they simply don't need it for knowledge. Milton's fallen angels immediately and desperately lapse into discursive reasoning. At first they
seem relatively competent, for the debate in hell proceeds dialectically toward Mammon's reasonable advice to 'compose our present evils, with
regard / Of what we are and where' (2.281-3), a formula reflecting both
self-awareness and a reflex to 'compose' parts into a more coherent whole.
This sage counsel, which is greeted with thunderous applause, then confronts Beelzebub's deceptive countenance and the fact that Satan has been
ready with his own plan from the start (379ff.); not really designed to reason through, as Aquinas would put it, from things known to a thing
unknown — the best course of action — the debate has been a sham, a performance accommodated to its audience in Satanic parody of the highly
accommodated debate between Father and Son in heaven. One is not surprised to find this example of discursive futility followed by another:

> . . . In discourse more sweet
> (For eloquence the soul, song charms the sense,)
> Others sat apart on a hill retired,
> In thoughts more elevate, and reasoned high
> Of providence, foreknowledge, will, and fate,
> Fixed fate, free will, foreknowledge absolute,
> And found no end, in wandering mazes lost. (2.555-62)

It is precisely through their impaired intuition and the resulting reliance
on discursive reason, which is insufficient to grasp these crucial Miltonic
issues, that the devils' fate comes to resemble that of the wandering
Aeneadae.

Expressive countenances are no less important on earth, from our first
parents' entrance as Satan reads 'in their looks divine / The image of their
glorious maker' (4.291-2) to their final glance backward toward the garden's 'gate / With dreadful faces thronged and fiery arms' (12.643-4).
Facial expression occurs at a macrocosmic level as well. The devils inhabit
a landscape of bodily fragmentation, as befits a suburb of chaos. Heaven's
face appears there only in simile, and only as it is being obscured:

> Thus they their doubtful consultations dark
> Ended rejoicing in their matchless chief:
> As when from mountain tops the dusky clouds
> Ascending, while the north wind sleeps, o'erspread

Heaven's cheerful face, the louring element
Scowls o'er the darkened landscape snow, or shower. (2.486-91)

In paradise, in contrast, 'fair morning first smiles on the world' (5.124), and in heaven 'the face of brightest heaven' alternates between full resplendence and 'grateful twilight (for night comes not there / In darker veil)' (5.644-6). These expressions might simply be classified as poeticisms were they not part of an elaborate and systematic pattern of imagery tied to the discursive / intuitive opposition. The facial image and its expression of felicity are one of the principal means by which the poem signifies the assertion of cosmic order upon chaos. Satan's rebellion reduces heaven itself to chaos until the divine command restores order:

> At his command the uprooted hills retired
> Each to his place, they heard his voice and went
> Obsequious, heaven his wonted face renewed,
> And with fresh flowerets hill and valley smiled. (6.781-4)

In the creation of the world waters spread 'over all the face of earth' (7.278). The grass then clads 'her universal face with pleasant green' (316). Finally, with all her parts in place, 'earth in her rich attire / Consummate lovely smiled' (501-2).

This use of the face as a primary signifier of order reveals that if Milton in recasting epic pondering looks back in time for the scholastic distinction of intuitive and discursive cognition, he also looks forward to anticipate insights of various forms of modern psychology. Cognitive science in our time has produced a vast literature on the perception of faces, a subject that offers insight into both early childhood development and the perception of forms.[44] The maternal face is the first perceptual gestalt whereby the infant creates a whole out of parts and finds inscribed in that whole the expression of approval or disapproval. Lacanian psychoanalysis recognizes a related process in the mirror stage, when the infant recognizes that the parts of the heretofore fragmentary *corps morcelé* compose a unified body. Claudia M. Champagne develops a fine Lacanian reading of Adam's progress from bodily fragmentation through his visual perception of Eve as 'an image of the human form in its entirety', and others have noted the relevance of Lacanian ideas to Eve's mirror scene.[45] D. W. Winnicott observes that 'in individual emotional development the precursor of the mirror is the mother's face'.[46] Adam's development proceeds in plodding sequence, from fragmentation, to perceiving Eve 'in herself complete' (8.548), through the insecurity this perception entails (most notably in the separation scene), and eventually to an acceptance of the 'paradise within thee, happier far' (12.587). Eve, in contrast, true to the privileged position she holds in the poem through her association with intuition, in the answering looks of a human face divine immediately unites parts into a meaningful whole.

Adam and Eve are aligned according to the discursive / intuitive distinction from birth. In the awakening scene examined previously, Adam on rising views a succession of external objects, then turns to a successive 'limb by limb' survey of himself, and finally becomes a literal embodiment of 'discourse' by running about with lively vigour. Eve instinctively turns from movement to stasis. While Adam rejoices in the murmuring stream and the movement of animals, she prefers the pool's pure stillness and her own theophanic countenance communicating god-like presence in the perceived sky. In the perceptual equivalent of divine creation, she perceives a 'shape' within the watery gleam. The shape soon returns, like the maternal countenance to the infant's gaze, bearing answering looks of sympathy and love. Running counter to the negative implications that the scene undeniably creates and that dominate commentary is a more fundamental identification of Eve with the angelic mode of cognition. We should also note that both Adam and Eve are subsequently subjected to the cognitive modes that complement their primary identification. Adam is granted sight of the 'shape divine' (8.295), while Eve is warned by the divine Logos and led by this invisible presence from what she only retrospectively labels vain desire. Nevertheless, whether we read the coming-into-being scenes as representing nature or nurture, innate characteristics or conditioned response (and Milton typically has it both ways), our first parents maintain their earliest and most basic identification.

Much of Adam's long discourse with Raphael, like his later long discourse with Michael, takes place in Eve's absence. She departs at the beginning of Book 8 in order to hear the answer to Adam's question on astronomy later from her spouse. Such is the conjugal plot, but the scene continues the poem's argument about cognitive modes as well. She leaves because she reads Adam's face: 'So spoke our sire, and by his countenance seemed / Entering on studious thoughts abstruse, which Eve / Perceiving where she sat retired in sight' (8.39-41), rose to visit her flowers. Lest we misunderstand, and suppose her to lack Adam's facility, Milton adds a very Thomistic anticipation: 'Yet went she not, as not with such discourse / Delighted, or not capable her ear / Of what was high' (48-50). Adam later observes that 'wisdom in discourse with her / Looses discountenanced' (8.552-3). Milton's spelling here allows him to assign Eve victory (loses) over a competitor who like a Homeric hero soundly struck comes undone (looses) and loses the signifier of her ordered unity. The implications are again ambiguous, but Eve's association with heavenly cognition is maintained. Adam also declares to the angel that 'sweeter thy discourse is to my ear / Than fruits of palm-tree' (8.211-12), an observation strangely qualified when the narrator begins the next book dismissing Adam's rather futile discussion as 'venial discourse unblamed' (9.5). Does Eve share her author's superior indifference when she then prefers solitary labour to the more usual arrangement lest 'object new / Casual discourse draw on' (9.222-3)? Despite their prelapsarian innocence, 'casual' and 'venial' point proleptically toward a period of impaired cognition, and their association with Adam and his cognitive mode is compromising. Given such repeated indications that Eve is more advanced upon the scale of nature and more capable of an angelic form of cognition, if one accepts that the poem recounts a fortunate Fall into a 'paradise within' which is 'happier far' (12.587) than what preceded it (though it must be noted that the author leaves unanswered the implied question 'happier far than what?'), one might also begin to suspect that even before her final instructive dream Eve intuits the providential plan much more clearly than do her readers.

Murray Krieger writes of the critic's need to remain alert to the literary text's 'peculiar and paradoxical nature':

> it is an object that, as a verbal sequence, is experienced temporally; but, because it is a fixed and invariant sequence, it has formal characteristics that provoke him to claim to find spatial interrelationships within it. This is to define literary form as the imposition of spatial structures upon a temporal ground. But the critic cannot permit his own impositions of spatial structures to deceive him: the object and its structures are in movement and so are the structures of his consciousness, which interacts with it.[47]

Raphael's two types of reasoning are also the two ways we experience this text and all texts. To rephrase and amplify a claim made earlier in this chapter, a unique feature of *Paradise Lost* is the extent to which it manages to invite 'the imposition of spatial structures upon a temporal ground', to dramatize our inability to do so with confidence, and at the same time to incorporate these two processes into a rhetorical program. When we acknowledge that Milton portrays human progress as motivated by an aspiration to angelic intuition, we can see that every device problematizing or transcending the normal successive orders of language and narrative participates in his epic's programmatic didacticism. To merely list such devices would be to synthesize and summarize an unassimilable wealth of accumulated critical insight. Small-scale effects include, to cite as exemplary only one among so many others, the opening lines' layering of alternative discourses onto the surface syntax. David Daiches finds that alliteration in 'Of Man's First Disobedience, and the Fruit / Of that Forbidden Tree' (1.1-2) 'forces these words together: we think of "first fruit", then — "forbidden"; through acoustical means the echo of Leviticus 23 deepens our understanding of the primal scene'.[48] Every reader will have his or her own set of similar instances. On a larger scale, the apparently endless patterning that scholarship continues to unearth also serves to reorient the reader from a diachronic to a synchronic perspective and to provide evidence that beneath irregularity lies a regularity imitative and symbolic of the providential order. I would point only to

Gunnar Qvarnström's elaboration of the epic's Christocentric symmetries in *The Enchanted Palace*, and to the recovery of its precise and patterned chronology by Qvarnström and Fowler, intricately rendered shapes within the text's watery gleam that would astonish early readers, who believed Milton to be careless of such matters.[49] On the other hand, the notion that the reader repeatedly errs and then re-evaluates or is 'surprised by sin' has become, justifiably, perhaps the dominant shared assumption of Milton studies, and Raphael would surely claim that this too is part of the program. This process reminds us that every perceived critical Pandemonium rises tenuously 'like an exhalation' (1.711). Ever aspiring toward a sublime view we can never adequately attain, we find that we are inevitably like discursive Adam even as we strive to be like intuitive Eve.

Notes

1. Rudat (1979) and Martindale (1986), pp. 3-4. Martindale does not cite Rudat's article. Martindale uses this as an example of an allusion 'beyond dispute', in contrast to many others proposed by scholars who have 'something of a vested interest in exaggerating the learning of *Paradise Lost* and multiplying sources and allusions' (p. 1). His principal target is Francis Blessington's Paradise Lost *and the Classical Epic*, but he also finds Blessington's approach to allusion 'characteristic of much modern criticism'. My generic approach is compatible with Martindale's contention that Milton more often 'evokes a whole tradition as much as any particular passage or author' (p. 5), but I also believe it is difficult to exaggerate the learning of *Paradise Lost*. I also find Milton's allusions often to be more precise than does Martindale. He rejects, for example, Blessington's proposal that the 'great consult' of devils in Book 2 alludes to *Iliad* 2, claiming that it 'alludes to no one particular source within a rich tradition'. But does it not allude to a number of particular sources, including (and I think most significantly) the *Iliad*, as well as more generally to the epic tradition of assemblies? Citations of *Paradise Lost* are from the edition by Alastair Fowler (1981). All other citations of Milton's works are from the Columbia *Works* (1931-38) with volume and page numbers.
2. Rudat (1981).
3. Consider the use of 'undergo' in 1.155, 10.126, 10.575.
4. The Columbia edition index lists twenty-four specific references to Hercules in the prose works, to which one must add a number of more oblique and periphrastic instances.
5. For an able discussion of square and circle symbolism, see Heninger (1974), pp. 104-15. More specifically, Milton may be thinking here of the ending of the *Paradiso* (33.133-9), where the gazing Dante compares his inability to comprehend the divine image to the geometer's inability to square the circle. I wish to acknowledge that the spatiality of Milton's epic has received a great deal of attention. Of the many treatments of the vertical dimension, the most detailed remain Jackson Cope's chapter on 'Scenic Structure' (1962) and Hainsworth (1983) on 'Ups and Downs'. Most influential on horizontal aspects have been MacCaffrey (1959), pp. 188-206; Fish (1967), pp. 130-42; and Parker (1979), pp. 114-58. Michael Lieb (1981) offers illuminating chapters

on 'Place', 'Mount', and 'Presence' that bear on my theme. Jason Rosenblatt (1990) also writes insightfully on 'Milton's spiritual geography'.

6. On Aquinas' acceptance, and authorization for the later Middle Ages, of Aristotle's view that the north was the bottom of the world, see Freccero (1986, ch. 4). In his *Commentarium in Zachariam* (Book 3, ch. 14, cols. 1525-6), Jerome writes of the division of peoples 'some to the East and South, that is to the right: some to the North and West, that is, to the left' ('ut alii ad Orientem et Austrum, id est, ad dextram: alii ad Aquilonem et Occidentem, ad sinistram').

7. It is interesting to note that Milton's infinitely divisible continuum is contemporary with the development of mathematical calculus by Newton and Leibniz. Both mathematicians were seeking means to reconcile infinitesimal, infinite, and finite-quantifiable units. Satan's illusion that 'one step higher' would set him highest might be seen as a mathematical failure: as a result of his impaired intuition, he lacks the operations of integration that would reconcile God's position above all height to what from the Divinity's perspective is a set of infinitesimal steps.

8. Kathleen Swaim (1986, pp. 75-6) describes the poem's process of emanation and return precisely: 'The cosmic relationship of sun to elements below it is a two-way process; the sun gives and receives — gives of its own nature, receives those portions or emanations of lower natures that are most like itself. In plants these are the odorous spirits that bright consummate flowers breathe (481-82); in humans these are such gestures of praise as the morning hymn in Book 5'.

9. John Lightfoot, *De Creatione*, in *Works* (1822), vol. 3, p. 412. For another example of the standard formula, see vol. 7, p. 370. Swaim (1986, p. 74) observes a related pattern of directional conflict: 'It is especially significant that the hierarchy of Adam's pre-Raphaelean morning hymn moves from high to low. That pattern governs Adam's other pre-Raphaelean hierarchy of the psychological faculties also, the descending line of reason, fancy, the senses. The principle of hierarchic descent from heaven to earth is characteristic of Adam's untutored thought; it is inseparable from his consciousness of himself as humble and grateful dust. Raphael's hierarchies, however, move in the precisely opposite direction, from down to up, from root to flower and fruit, from vegetable spirits to angelic intuitive reason, from animal to angelic and even cosmic digestion, in general from earth to Heaven, not from Heaven to earth. The accumulation of Raphael's hieararchies argues an intention to reverse the direction of Adam's hierarchical awareness'. Perhaps Raphael's attempted reversal is incomplete, leaving Adam both confused and unaware of his confusion.

10. Addison, *Spectator* 321, (1721, vol. 3, p. 176). Natalie Davis (1978) locates this topos within the larger Renaissance fascination with 'The World Upside Down'. In this passage Milton allows Eve to redeem Lilith, in Jewish tradition Adam's first wife who insisted on equality and refused to lie with Adam in the missionary position. See Roslyn Jacks' chapter (1980) on Lilith for additional background. Note also Milton's avoidance of vertical positioning as the pair 'straight side by side were laid' (4.741). Rudat (1985) notes that Pope alludes to Milton's submissive Eve in 'The Rape of the Lock', reversing what Rudat sees as the proper Miltonic categories when Belinda 'insults' and 'subdues' her male foe. Martindale (1986, p. 89) at least acknowledges 'a curious

surrealism' in 'clouds that shed May flowers', but Leslie Moore (1990, p. 68) is the only modern critic I know of to find significance in the passage's spatial contradiction. Locating Adam within the sublime and Eve within the beauti- ful, she believes that 'given Addison's placement of Adam and Eve in different aesthetic realms, a mutual subordination is hardly possible, for the lines offer an image of submissive beauty smiled upon — and supported — by a superior aesthetic mode'.

11. C. A. Patrides (1982, pp. 83-9) discusses this etymology and outlines Renaissance ideas on the upright human stature.

12. Adelman (1978), p. 68.

13. See below for a discussion of the theology of the divine face.

14. As Purvis Boyette (1976) observes, Eve's Graces mark a very specific point of contact with Renaissance Neoplatonism as figures of emanation and return.

15. See, for example, Burden (1967), p. 130.

16. Hammill (1980) usefully surveys the relevant traditions of celestial ascent.

17. Dryden (1962), vol. 2, p. 165.

18. Wyatt (1981), pp. 208-9. Wyatt blends the original biblical contexts with the Petrarchist, but as the Petrarchan mistress shed her religiosity, a more strictly erotic-secular heart imagery flourished in the Elizabethan miscellanies, most notably in the *Paradise of Dainty Devices* of 1576. In contrast to Milton's si- multaneously vertical-biblical and horizontal-secular sense of the heart's hardening and softening, Spenser uses the imagery strictly in the latter way. Donne's reworking of biblical and Petrarchist heart imagery is most thorough in the *Holy Sonnets*. Among seventeenth-century poets George Herbert uses the omphalic heart most extensively, developing in *The Temple* a wide range of associations of the heart with sacred spatiality. Wyatt (e.g., in 'Go burning sighes unto the frozen heart'), Surrey, and other mid-century lyricists employ both the freezing-thawing heart and writing upon the heart in secular, erotic contexts. Again, seventeenth-century poets recover and develop the biblical context for both images, as, for example, in Herbert's 'The Altar'.

19. For a thorough and insightful history of the 'society of the marriage bed', see Turner (1987).

20. Turner (1987), p. 200.

21. For discussions of Milton's material-spiritual monism, see Fallon (1991) and Marjara (1992). On the all-in-all soul, see Waddington (1990).

22. Georgia Crampton (1974) exhaustively documents the *agere et pati* tradition. She cites the Castiglione passage, which comes from Hoby's 1561 translation.

23. Scarry (1985), p. 52.

24. Ricoeur (1966), p. 469.

25. Burden (1967), pp. 111-12

26. MacCaffrey (1959), p. 53.

27. I offer as corroboration of my inability to locate other occurrences of 'intu- ition' and 'discursive' the Columbia edition indexes and the concordances of Cooper (1923), Ingram and Swaim (1972), and Sterne and Kollmeier (1985).

28. Wide-ranging treatments of the subject in the Scholastics can be found in Day (1947), Klubertanz (1952) and Schmidt (1966). I quote Aquinas from the very literal translation of Anton Pegis (1945). Peter Fiore's balanced article on Aquinas in *A Milton Encyclopedia* (ed. Hunter, 1978-83) traces Milton's debt; his emphasis on Milton's acceptance of the Thomistic idea that 'the higher

form always contained within itself the functions of the lower form' is relevant to my argument. See also the encyclopedia articles by Willis Monie on 'Reason', and Donald Roberts on 'Philosophy, Milton's'. Curry (1966, pp. 167-71) argues convincingly for the influence of Duns Scotus on Milton's scale of nature.

29. Calvin 1.2.1. Calvin's *Institutes* is cited by book, chapter, and paragraph from the Battles translation (1960). Other works of Calvin are cited by volume and page from the Baum edition in my own translations. The studies by Dowey (1952) and Parker (1959) remain the standard treatments of this aspect of Calvin's thought.

30. Calvin (1960), 3.2.14

31. Cf. Schmidt (1966), p. 242.

32. Schmidt (1966), p. 208.

33. Aquinas (1945), vol. 1, p. 543.

34. Aquinas, vol. 1, p. 541.

35. Aquinas, vol. 2, p. 424.

36. Aquinas, vol. 1, pp. 542-3.

37. Duns Scotus modifies Aquinas' position on this issue in his *Opus Oxoniense* (II, d.1, q.5). See Day (1947), p. 84.

38. For the best development of the commonplace that Christian epic is oxymoronic for Milton, see Robert Crosman's *Reading* Paradise Lost (1980).

39. Fowler's edition, p. 142.

40. Fowler's edition, p. 302.

41. Levine (1983), p. 101. Levine surveys Homer's use of smiling and laughter and the considerable scholarship on the subject. More concerned with *lacrimae rerum*, Vergil has not stimulated equivalent interest. The Mezentius passage offers an ominous variation on the *olli subridens* formula: 'to this laughing amidst his wrath Mezentius:' 'ad quae subridens mixta Mezentius ira' (10.742). The scene closely parallels the interchange between dying Hector and triumphant Achilles in *Il.*, 22.365ff., but Achilles does not smile. There is also, of course, biblical precedent for a God who mocks his foes; cf. Empson (1961), p. 121. Grandsen (1967, p. 284) links *Aen.*, 12.829 and *PL.*, 5.718. Schaar (1982, pp. 139-41) adds Camoens, Marino, and Dante as 'infracontexts'.

42. Brockington (1950) discusses biblical uses of God's face. Prestige (1936, pp. 55-7 and 158-61) explores patristic developments. I have located no study treating later medieval and Renaissance usages or Milton's interest, though many studies touch in some way on the related but more general idea of the image of God.

43. Calvin's *Commentary on Deuteronomy*, 5.4, XXIV.211. See also *Institutes* I.i.2.

44. Vicki Bruce's 1991 collection, a special edition of *The European Journal of Cognitive Psychology*, contains extensive bibliography on the subject. Patricia Webbink's 1986 book contains an efficiently complementary bibliography of studies extending beyond the strictly scientific literature.

45. Champagne (1991), p. 54. Eve receives brief Lacanian treatment as well in Zimmerman (1981), Earl (1985), Shullenberger (1986), and Snider (1986). Is not Eve's 'swelling Breast' (4.495) as she leans over Adam immediately following her account of the mirror scene a suggestion of her maternal function?

46. Winnicott (1982), p. 111.

47. Krieger (1976), p. 39.

48. Daiches (1960), p. 56.

49. Qvarnström (1967), chapter 1 and Fowler's edition, pp. 25-8.

Bibliography

Each of the six poems considered in this study has stimulated such an enormous volume of scholarship that even listing indispensable secondary literature would expand a bibliography beyond practical limits. The following is merely a list of works cited.

Primary Sources

Apollonius Rhodius (1921), *Argonautica*, trans. R. C. Seaton, Loeb Classical Library, William Heinemann, London.

Aquinas, Thomas (1945), *Basic Writings of Thomas Aquinas*, trans. Anton C. Pegis, 2 vols., Random House, New York.

Ariosto, Ludovico (1971), *Orlando Furioso*, ed. Lanfranco Caretti, Einaudi, Turin.

—— (1974), *Orlando Furioso*, trans. Guido Waldman, Oxford University Press, Oxford.

Aristotle (1986), *De Anima*, trans. Hugh Lawson-Tancred, Penguin, Harmondsworth.

—— (1939), *The Nicomachaean Ethics*, trans. H. Rackham, Loeb Classical Library, William Heinemann, London.

—— (1982), *The Poetics*, trans. W. Hamilton Frye, Loeb Classical Library, William Heinemann, London.

—— (1989), *Posterior Analytics*, trans. Hugh Tredennick, Loeb Classical Library, William Heinemann, London.

Arnobius of Sicca (1949), *The Case Against the Pagans*, trans. George E. McCracken, Newman Press, Westminster.

Boethius (1962), *The Consolation of Philosophy*, trans. H. F. Stewart, Loeb Classical Library, William Heinemann, London.

Boiardo, Matteo Maria (1963), *Orlando Innamorato*, ed. Aldo Scaglione, Classici UTET, Turin.

—— (1989), *Orlando Innamorato*, trans. Charles Stanley Ross, University of California Press, Berkeley.

Calvin, Jean (1863-1900), *Calvini opera quae supersunt omnia*, ed. G. Baum et al, 59 vols., Schwetschke, Brunsvigae.

—— (1960), *Institutes of the Christian Religion*, trans. Ford Lewis Battles, ed. John T. McNeill, Westminster Press, Philadelphia.

Cartari, Vincenzo (1979), *Imagini de i Dei degli Antichi*, reprint of the 1615 Padua ed., Garland, New York.

Castiglione, Baldassare (1966), *The Book of the Courtier*, trans. Sir Thomas Hoby, Dutton, London.

Chaucer, Geoffrey (1957), *The Works of Geoffrey Chaucer*, ed. F. N. Robinson, Houghton Mifflin, Boston.

Cicero (1975), *De Officiis*, trans. Walter Miller, Loeb Classical Library, William Heinemann, London.

—— (1958), *Speeches*, trans. Robert Gardner, 2 vols., Loeb Classical Library, William Heinemann, London.

Conti, Natale (Natalis Comes) (1976), *Mythologiae, sive explicationum fabularum libri decem*, reprint of the 1567 Venice ed., Garland, New York.

Dante Alighieri (1893), *Il Convito di Dante Alighieri e le Epistole*, G. Barbera, Florence.

Dante Alighieri (1970-75), *The Divine Comedy*, trans. Charles S. Singleton, 3 vols., Princeton University Press, Princeton.

Diodorus Siculus (1956-57), *Bibliotheca Historica*, trans. John Skelton, ed. F. M. Salter and H. L. R. Edwards, 2 vols., Early English Text Society, London.

Donne, John (1964), *The Divine Poems*, ed. Helen Gardner, Clarendon, Oxford.

Duns Scotus, John (1912), *Commentaria Oxoninensia ad IV libros magistri sententiarium*, ed. Mariano Fernandez Garcia, Ad Claras Aquas, S. Bonaventura.

Giraldi Cinthio (1968), *On Romances*, trans. Henry L. Snuggs, University of Kentucky Press, Lexington.

Homer (1917-19), *Opera: Odyssey*, vols. 3-4, ed. T. W. Allen, Oxford Classical Texts, Oxford.

—— (1920), *Opera: Iliad*, vols. 1-2, ed. D. B. Monro and T. W. Allen, Oxford Classical Texts, Oxford.

—— (1951), *The Iliad of Homer*, trans. Richmond Lattimore, University of Chicago Press, Chicago.

—— (1965), *The Odyssey of Homer*, trans. Richmond Lattimore, Harper and Row, New York.

Herbert, George (1964), *The Works of George Herbert*, ed. F. E. Hutchinson, Clarendon, Oxford.

Hooker, Richard (1925), *Of the Laws of Ecclesiastical Polity*, 2 vols., Dutton, New York.

Jerome (1884), *Commentarium in Zachariam*, Patrologia Latina, vol. 25, ed. J-P. Migne, Garnier, Paris.

Landino, Cristoforo (1980), *Disputationes Camaldulenses*, ed. Peter Lohe, Sansoni, Florence.

Langland, William (1978), *Piers Plowman by William Langland: an Edition of the C-Text*, ed. Derek Pearsall, University of California Press, Berkeley.

Lightfoot, John (1822), *Works*, John Rogers Pitman, London.

Livy (1967), *History*, trans. B. O. Foster, Loeb Classical Library, William Heinemann, London.

Milton, John (1931-40), *The Works of John Milton*, gen. ed. Frank Allen Patterson, 18 vols., Columbia University Press, New York.

—— (1953-82), *Complete Prose Works of John Milton*, gen. ed. Don M. Wolfe, 8 vols., Yale University Press, New Haven.

—— (1971), *Paradise Lost*, ed. Alastair Fowler, Longman, London.

Ovid (1916), *Metamorphoses*, trans. Frank J. Miller, 2 vols., Loeb Classical Library, William Heinemann, London.

—— (1931) *Fasti*, trans. J. G. Frazer, Loeb Classical Library, William Heinemann, London.

The Paradise of Dainty Devices, ed. Hyder Edward Rollins, Harvard University Press, Cambridge.

Peletier du Mans, Jacques (1930), *L'art poétique*, ed. Andre Boulanger, Société d'édition Les Belles Lettres, Paris.

Petrarca, Francesco (1926), *L'Africa: Edizione critica*, ed. Nicola Festa, Sansoni, Florence.

Plato, *The Collected Dialogues of Plato* (1961), eds. Edith Hamilton and Huntington Cairns, Princeton University Press, Princeton.

Pulci, Luigi (1939), *Morgante Maggiore*, ed. Franco Ageno, Mondadori, Milan.

Ronsard, Pierre de (1950), *Oeuvres complètes*, ed. Gustave Cohen, 2 vols., Gallimard, Paris.

Salutati, Coluccio (1951), *De laboribus Herculis*, ed. B. L. Ullman, 2 vols., Thesaurus Mundi, Turicia.

Seneca, Lucius Annaeus (1970), *Tragedies*, trans. Frank Justus Miller, 2 vols., Loeb Classical Library, William Heinemann, London.

Shakespeare, William (1974), *The Riverside Shakespeare*, ed. G. Blakemore Evans, Houghton Mifflin, Boston.

Sidney, Sir Philip (1977), *Arcadia*, ed. Maurice Evans, Penguin, Harmondsworth.

Smith, Gregory, ed. (1904), *Elizabethan Critical Essays*, Oxford University Press, Oxford.

Spenser, Edmund (1932-49), *The Works of Edmund Spenser: A Variorum Edition*, ed. Edwin Greenlaw et al., 9 vols., Johns Hopkins University Press, Baltimore.

—— (1977), *The Faerie Queene*, ed. A. C. Hamilton, Longman, London.

Swift, Jonathan (1967), *Gulliver's Travels*, Penguin, London.

Tasso, Torquato (1961), *Gerusalemme liberata*, ed. Bartolo Tommaso Sozzi, Feltrinelli, Milan.

—— (1973), *Discourses on the Heroic Poem*, trans. Mariella Cavalchini and Irene Samuel, Clarendon, Oxford.

Vergil (1969), *Opera*, ed. R. A. B. Mynors, Clarendon, Oxford.

Vida, Marco Girolamo (1978), *The Christiad*, eds. Gertrude C. Drake and Clarence Allen Forbes, Southern Illinois University Press, Carbondale.

Vitruvius (1970), *De architectura*, trans. F. Granger, 2 vols., Loeb Classical Library, William Heinemann, London.

Wyatt, Sir Thomas (1981), *The Complete Poems*, ed. R. A. Rebholz, Yale University Press, New Haven.

Secondary Sources

Addison, Joseph (1721), *Works*, 8 vols., Thomas Tickell, London.

Adelman, Janet (1978), 'Creation and the Place of the Poet in *Paradise Lost*', in Martz, Louis L. and Aubrey Williams (eds.), *The Author in His Work: Essays on a Problem in Criticism*, Yale University Press, New Haven.

Adkins, Arthur W. H. (1963), 'Friendship and Self-Sufficiency in Homer and Aristotle', *Classical Quarterly*, vol. 13, pp. 30-45.

Ajam, Laurent (1982), 'Le forêt dans l'oeuvre de Chrétien de Troyes', *Europe*, vol. 642, pp. 120-5.

Alpers, Paul J. (1967), *The Poetry of the* Faerie Queene, Princeton University Press, Princeton.

—— (1979), *The Singer of the Eclogues: A Study of Virgilian Pastoral*. University of California Press, Berkeley.

Anderson, Andrew Runni (1928), 'Heracles and His Successors', *Harvard Studies in Classical Philology*, vol. 39, pp. 7-58.

Anderson, Donald K. (1972), 'Donne's "Hymne to God my God, in my Sicknesse" and the T-in-O Maps', *South Atlantic Quarterly*, vol. 71, pp. 456-72.

Anderson, William S. (1971), 'Two Passages from Book XII of the *Aeneid*', *California Studies in Classical Antiquity*, vol. 4, pp. 49-65.

Aptekar, Jane (1969), *Icons of Justice: Iconography and Thematic Imagery in Book 5 of the* Faerie Queene, Columbia University Press, New York.

Arend, Walter (1933), *Die typischen Scenen bei Homer*, Weidemannsche Buchhandlung, Berlin.

Armstrong, James I. (1958), 'The Arming Motif in the *Iliad*', *American Journal of Philology*, vol. 79, pp. 337-54.

Ascoli, Albert R. (1987), *Ariosto's Bitter Harmony: Crisis and Evasion in the Italian Renaissance*, Princeton University Press, Princeton.

Auerbach, Erich (1953), *Mimesis: The Representation of Reality in Western Literature*, trans. Willard R. Trask, Princeton University Press, Princeton.

Austin, Norman (1975), *Archery at the Dark of the Moon: Poetic Problems in Homer's* Odyssey, University of California Press, Berkeley.

Bakhtin, Mikhail (1981), *The Dialogic Imagination*, trans. C. Emerson and ed. M. Holquist, University of Texas Press, Austin.

Baldassarri, Guido (1982), *Il Sonno di Zeus: Sperimentazione narrativa del poema rinascimentale e tradizione omerica*, Bulzone Editore, Rome.

Barkan, Leonard (1975), *Nature's Work of Art*, Yale University Press, New Haven.

Baybak, Michael, Paul Delany, and A. Kent Hieatt (1969), 'Placement "In the Middest" in *The Faerie Queene*', *Papers on Language and Literature*, vol. 5., pp. 227-34.

Beazley, C. Raymond (1906), *The Dawn of Modern Geography*, Oxford University Press, Oxford.

Benveniste, Emile (1973), *Indo-European Language and Society*, trans. Elizabeth Palmer, University of Miami Press, Coral Gables.

Berger, Harry, Jr. (1966), 'Spenser's *Faerie Queene*, Book I: Prelude to Interpretation', *Southern Review*, vol. 2, pp. 18-49.

Beye, Charles R. (1993), *Ancient Epic Poetry: Homer, Apollonius, Virgil*, Cornell University Press, Ithaca.

Blessington, Francis C. (1979), Paradise Lost *and the Classical Epic*, Routledge and Kegan Paul, London.

Bloomfield, Morton W. (1970), 'Episodic Motivation and Marvels in Epic and Romance', in *Essays and Explorations: Studies in Ideas, Language and Literature*, Harvard University Press, Cambridge, pp. 97-128.

Boyette, Purvis (1976), 'Milton's Eve and the Neoplatonic Graces', *Renaissance Quarterly*, vol. 20, pp. 341-4.

Bremmer, Jan N. (1983), *The Early Greek Concept of the Soul*, Princeton University Press, Princeton.

Brockington, L. H. (1950), 'Presence', in Richardson, Alan (ed.), *A Theological Word Book of the Bible*, Macmillan, New York.

Bruce, Vicki, ed. (1991), *Face Recognition*, Lawrence Erlbaum, London.

Brundage, James A. (1966), 'Cruce Signari: The Rite for Taking the Cross in England', *Traditio*, vol. 22, pp. 289-310.

Bruneau, Philipe (1970), *Recherches sur les cultes de Délos à l'époque hellenestique et à l'époque impériale*, Boccard, Paris.

Burden, Dennis H. (1967), *The Logical Epic: A Study of the Argument of* Paradise Lost, Harvard University Press, Cambridge.

Butterworth, Edric A. S. (1970), *The Tree at the Navel of the World*, Walter De Gruyter, Berlin.

Carne-Ross, D. S. (1966), 'The One and the Many: A Reading of the *Orlando Furioso*, Cantos 1 and 8', *Arion*, vol. 5, pp. 195-234.

Champagne, Claudia M. (1991), 'Adam and His Other Self in *Paradise Lost*: A Lacanian Study in Psychic Development', *Milton Quarterly*, vol. 25, pp. 48-59.

Cheney, Donald (1966), *Spenser's Image of Nature: Wild Man and Shepherd in the* Faerie Queene, Yale University Press, New Haven.

Clausen, Wendell (1987), *Vergil's* Aeneid *and the Tradition of Hellenistic Poetry*, University of California Press, Berkeley.

Colie, Rosalie (1966), *Paradoxia Epidemica: the Renaissance Tradition of Paradox*, Princeton University Press, Princeton.

—— (1973), *The Resources of Kind: Genre Theory in the Renaissance*, University of California Press, Berkeley.

Commager, Steele (1981), 'Fateful Words: Some Conversations in *Aeneid* 4', *Arethusa*, vol. 14, pp. 101-14.

Cooper, Lane (1923), *A Concordance of the Latin, Greek, and Italian Poems of John Milton*, Max Niemeyer, Halle.

Cope, Jackson (1962), *The Metaphoric Structure of* Paradise Lost, Johns Hopkins University Press, Baltimore.

Copley, Frank Olin (1956), *Exclusus Amator: A Study in Latin Love Poetry*. American Philological Association, Madison.

Craig, Martha (1967), 'The Secret Wit of Spenser's Language', in Alpers, Paul J., (ed.), *Elizabethan Poetry: Modern Essays in Criticism*, Oxford University Press, New York, pp. 447-72.

Crampton, Georgia (1974), *The Condition of Creatures: Suffering and Action in Chaucer and Spenser*, Yale University Press, New Haven.

Crosman, Robert (1980), *Reading* Paradise Lost, Indiana University Press, Bloomington.

Crotty, Kevin (1994), *The Poetics of Supplication: Homer's* Iliad *and* Odyssey, Cornell University Press, Ithaca.

Cuillandre, Joseph (1943), *La Droite et la gauche dans les poèmes homeriques en concordance avec la doctrine pythagoricienne et la tradition celtique*, Imprimeries Réunies, Rennes.

Cunliffe, Richard J. (1963), *Lexicon of the Homeric Dialect*, University of Oklahoma Press, Norman.

Curry, Walter Clyde (1966), *Milton's Ontology, Cosmogony, and Physics*, University of Kentucky Press, Lexington.

Daiches, David (1960), 'The Opening of *Paradise Lost*', in Kermode, Frank (ed.), *The Living Milton: Essays by Various Hands*, Routledge and Kegan Paul, London, pp. 55-69.

Davis, Natalie Zemon (1978), 'Women on Top: Sexual Inversion and Political Disorder in Early Modern Europe', in Babcock, Barbara A. (ed.), *The Reversible World: Symbolic Inversion in Art and Society*, Cornell University Press, Ithaca, pp. 147-90.

Day, Sebastian J. (1947), *Intuitive Cognition: A Key to the Significance of the Later Scholastics*, The Franciscan Institute, St. Bonaventure.

Detienne, Marcel and Jean-Pierre Vernant (1978), *Cunning Intelligence in Greek Culture and Society*, trans. Janet Lloyd, Humanities Press, Atlantic Highlands.

Di Cesare, Mario A. (1974), *The Altar and the City: A Reading of Vergil's Aeneid*, Columbia University Press, New York.

Dodds, E. R. (1951), *The Greeks and the Irrational*, University of California Press, Berkeley.

Donato, Eugenio (1972), '"Per Selve e Boscherecci Labirinti": Desire and Narrative Structure in Ariosto's *Orlando Furioso*', *Barocco*, vol. 4, pp. 17-34.

Doob, Penelope Reed (1990), *The Idea of the Labyrinth from Classical Antiquity through the Middle Ages*, Cornell University Press, Ithaca.

Doroszlaï, Alexandre (1991), 'Les sources cartographiques et le *Roland Furieux*: quelques hypothèses autour de l' "espace réel" chez l'Arioste', in Doroszlaï, et al (eds.), *Espaces réels et espaces imaginaires dans le* Roland Furieux, Université de la Sorbonne Nouvelle, Paris.

Dougherty, James (1980), *The Fivesquare City: The City in the Religious Imagination*, University of Notre Dame Press, Notre Dame.

Dowey, Edward A. (1952), *The Knowledge of God in Calvin's Theology*, Columbia University Press, New York.

Dronke, Peter (1981), 'Arbor Caritatis', in Heyworth, P. (ed.), *Medieval Studies for J. A. W. Bennett*, Clarendon, Oxford, pp. 207-53.

Dryden, John (1962), *Of Dramatic Poesy, and Other Critical Essays*, 2 vols., Dent, London.

Duckworth, George E. (1962), *Structural Patterns and Proportions in Vergil's Aeneid*, University of Michigan Press, Ann Arbor.

Durling, Robert M. (1965), *The Figure of the Poet in Renaissance Epic*, Harvard University Press, Cambridge.

DuRocher, Richard J. (1985), *Milton and Ovid*, Cornell University Press, Ithaca.

Earl, James W. (1985), 'Eve's Narcissism', *Milton Quarterly*, vol. 19, pp. 14-16.

Edgeworth, Robert J. (1986), 'The Ivory Gate and the Threshold of Apollo', *Classica et Mediaevalia*, vol. 37, pp. 145-60.

Eliade, Mircea (1959), *The Sacred and the Profane: The Nature of Religion*, trans. Willard R. Trask, Harcourt, Brace and World, New York.

—— (1988), *Symbolism, the Sacred, and the Arts*, ed. Diane Apostolos-Cappadona, Crossroad, New York.

Empson, William (1961), *Milton's God*, Revised ed., Chatto and Windus, London.

Eriksen, Roy (1991), 'God Enthroned: Expansion and Continuity in Ariosto, Tasso, and Milton', in Di Cesare, Mario A. (ed.), *Milton in Italy: Contexts, Images, Perspectives*, Medieval and Renaissance Texts and Studies, Binghamton, pp. 405-25.

Ernout, A. and A. Meillet (1967), *Dictionnaire etymologique de la langue Latine*, Klingsleck, Paris.

Fallon, Stephen M. (1991), *Milton Among the Philosophers: Poetry and Materialism in Seventeenth-Century England*, Johns Hopkins University Press, Baltimore.

Feeney, D. C. (1991), *The Gods in Epic*, Clarendon, Oxford.

Fenichel, Otto (1945), *The Psychoanalytic Theory of Neurosis*, Norton, New York.

Fichter, Andrew (1982), *Poets Historical: Dynastic Epic in the Renaissance*. Yale University Press, New Haven.

Fish, Stanley (1967), *Surprised by Sin: The Reader in* Paradise Lost, Macmillan, London.

Fletcher, Angus (1971), *The Prophetic Moment: An Essay on Spenser*, University of Chicago Press, Chicago.

Flori, Jean (1979), 'Les origines de l'adoubement chevaleresque', *Traditio*, vol. 35, pp. 209-72.

Fowler (1982), *Kinds of Literature: An Introduction to the Theory of Genres*, Harvard University Press, Cambridge.

Freccero, John (1986), *Dante: The Poetics of Conversion*, Harvard University Press, Cambridge.

Galinsky, G. Karl (1966), 'The Hercules-Cacus Episode in *Aeneid* VIII', *American Journal of Philology*, vol. 87, pp. 18-51.

—— (1972), *The Herakles Theme*, Rowman and Littlefield, Totowa.

Gardner, Edmund G. (1968), *The King of Court Poets: A Study of the Work, Life and Times of Lodovico Ariosto*, Greenwood Press, New York.

Gehring, August (1970), *Index Homericus*, Georg Olms Verlag, Hildesheim.

Goldberg, Jonathan (1981), *Endlesse Worke: Spenser and the Structures of Discourse*, Johns Hopkins University Press, Baltimore.

Gould, John (1973), '*HIKETEIA*', *Journal of Hellenic Studies*, vol. 93, pp. 74-103.

Grandsen, K. W. (1967), 'Paradise Lost *and the* Aeneid', *Essays in Criticism*, vol. 17, pp. 281-303.

—— (1973), 'Typology, Symbolism, and Allegory in the *Aeneid*', *Proceedings of the Virgil Society*, vol. 13, pp. 14-27.

Graves, Robert (1961), *The Greek Myths*, 2 vols., Penguin, Baltimore.

Green, Arthur (1977), 'The *Zaddiq* as *Axis Mundi* in Later Judaism', *Journal of the American Academy of Religion*, vol. 45, pp. 327-47.

Greene, Thomas M. (1963), *The Descent from Heaven: A Study in Epic Continuity*, Yale University Press, New Haven.

Greenhill, Eleanor Simmons (1954), 'The Child in the Tree: A Study of the Cosmological Tree in Christian Tradition', *Traditio*, vol. 10, pp. 323-71.

Griffin, Robert (1974), *Ludovico Ariosto*, Twayne, New York.

Hainsworth, J. D. (1983), 'Ups and Downs in *Paradise Lost*', *Essays in Criticism*, vol. 33, pp. 99-107.

Hainsworth, J. B. (1991), *The Idea of Epic*, University of California Press, Berkeley.

Halperin, David M. (1983), *Before Pastoral: Theocritus and the Ancient Tradition of Bucolic Poetry*, Yale University Press, New Haven.

Hammill, Carrie (1980), *The Celestial Journey and the Harmony of the Spheres in English Literature, 1300-1700*, Texas Christian University Press, Fort Worth.

Hanning, Robert W. (1977), *The Individual in Twelfth-Century Romance*, Yale University Press, New Haven.

Hardie, Philip (1983), 'Atlas and Axis', *Classical Quarterly*, vol. 33, pp. 220-8.

—— (1985), 'Imago Mundi: Cosmological and Ideological Aspects of the Shield of Achilles', *Journal of Hellenic Studies*, vol. 105, pp. 11-31.

—— (1986), *Virgil's Aeneid: Cosmos and Imperium*, Clarendon, Oxford.

—— (1993), *The Epic Successors of Virgil*, Cambridge University Press, Cambridge.

Heninger, S. K., Jr. (1974), *Touches of Sweet Harmony: Pythagorean Cosmology and Renaissance Poetics*, The Huntington Library, San Marino.

Hersey, George (1988), *The Lost Meaning of Classical Architecture*, MIT Press, Cambridge.

Hill, Thomas D. (1978), 'The Theme of the Cosmological Cross in Two Old English Cattle Charms', *Notes and Queries*, n.s. vol. 25, pp. 488-9.

Holm, Jean, and John Bowker, eds. (1994), *Sacred Place*, Pinter, London.

Hughes, Merritt (1953), 'The Arthurs of *The Faerie Queene*', *Etudes Anglaises*, vol. 6, pp. 193-213.

Hunter, William B., Jr., gen. ed., (1978-83), *A Milton Encyclopedia*, 9 vols., Bucknell University Press, Lewisburg.

Hurley, Margaret (1975), 'Saints' Legends and Romance Again: Secularization of Structure and Motif', *Genre*, vol. 8, pp. 60-73.

Ingram, William, and Kathleen Swaim, eds. (1972), *A Concordance to Milton's English Poetry*, Clarendon, Oxford.

Jacks, Roslyn (1980), *Women and Judaism: Myth, History, and Struggle*,

Doubleday, Garden City.

Jakobson, Roman (1978), 'The Dominant', in Matejka, Ladislav and Krystyna Pomorska (eds.), *Readings in Russian Poetics: Formalist and Structuralist Views*, University of Michigan Press, Ann Arbor, pp. 82-7.

Janko, Richard (1992), *The Iliad: A Commentary, Volume IV: Books 13-16*, Cambridge University Press, Cambridge.

Javitch, Daniel (1978), 'Rescuing Ovid from the Allegorizers', Comparative Literature, vol. 30, pp. 97-107.

—— (1980), '*Cantus Interruptus* in the *Orlando Furioso*', *Modern Language Notes*, vol. 95, pp. 66-80.

—— (1984), 'The *Orlando Furioso* and Ovid's Revision of the *Aeneid*', *Modern Language Notes*, vol. 99, pp. 1023-36.

—— (1988), 'Narrative Discontinuity in the *Orlando Furioso* and its Sixteenth Century Critics', *Modern Language Notes*, vol. 103, pp. 51-74.

—— (1991), *Proclaiming a Classic: The Canonization of* Orlando Furioso, Princeton University Press, Princeton.

Jung, Marc-René (1966), *Hercule dans la Littérature Française du XVIe Siècle*, Droz, Geneva.

Kates, Judith (1983), *Tasso and Milton: The Problem of Christian Epic*, Bucknell University Press, Lewisburg.

Kermode, Frank (1971), *Shakespeare, Spenser, Donne*, Routledge and Kegan Paul, London.

Kirk, G. S. (1974), *The Nature of Greek Myths*, Penguin, London.

—— (1985), *The Iliad: A Commentary, Volume I: Books 1-4*, Cambridge University Press, Cambridge.

Klubertanz, George P. (1952), *The Discursive Power*, The Modern Schoolman, St. Louis.

Knauer, Georg Nicolaus (1964), *Die Aeneis und Homer: Studien zur poetischen Technik Vergils mit Listen der Homerzitate in der Aeneis*, Vandenhoeck & Ruprecht, Gottingen.

Kohler, Erich (1956), *L'Aventure Chevaleresque*, Gallimard, Paris.

Krieger, Murray (1976), *Theory of Criticism: A Tradition and Its System*, Johns Hopkins University Press, Baltimore.

Lamberton, Robert (1986), *Homer the Theologian: Neoplatonist Allegorical Reading and the Growth of the Epic Tradition*, University of California Press, Berkeley.

Leclercq, Jean (1958), 'Le cloître est-il un paradis?', in Fumasoni-Biondi, Pietro (ed.), *Le message des moines à notre temps*, Fayard, Paris, pp. 141-59.

Levine, Daniel B. (1983), 'Homeric Laughter and the Unsmiling Suitors', *The Classical Journal*, vol. 78, pp. 97-104.

Lewalski, Barbara Kiefer (1979), *Protestant Poetics and the Seventeenth-Century Religious Lyric*, Princeton University Press, Princeton.

Lewis, C. S. (1958), *The Allegory of Love*, Macmillan, London.

Lieb, Michael (1981), *Poetics of the Holy: A Reading of* Paradise Lost, University of North Carolina Press, Chapel Hill.

Lloyd, G. E. R. (1966), *Polarity and Analogy: Two Types of Argumentation in Early Greek Thought*, Cambridge University Press, Cambridge.

Lloyd, Robert B. (1972), '*Superbus* in the *Aeneid*', *American Journal of Philology*, vol. 93, pp. 125-32.

Lyne, R. O. A. M. (1987), *Further Voices in Vergil's* Aeneid, Clarendon, Oxford.

MacCaffrey, Isabel G. (1959), Paradise Lost *as Myth*, Harvard University Press, Cambridge.

—— (1976), *Spenser's Allegory: The Anatomy of Imagination*, Princeton University Press, Princeton.

MacIntyre, Jean (1966), 'Spenser's Herculean Heroes', *Humanities Association Bulletin*, vol. 17, pp. 5-12.

Mack, Sarah (1978), *Patterns of Time in Vergil*, Archon, Hamden.

Marinelli, Peter V. (1987), *Ariosto and Boiardo: The Origins of* Orlando Furioso, University of Missouri Press, Columbia.

Marjara, Harinder Singh (1992), *Contemplation of Created Things: Science in* Paradise Lost, University of Toronto Press, Toronto.

Manuel, Frank (1965), *Shapes of Philosophical History*, Stanford University Press, Stanford.

Martindale, Charles (1986), *John Milton and the Transformation of Ancient Epic*, Routledge and Kegan Paul, London.

Martz, Louis L. (1980), *Poet of Exile: A Study of Milton's Poetry*, Yale University Press, New Haven.

McDannell, Colleen and Bernhard Lang (1988), *Heaven: A History*, Yale University Press, New Haven.

Menard, Philippe (1976), 'Le chevalier errant dans la littérature arthurienne: recherches sur les raisons du départ et de l'errance', in *Voyage, Quête, Pèlerinage dans la littérature et la civilisation médiévales*, CUER MA, Provence, pp. 313-22.

Miller, David Lee (1988), *The Poem's Two Bodies: The Poetics of the 1590* Faerie Queene, Princeton University Press, Princeton.

Miller, Jacqueline (1986), 'The Omission in Red Cross Knight's Story: Narrative Inconsistencies in the *Faerie Queene*', *ELH*, vol. 53, pp. 279-88.

Mills, Donald H. (1983), 'Sacred Space in Vergil's *Aeneid*', *Vergilius*, vol. 29, pp. 34-46.

Moore, Leslie (1990), *Beautiful Sublime: The Making of* Paradise Lost, *1701-1734*, Stanford University Press, Stanford.

Morris, Colin (1972), *The Discovery of the Individual: 1050-1200*, Harper and Row, New York.

Müller, Werner (1961), *Die heilige Stadt: Roma Quadrata, himmlisches Jerusalem und die Mythe vom Weltnabel*, W. Kohlhammer, Stuttgart.

Murrin, Michael (1980), *The Allegorical Epic: Essays in its Rise and Decline*, University of Chicago Press, Chicago.

Murtaugh, Kristin O. (1980), *Ariosto and the Classical Simile*, Harvard University Press, Cambridge.

Nagy, Gregory (1979), *The Best of the Achaeans*, Johns Hopkins University Press, Baltimore.

Needham, Rodney, ed. (1973), *Right and Left*, University of Chicago Press, Chicago.

Nelson, William (1963), *The Poetry of Edmund Spenser*, Columbia University Press, New York.

Newman, John K. (1986), *The Classical Epic Tradition*, University of Wisconsin Press, Madison.

Nohrnberg, James (1976), *The Analogy of the* Faerie Queene, Princeton University Press, Princeton.

Olschki, Leonardo (1913), *Paris nach den altfranzosischen nationalen Epen. Topographie, Stadtgeschicte und lokale Sagen*, C. Winter, Heidelberg.

Onians, R. B. (1951), *The Origins of European Thought About the Body, the Mind, the Soul, the World, Time, and Fate*, Cambridge University Press, Cambridge.

Otis, Brooks (1963), *Virgil: A Study in Civilized Poetry*, Clarendon, Oxford.

Panofsky, Erwin (1930), *Hercules am Scheidewege*, B. G. Teubner, Leipzig.

Parker, Patricia A. (1979), *Inescapable Romance: Studies in the Poetics of a Mode*, Princeton University Press, Princeton.

Parker, T. H. L. (1959), *Calvin's Doctrine of the Knowledge of God*, Eerdmans, Grand Rapids.

Patrides, C. A. (1982), *Premises and Motifs in Renaissance Thought and Literature*, Princeton University Press, Princeton.

Pedrick, Victoria (1982), 'Supplication in the *Iliad* and the *Odyssey*', *Transactions of the American Philological Association*, vol. 112, pp. 125-40.

Prestige, G. L. (1936), *God in Patristic Thought*, SPCK, London.

Pucci, Pietro (1987), *Odysseus Polytropos: Intertextual Readings in the* Odyssey *and the* Iliad, Cornell University Press, Ithaca.

Putnam, Michael C. J. (1965), *The Poetry of the* Aeneid: *Four Studies in Imaginative Unity and Design*, Harvard University Press, Cambridge.

Quilligan, Maureen (1983), *Milton's Spenser: The Politics of Reading*, Cornell University Press, Ithaca.

Quint, David (1979), 'The Figure of Atlante: Ariosto and Boiardo's Poem', *Modern Language Notes*, vol. 94, pp. 77-91.

—— (1993), *Epic and Empire*, Princeton University Press, Princeton.

Qvarnström, Gunnar (1967), *The Enchanted Palace: Some Structural Aspects of* Paradise Lost, Almqvist and Wiksell, Stockholm.

Rahner, Hugo (1963), *Greek Myths and Christian Mystery*, trans. Brian Battershaw, Harper & Row, New York.

Reid, David (1991), 'Tasso and Milton on How One Sees Oneself', in Di Cesare, Mario A. (ed.), *Milton in Italy: Contexts, Images, Perspectives*, Medieval and Renaissance Texts and Studies, Binghamton, pp. 445-61.

Ricoeur, Paul (1966), *Freedom and Nature: The Voluntary and the Involuntary*, trans. Erazim V. Kohak, Northwestern University Press, Evanston.

Rosenberg, D. M. (1981), *Oaten Reeds and Trumpets: Pastoral and Epic in Virgil, Spenser, and Milton*, Bucknell University Press, Lewisburg.

Rosenblatt, Jason P. (1990), 'Eden, Israel, England: Milton's Spiritual Geography', in McVeagh, John (ed.), *All Before Them: 1660-1780*, Ashfield Press, London, pp. 49-63.

Rowse, A. L. (1955), *The Expansion of Elizabethan England*, Macmillan, London, 1955.

Rudat, Wolfgang E. H. (1979), 'Milton's Satan and Virgil's Juno: The "Perverseness" of Disobedience in *Paradise Lost*', *Renaissance and Reformation*, vol. 15, pp. 77-82.

—— (1981), 'Milton's Dido and Aeneas: The Fall in *Paradise Lost* and the Vergilian Tradition', *Classical and Medieval Literature*, vol. 2, pp. 33-46.

—— (1985), 'Pope's Belinda, Milton's Eve, and the Missionary Position', *American Notes and Queries*, vol. 23, pp. 103-4.

Russo, Joseph, Manuel Fernandez-Galiano, and Alfred Heubeck, eds. (1992), *A Commentary on Homer's Odyssey: Volume III, Books XVII-XXIV*, Clarendon, Oxford.

Rykwert, Joseph (1988), *The Idea of a Town: The Anthropology of Urban Form in Rome, Italy and the Ancient World*, MIT Press, Cambridge.

Saccone, Eduardo (1974), *Il soggetto del Furioso*, Liguori, Naples.

Scarry, Elaine (1985), *The Body in Pain: The Making and the Unmaking of the World*, Oxford University Press, Oxford.

Schaar, Claes (1982), *'The Full Voic'd Quire Below': Vertical Context Systems in Paradise Lost*, CWK Gleerup, Lund.

Schmidt, Robert W. (1966), *The Domain of Logic According to Saint Thomas Aquinas*, Martinus Nijhoff, The Hague.

Schwartz, Barry (1981), *Vertical Classification: A Study in Structuralism and the Sociology of Knowledge*, University of Chicago Press, Chicago, 1981.

Scully, Stephen (1990), *Homer and the Sacred City*, Cornell University Press, Ithaca.

Segal, Charles (1971), *The Theme of the Mutilation of the Corpse in the Iliad*, E. J. Brill, Leiden.

—— (1974), 'Transition and Ritual in Odysseus' Return', in Cook, Albert (ed.), *Homer: The Odyssey*, Norton, New York, pp. 465-86.

Shapiro, Marianne (1983), 'From Atlas to Atlante', *Comparative Literature*, vol. 35, pp. 323-50.

—— (1988), *The Poetics of Ariosto*, Wayne State University Press, Detroit.

Shullenberger, William (1986), 'Wrestling with the Angel: *Paradise Lost* and Feminist Criticism', *Milton Quarterly*, vol. 20, pp. 69-85.

Siebenhuner, Herbert (1954), *Das Kapitol in Rom: Idee und Gestalt*, Kosel, Munich.

Sklute, Larry (1953), 'The Ambiguity of Ethical Norms in Courtly Romance', *PMLA*, vol. 68, pp. 1160-82.

Small, Jocelyn Penny (1982), *Cacus and Marsyas in Etrusco-Roman Legend*, Princeton University Press, Princeton.

Smith, Jonathan Z. (1987), *To Take Place: Toward Theory in Ritual*, Chicago University Press, Chicago, 1987.

Smith, Roland M. (1955), 'Origines Arthurianae: The Two Crosses of Spenser's Red Cross Knight', *Journal of English and Germanic Philology*, vol. 54, pp. 670-83.

Snell, Bruno (1953), *The Discovery of the Mind: The Greek Origins of European Thought*, trans. T. G. Rosenmeyer, Harvard University Press, Cambridge.

Snider, Alvin (1986), 'The Self-Mirroring Mind in Milton and Traherne', *University of Toronto Quarterly*, vol. 55, pp. 313-27.

Stallybrass, Peter (1991), 'The World Turned Upside Down: Inversion, Gender and the State', in Wayne, Valerie (ed.), *The Matter of Difference: Materialist Feminist Criticism of Shakespeare*, Cornell University Press, Ithaca, pp. 201-20.

Stanley, Keith (1993), *The Shield of Homer: Narrative Structure in the Iliad*, Princeton University Press, Princeton.

Steadman, John M. (1974), *The Lamb and the Elephant: Ideal Imitation and the Context of Renaissance Allegory*, Huntington Library, San Marino.

Sterne, Laurence and Harold H. Kollmeier, eds. (1985), *A Concordance to the English Prose of John Milton*, Medieval and Renaissance Texts and Studies, Binghamton.

Stinger, Charles L. (1981), '*Roma triumphans*: Triumphs in the Thought and Ceremonies of Renaissance Rome', *Museum Helveticum*, vol. 19, pp. 189-201.

—— (1985), *The Renaissance in Rome*, Indiana University Press, Bloomington.

Swaim, Kathleen M. (1986), *Before and After the Fall: Contrasting Modes in Paradise Lost'*, University of Massachusetts Press, Amherst.

Taplin, Oliver (1992), *Homeric Soundings: The Shaping of the Iliad*, Clarendon, Oxford.

Terrien, Samuel (1970), 'The Omphalos Myth and Hebrew Religion', *Vetus Testamentum*, vol. 20, pp. 315-38.

Tieche, M. (1945), 'Atlas als Personifikation der Weltachse', *Museum Helveticum*, vol. 2, pp. 65-86.

Turner, James Grantham (1987), *One Flesh: Paradisal Marriage and Sexual Relations in the Age of Milton*, Clarendon, Oxford.

Tuve, Rosemond (1966), *Allegorical Imagery: Some Medieval Books and their Posterity*, Princeton University Press, Princeton.

Van de Velde, Carl (1965), 'The Labours of Hercules: a Lost Series of Paintings by Frans Floris', *The Burlington Magazine*, vol. 108, pp. 114-23.

Van Wees, Hans (1986), 'Leaders of Men? Military Organization in the *Iliad*', *Classical Quarterly*, vol. 36, pp. 285-303.

—— (1988), 'Kings in Combat: Battles and Heroes in the *Iliad*,' *Classical Quarterly*, vol. 38, pp. 1-24.

—— (1994), 'The Homeric Way of War: The *Iliad* and the Hoplite Phalanx (I)', *Greece and Rome*, vol. 41, pp. 1-18.

Vernant, Jean-Pierre (1983), *Myth and Thought Among the Greeks*, Routledge and Kegan Paul, London.

Vivante, Paolo (1982), *The Epithets in Homer: A Study in Poetic Values*, Yale University Press, New Haven.

Von Simson, Otto (1962), *The Gothic Cathedral*, Bollingen, New York.

Waddington, Raymond B. (1990), '"All in All": Shakespeare, Milton, Donne and the Soul-in Body Topos', *English Literary Renaissance*, vol. 20, pp. 40-68.

Warton, Thomas (1762), *Observations on the Fairy Queen of Spenser*, R. and J. Dodsley, London, 1969 reprint by Gregg International Publishers, Westmead, Farnborough, Hants.

Waters, Lindsay (1981), 'Milton, Tasso, and the Renaissance Grand Style: Syntax and its Effect on the Reader', *Stanford Italian Review*, vol. 2, pp. 81-92.

Webber, Joan M. (1979), *Milton and His Epic Tradition*, University of Washington Press, Seattle.

Webbink, Patricia (1986), *The Power of the Eyes*, Springer, New York.

Weinberg, Bernard (1961), *A History of Literary Criticism in the Italian Renaissance*, 2 vols., University of Chicago Press, Chicago.

Wensinck, A. J. (1916), *The Idea of the Western Semites Concerning the Navel of the Earth*, E. J. Brill, Leiden.

Wetmore, Monroe Nichols (1911), *Index verborum Vergilianus*, Yale University Press, New Haven.

White, Michael J. (1992), *The Continuous and the Discrete: Ancient Physical Theories from a Contemporary Perspective*, Clarendon, Oxford.

Wind, Edgar (1958), *Pagan Mysteries in the Renaissance*, Norton, New York.

Winnicott, D. W. (1982), *Playing and Reality*, Tavistock, New York.

Wofford, Susanne Lindgren (1992), *The Choice of Achilles: The Ideology of Figure in the Epic*, Stanford University Press, Stanford.

Yardley, J. C. (1981), 'Evander's *altum limen*: Virgil *Aen*. 8.461-2', *Eranos*, vol. 79, pp. 147-8.

Yarnall, Judith (1994), *Transformations of Circe: The History of an Enchantress*, University of Illinois Press, Urbana.

Zanker, Paul (1988), *The Power of Images in the Age of Augustus*, trans. Alan Shapiro, University of Michigan Press, Ann Arbor.

Zarker, John W. (1972), 'The Hercules Theme in the *Aeneid*', *Vergilius*, vol. 18, pp. 34-48.

Zatti, Sergio (1983), *L'uniforme cristiano e il multiforme pagano*, Il Saggiatore, Milan.

Zimmerman, Shari A. (1981), 'Milton's *Paradise Lost*: Eve's Struggle for Identity', *American Imago*, vol. 38, pp. 247-67.

Index